D1489251

TRADE AND DEVELOPMENT REPORT, 2013

Report by the secretariat of the
United Nations Conference on Trade and Development

UNITED NATIONS
New York and Geneva, 2013

Note

- Symbols of United Nations documents are composed of capital letters combined with figures. Mention of such a symbol indicates a reference to a United Nations document.

- The designations employed and the presentation of the material in this publication do not imply the expression of any opinion whatsoever on the part of the Secretariat of the United Nations concerning the legal status of any country, territory, city or area, or of its authorities, or concerning the delimitation of its frontiers or boundaries.

- Material in this publication may be freely quoted or reprinted, but acknowledgement is requested, together with a reference to the document number. A copy of the publication containing the quotation or reprint should be sent to the UNCTAD secretariat.

UNCTAD/TDR/2013

UNITED NATIONS PUBLICATION

Sales No. E.13.II.D.3

ISBN 978-92-1-112867-3
eISBN 978-92-1-0546284-3
ISSN 0255-4607

Contents

List of tables

List of boxes

List of charts

Classification by country or commodity group

The classification of countries in this *Report* has been adopted solely for the purposes of statistical or analytical convenience and does not necessarily imply any judgement concerning the stage of development of a particular country or area.

The major country groupings used in this *Report* follow the classification by the United Nations Statistical Office (UNSO). They are distinguished as:

» Developed or industrial(ized) countries: the countries members of the OECD (other than Chile, Mexico, the Republic of Korea and Turkey) plus all other EU member countries.

» Transition economies refers to South-East Europe, the Commonwealth of Independent States (CIS) and Georgia.

» Developing countries: all countries, territories or areas not specified above.

The terms "country" / "economy" refer, as appropriate, also to territories or areas.

References to "Latin America" in the text or tables include the Caribbean countries unless otherwise indicated.

References to "sub-Saharan Africa" in the text or tables include South Africa unless otherwise indicated.

For statistical purposes, regional groupings and classifications by commodity group used in this *Report* follow generally those employed in the *UNCTAD Handbook of Statistics 2012* (United Nations publication, sales no. B.12.II.D.1) unless otherwise stated. The data for China do not include those for Hong Kong Special Administrative Region (Hong Kong SAR), Macao Special Administrative Region (Macao SAR) and Taiwan Province of China.

Other notes

References in the text to *TDR* are to the *Trade and Development Report* (of a particular year). For example, *TDR 2012* refers to *Trade and Development Report, 2012* (United Nations publication, sales no. E.12.II.D.6).

The term "dollar" ($) refers to United States dollars, unless otherwise stated.

The term "billion" signifies 1,000 million.

The term "tons" refers to metric tons.

Annual rates of growth and change refer to compound rates.

Exports are valued FOB and imports CIF, unless otherwise specified.

Use of a dash (–) between dates representing years, e.g. 1988–1990, signifies the full period involved, including the initial and final years.

An oblique stroke (/) between two years, e.g. 2000/01, signifies a fiscal or crop year.

A dot (.) indicates that the item is not applicable.

Two dots (..) indicate that the data are not available, or are not separately reported.

A dash (-) or a zero (0) indicates that the amount is nil or negligible.

Decimals and percentages do not necessarily add up to totals because of rounding.

Abbreviations

BIS	Bank for International Settlements
CIS	Commonwealth of Independent States
ECB	European Central Bank
ECLAC	Economic Commission for Latin America and the Caribbean
EIB	European Investment Bank
ERM	European Exchange Rate Mechanism
ESCAP	Economic and Social Commission for Asia and the Pacific
EU	European Union
FAO	Food and Agriculture Organization of the United Nations
FDI	foreign direct investment
FSB	Financial Stability Board
GDP	gross domestic product
IEA	International Energy Agency
ILO	International Labour Organization (or Office)
IMF	International Monetary Fund
LDC	least developed country
LLR	lender of last resort
ODA	official development assistance
OECD	Organisation for Economic Co-operation and Development
OPEC	Organization of the Petroleum Exporting Countries
PPP	purchasing power parity
REER	real effective exchange rate
SME	small and medium-sized enterprise
TDR	Trade and Development Report
TNC	transnational corporation
UNCTAD	United Nations Conference on Trade and Development
UN-DESA	United Nations Department of Economic and Social Affairs
UNSD	United Nations Statistics Division
USDA	United States Department of Agriculture
WTO	World Trade Organization

OVERVIEW

Five years after the onset of the global financial crisis the world economy remains in a state of disarray. Strong expansionary monetary policies in the major developed economies have not succeeded in fostering credit creation and strengthening aggregate demand. Fiscal austerity and wage compression in many developed countries are further darkening the outlook, not only for the short term, but also for the medium term. The burden of adjustment of the global imbalances that contributed to the outbreak of the financial crisis remains with the deficit countries, thus strengthening deflationary forces in the world economy.

The dominance of finance over real economic activities persists, and may even have increased further. Yet financial reforms at the national level have been timid at best, advancing very slowly, if at all. In 2008 and 2009, policymakers of several economically powerful countries had called for urgent reforms of the international monetary and financial system. However, since then, the momentum in pushing for reform has all but disappeared from the international agenda. Consequently, the outlook for the world economy and for the global environment for development continues to be highly uncertain.

Some developing and transition economies have been able to mitigate the impact of the financial and economic crises in the developed countries by means of expansionary macroeconomic policies. But with the effects of such a response petering out and the external economic environment showing few signs of improvement, these economies are struggling to regain their growth momentum.

Prior to the Great Recession, exports from developing and transition economies grew rapidly owing to buoyant consumer demand in the developed countries, mainly the United States. This seemed to justify the adoption of an export-oriented growth model. But the expansion of the world economy, though favourable for many developing countries, was built on unsustainable global demand and financing patterns. Thus, reverting to pre-crisis growth strategies cannot be an option. Rather, in order to adjust to what now appears to be a structural shift in the world economy, many developing and transition economies are obliged to review their development strategies that have been overly dependent on exports for growth.

It is not a new insight that growth strategies that rely primarily on exports must sooner or later reach their limits when many countries pursue them simultaneously: competition among economies based on low unit labour costs and taxes leads to a race to the bottom, with few development gains but potentially disastrous social consequences. At the present juncture, where growth of demand from developed countries is expected to remain weak for a protracted period of time, the limitations of such a growth strategy are becoming even more obvious. Therefore, a rebalancing of the drivers of growth, with greater weight given to domestic demand, is indispensable. This will be a formidable challenge for all developing countries, though more difficult for some than for others. In any case, it will require a new perspective on the role of wages and the public sector in the development process. Distinct from export-led growth, development strategies that give a greater role than in the past to domestic demand for growth can be pursued by all countries simultaneously without beggar-thy-neighbour effects, and without counterproductive wage and tax competition. Moreover, if many trade partners in the developing world manage to expand their domestic demand simultaneously, they can spur South-South trade.

No sustained recovery of the world economy in sight

The global economy is still struggling to return to a strong and sustained growth path. The rate of world output, which was 2.2 per cent in 2012, is forecast to grow at a similar rate in 2013. As in previous years, developed countries are expected to show the poorest performance, with around 1 per cent increase in gross domestic product (GDP). Developing and transition economies are likely to grow by almost 5 per cent and 3 per cent respectively.

Economic activity in many developed countries and a number of emerging market economies is still suffering from the impacts of the financial and economic crisis that started in 2008, and from the unsustainable financial processes and domestic and international imbalances that led to it. However, continuing weak growth in several countries may also be partly due to their current macroeconomic policy stance.

In the European Union (EU), GDP is expected to shrink for the second consecutive year. Economic contraction is likely to be more severe in the euro area than in other EU countries. Private demand remains subdued, especially in the periphery economies, due to high unemployment, wage compression, low consumer confidence and the still incomplete process of balance sheet consolidation. Given the ongoing process of deleveraging, expansionary monetary policies have failed to induce banks to provide much-needed new credit to the private sector that could reinvigorate demand. In this context, the increased tendency towards fiscal tightening makes a quick return to a higher growth trajectory highly unlikely. Indeed, attempts to resolve the crisis in the euro area through fiscal austerity may backfire badly, as it adds a deflationary impulse to already weak private demand. The countries in the euro zone that have been suffering the most from the crisis continue to operate under extremely adverse conditions, while growth in the surplus countries has largely relied on strong exports. Since governments in the latter countries have been reluctant to stimulate domestic demand by other means than monetary policy, disequilibrium within the zone persists.

At the global level, it is notable that Japan is bucking the current austerity trend by providing strong fiscal stimulus and monetary expansion that are aimed at reviving economic growth and curbing deflationary trends. These measures could help maintain its GDP growth at close to 2 per cent in 2013. The United States is expected to grow at a similar rate, but based on a different set of factors. Partly owing to significant progress made in the consolidation of its banking sector, private domestic demand has begun to recover. On the other hand, cuts in public spending, including for needed investment in infrastructure, are having a contractionary effect. Since the net outcome of these opposing tendencies is unclear, there is also considerable uncertainty about whether the expansionary monetary policy stance will be maintained.

Growth in many developing countries driven by domestic demand

Developing countries are expected to grow by between 4.5 and 5 per cent in 2013, similar to 2012. In many of them, growth has been driven more by domestic demand than by exports, as external demand from developed economies has remained weak. In addition, short-term capital inflows, attracted by higher interest rates than in the major developed countries, have been exerting appreciation pressure on the currencies of several emerging market economies, thus weakening their export sectors.

As before, in 2012 output growth was strong in East, South and South-East Asia, at 5.3 per cent, but recently there has been a slowdown, reflecting weak demand from some of the major export markets. In China, the contribution of net exports to GDP growth declined further, while fixed investment and private consumption, as a result of faster wage growth, continued to drive output expansion. Domestic demand, encouraged by various incomes policy measures in a number of other countries in the region, such as India, Indonesia, the Philippines and Thailand, is also supporting output growth, which may therefore accelerate moderately in the region as a whole in 2013.

Economic growth in West Asia slowed down dramatically, from 7.1 per cent in 2011 to 3.2 per cent in 2012, a level that is expected to be maintained in 2013. Weaker external demand, especially from Europe, affected the entire region, most prominently Turkey, whose growth rate dropped sharply from around 9 per cent in 2010 and 2011 to 2.2 per cent in 2012. The Gulf Cooperation Council (GCC) countries maintained large public spending programmes to support domestic demand and growth, despite scaling back their oil production during the last quarter of 2012 to support oil prices.

Growth in Africa is expected to slow down in 2013, owing to weaker performance in North Africa, where political instability in some countries has been mirrored in recent years by strong fluctuations in growth. In sub-Saharan Africa, by contrast, GDP growth has remained stable, at above 5 per cent, owing to continued high earnings from exports of primary commodities and relatively strong public and private investment in some countries. However, the two largest economies of the region, Nigeria and South Africa, face considerable downside risks due to faltering external demand and some weaknesses on the supply side. In addition, several least developed countries (LDCs) of the region remain vulnerable to sudden and drastic swings in demand for certain commodities.

Growth is also expected to remain relatively stable in Latin America and the Caribbean, at around 3 per cent, on average, as a slowdown in some countries, including Mexico, is likely to be offset by faster growth in Argentina and Brazil. Overall, growth in the region is being driven by domestic demand, based on public and private consumption.

The transition economies have experienced a downward trend in their economic performance. Under the impact of the continuing crisis in much of Western Europe, most of the transition economies of South-Eastern Europe entered into recession in 2012. The members of the Commonwealth of Independent State (CIS) maintained a growth rate of over 3 per cent in 2012 based on sustained domestic demand, but this is expected to slow down slightly in 2013. The economic outlook for the region remains closely linked to the performance of the economy of the Russian Federation and to commodity price developments.

As the rapid expansion of developing economies as a group has further increased their weight in the world economy, a new pattern of global growth seems to be emerging. While developed countries remain the main export markets for developing countries, the share of the latter's contribution to growth in the world economy has increased, from 28 per cent in the 1990s to about 40 per cent in the period 2003–2007, and to close to 75 per cent since 2008. However, more recently, growth in these economies has decelerated. If developing countries can increase the role of domestic demand and South-South trade in their development strategies, they may continue to grow at a relatively fast pace, with increasing potential to rely on each other for the expansion of aggregate demand. However, they cannot be expected to lift developed countries out of their sluggish growth pattern through higher imports from them.

Global trade expansion has virtually ground to a halt

International trade in goods and services has not returned to the rapid growth rate of the years preceding the crisis. After a sharp fall in 2008–2009 and a quick recovery in 2010, the volume of trade in goods expanded by only 5 per cent in 2011 and by less than 2 per cent in 2012, and it affected developed, developing and transition economies alike.

Sluggish economic activity in developed economies accounted for most of the slowdown in international trade. In 2012, European imports of goods shrank by almost 3 per cent in volume and by 5 per cent in value. Extremely weak intra-European trade was responsible for almost 90 per cent of the decline in European exports in 2012. Japan's exports have not yet recovered from their sharp fall caused by the earthquake of 2011, while the volume of its imports has continued to grow at a moderate pace. Among the major developed economies, only the United States maintained a positive growth rate in its international trade, although this appears to be slowing down in 2013.

Trade also decelerated considerably in developing and transition economies. Both exports and imports grew sluggishly in 2012 and the first months of 2013 in most developing regions. The sole exception was Africa, where exports recovered in countries previously affected by civil conflict. Export growth declined to 4 per cent in the developing countries as a whole. This slowdown included Asian countries that had previously played a major role in boosting international trade.

The rate of growth of China's exports, by volume, declined from an average annual rate of 27 per cent during the period 2002–2007 to 13 per cent in 2011 and to 7 per cent in 2012, a lower rate than its GDP growth. Concomitantly, China's imports, by volume, decelerated to 6 per cent in 2012 from 19 per cent, on average, between 2002 and 2007. Only regions exporting a large proportion of primary commodities (i.e. Africa, West Asia and, to a lesser extent, Latin America) saw a significant increase in their exports to China. Several exporters of manufactures in Asia registered a sizeable slowdown of growth in their external trade. This was the result not only of lower imports from Europe, but also of slower growth in some developing regions, in particular in East Asia.

The crisis of 2008–2009 has altered trade patterns in both developed and developing countries. Imports by all developed regions remain below their pre-crisis level, and only the United States has managed to increase its exports to a higher level than their previous peak of August 2008. On the other hand, exports from the group of emerging market economies were 22 per cent above their pre-crisis peaks, while the corresponding figure for their imports was 26 per cent higher. However, the pace of growth of trade of these economies has slowed down significantly: during the pre-crisis years, between 2002 and 2007, their export volume grew at an average annual rate of 11.3 per cent, but fell to only 3.5 per cent between January 2011 and April 2013. Growth in the volume of their imports also slowed down from 12.4 per cent to 5.5 per cent over the same period.

Overall, this general downward trend in international trade highlights the vulnerabilities developing countries continue to face at a time of lacklustre growth in developed countries. It is also indicative of a probably less favourable external trade environment over the next few years.

The particularities of a protracted downturn in developed countries

The difficulties of the developed countries as a group to find their way towards a path of sustained recovery following the recession of 2008–2009 suggests that the latest crisis is of quite a different nature than the cyclical crises of the past. From 2008 to 2012, global output growth averaged just 1.7 per cent. This is much slower than during any of the five-year periods that followed recessions in the global economy since the 1970s.

In this situation, expansionary policies would be needed to spur domestic demand and restore the confidence of households and firms. However, policymakers have instead been focusing their attention on restoring the confidence of financial markets. A central element of this strategy in developed countries has been fiscal austerity, based on the belief that high public debt ratios may eventually trigger a general aversion to sovereign debt, which could increase the risk premium and thereby impose a heavier debt burden on public finances. This strategy has not yielded the expected results. The outcome of fiscal contraction has negatively affected growth and job creation, as the expected increase in private demand has not materialized to compensate, or overcompensate, for the cuts in public spending. In addition, the fact that several countries that had strong trade relations with each other have been following austerity regimes at the same time has amplified their deflationary impact in the same way as simultaneous fiscal stimulus in 2009 generated very positive results. Moreover, monetary policies have proved ineffective in the sense that strong monetary expansion has not translated into an increase in loans to the private sector. This shows that, without the prospect of a growth in demand, the increasing availability of credit is not enough to stimulate private investment and create jobs.

Experience has shown that an expansionary fiscal policy can have a much stronger impact in such a situation, because this is precisely when it has a particularly strong multiplier effect. The legitimate objective of improving fiscal balances is more likely to be achieved through an expansion of aggregate demand, and thus the tax base, than by fiscal contraction which reduces income and employment growth. In addition, central bank operations that focus on reducing the risk of sovereign debt and maintaining low interest rates would enable a reduction in public debt servicing, and thereby lower medium- to long-term public debt ratios that are considered too high.

Structural reforms are needed, but what kinds?

Despite marked differences in economic performance across regions, in general, policies pursued over the past three years have not succeeded in resolving the crisis. There can be little doubt that, in addition to demand-enhancing policies, structural reforms are needed in many countries to lead their national economies and the global economy back to a path of sustained growth. Several proposals for reform have been made, in particular relating to the financial sector, the labour market, public finances and central banking, but not all of them have adequately addressed the causes of the crisis.

A major reason for the crisis has been the dominance of the financial sector over the real sector. Financial liberalization has resulted in governments being increasingly influenced by the belief that they need to maintain or regain the "confidence" of financial markets. The reforms adopted since 2008, which aim at improving supervision and capitalization of the banking system, are helpful but are unlikely to be sufficient to prevent activities of the financial markets from posing a threat to economic stability. Governments need to control financial markets more resolutely than in the past and limit the power of those markets over national, regional and global economies.

For many years preceding the financial and economic crisis, structural reform was virtually synonymous with introducing greater flexibility into the labour market, especially wage flexibility, and such reform is again suggested as a way out of the crisis. But a strategy aimed at strengthening the competitiveness of economies by reducing labour costs completely neglects the fact that wages are usually a major source of domestic demand. Moreover, when such a strategy is pursued by many countries at the same time, it leads to a race to the bottom, worsens income distribution and poses a threat to social cohesion. And greater inequality of income distribution was one of the factors that led to the crisis in the first place. Instead, an incomes policy aimed at accelerating consumption growth could contribute decisively to restoring national economies, and the global economy, to a stronger but also more balanced growth path.

Reforms aimed at fiscal consolidation may be necessary in many countries, but they need to consider the overall macroeconomic context. Public finances cannot be managed like the finances of a household because they inevitably have an impact on the entire economy and the spending behaviour of the private sector. Attempts to achieve fiscal consolidation in the short run have been unsuccessful at best, and counterproductive and procyclical at worst. Such consolidation can only be achieved after several years of sustained economic growth, and should not be considered a prerequisite for economic recovery.

Central banks of many developed countries have responded to the financial crisis, and, in the euro zone, to the crisis in some member States' public finances, with a number of unorthodox measures. But they may also have to find new ways of making credit available to non-financial agents to use in a way that generates demand, income and employment.

These various national reforms also require more determined international cooperation, including long overdue reform of the international monetary system, in order to achieve greater symmetry of adjustment efforts among deficit and surplus economies. In the present situation, several countries with large current account surpluses could probably do much more to help revive the world economy.

Developing and transition economies: better performance but continued vulnerability

One of the most significant changes in the shape of the world economy has been the increase in the share of developing countries in global GDP. The onset of the global economic and financial crisis initially reinforced this trend, as growth in developing countries in 2008–2009 decelerated less and recovered more rapidly than in developed countries. As a result, the share of developed countries in global GDP declined from 79 per cent in 1990 to about 60 per cent in 2012, while that of developing countries more than doubled, from 17 per cent to 36 per cent, over the same period. Most of this change occurred from 2004 onwards.

Nevertheless, economic developments in developed countries remain crucial for growth in developing countries. Indeed, the growth acceleration in the latter set of countries during the 1990s, and especially during the period 2003–2007, was associated with a larger proportion of international trade in the composition of their aggregate demand. Combined with the generally favourable external economic environment, such as growing imports by developed countries (especially the United States) and historically high commodity prices, particularly during the five years prior to the onset of the current crisis, the greater outward orientation of developing countries contributed to their growth.

However, an export-oriented growth strategy also implies greater vulnerability to a deterioration of the external environment, as has occurred since 2008. The international price and demand shocks during 2008–2009 had a severe impact on both exporters of primary commodities and exporters of manufactures. The subsequent rebound was more rapid and its beneficial impact greater on countries whose exports comprise a large proportion of primary commodities than for countries that export mainly manufactures.

Weaker demand from developed countries suggests that South-South trade may need to play a greater role in developing countries' growth strategy. In this respect, it offers greater potential than in the past, given that the share of South-South trade in total world trade increased from slightly less than 30 per cent in 1995 to slightly more than 40 per cent in 2012. Moreover, the share of manufactures in a developing country's exports to other developing countries and the value added in such trade are usually much higher than they are in its exports to developed countries, which is testimony to the potential developmental role of South-South trade.

Commodity price trends and outlook

Up to the financial crisis and the Great Recession of 2008–2009, rapid output growth in many developing and transition economies was the result of their strong increase in exports of manufactures to developed countries. This in turn contributed to higher export earnings of other developing countries that relied on exports of primary commodities. Since the turn of the millennium, these latter countries have also benefited from a trend change in the terms of trade. This change reflected not only an upward movement in the medium-term commodity price trend, interrupted only briefly in 2008–2009, but also a decline in world prices of certain manufactures, especially labour-intensive manufactures.

The increasing demand for commodities in rapidly growing developing countries, notably China, and the resulting higher price levels of many primary commodities, signifies a structural shift in physical market fundamentals. The upward trend in prices has also been supported by a slow supply response, as historically low price *levels* in the 1990s had led to a long period of underinvestment in production capacity for several key commodities, especially in the mineral and mining sectors. At the same time, the increasing presence of financial investors in commodity markets has accentuated the problem of price *volatility*. Projections about the further evolution of commodity prices are particularly difficult in the current uncertain global economic environment, but there is little doubt that the growth outlook for developing countries will have a significant impact on future commodity demand trends.

Continuing fast population growth and rising income in developing countries should lead to greater demand for several food items. Moreover, as production is unlikely to increase in line with the growing demand, including for biofuels, agricultural commodity prices could remain high over the next decade.

Demand conditions in the markets of many primary commodities that are used as inputs for the production of manufactures and for construction are determined by a number of factors. One factor is whether China succeeds in rebalancing its growth through an increase in domestic consumption. Another is whether other highly populated and rapidly growing developing countries will move to a more commodity-intensive phase of economic growth and industrialization. Even if China's GDP growth slows down, resulting in a lower use of some commodities, its ongoing industrialization and per capita income growth could continue to have a considerable impact on global markets, given the size of its economy. If, in addition, other large and highly populated developing countries also pursue a path of rapid industrialization, the demand prospects for industrial commodities, particularly metals, could remain robust. Infrastructure development associated with rapid urbanization also offers strong potential to increase demand for commodities.

In addition, rising living standards in many developing countries may boost demand for energy commodities in the medium term, despite improvements in energy efficiency that could contribute to a decline in energy use per unit of GDP. Oil prices could remain historically high, even if they fall slightly compared with their 2011–2012 levels, as demand from some of the rapidly growing developing countries will continue to rise and because the exploitation costs of new supplies are higher than those from conventional sources.

Overall, commodity prices may not rise as fast as they have over the past decade, but, following some downward adjustments in the short term, they should stabilize at a relatively high level in comparison with the early 2000s. However, this should not lead to complacency in the design of development strategies in natural-resource-rich countries. Their main challenge remains that of appropriating a fair share of the resource rents and channelling revenues towards investment in the real economy in order to spur the diversification and upgrading of production and exports.

Export-led growth strategies are reaching their limits

A key problem for policymakers in the developing and transition economies that have a large share of manufactures in their exports is that growth of exports and incomes in their countries is likely to be adversely affected by continued slow growth in developed countries' final expenditure for several years to come. In a number of these countries, production of manufactured goods for the world market has driven the expansion of their formal modern sectors, but in most of them domestic demand has not increased apace. This has been partly due to weak linkages between the export sector and the rest of the economy, and partly to the strategy of their firms and governments to strengthen the international competitiveness of their domestic producers by keeping wages low. Such a strategy will eventually reach its limit, as low wages dampen domestic demand growth, especially when many other countries pursue the same strategy simultaneously. Since the growth of demand in developed countries is likely to remain weak for an extended period of time, the limitations of such a strategy become even more acute. In these circumstances, continuing with export-led growth strategies through wage and tax competition would exacerbate the harm caused by slower growth in export markets and reduce any overall benefits.

The adoption of countercyclical macroeconomic policies can compensate for resulting growth shortfalls for some time. Indeed, most developing countries reacted to the decline in their net exports by increasing the share of government expenditure in GDP. There was also an increase of private consumption as a share of GDP in some of these countries, and of gross fixed capital formation as a share of GDP in some others. However, beyond such short-term responses, developing countries may need to take a more comprehensive and longer term perspective, involving a shift in development strategies that gives greater weight to domestic demand as an engine of growth. Such a move towards a more balanced growth path could compensate for the adverse impact of slower growing exports to developed countries. Moreover, this more balanced growth strategy could be pursued by all developing countries simultaneously without beggar-thy-neighbour effects. However, there are many challenges involved in moving towards a more balanced growth strategy. These include boosting domestic purchasing power, managing domestic demand expansion in a way that avoids an excessive increase in import demand, and nurturing the interrelationship between household and government expenditure, on the one hand, and investment on the other, to enable the sectoral composition of domestic production to adjust to new demand patterns, including through increased regional and South-South trade.

Hence, shifting the focus of development strategies to domestic markets does not mean minimizing the importance of the role of exports. Indeed, exports could expand further if several trade partners were to achieve higher economic growth at the same time.

Rebalancing domestic and external forces of growth

In seeking greater integration into a rapidly globalizing economy, the critical importance of domestic demand as a major impetus for industrialization is often overlooked. Growth of domestic demand accounts for about three quarters of the increase in domestic industrial output in large economies, and slightly more than half in small economies. Accelerating domestic demand growth could therefore be highly beneficial for output growth and industrialization, particularly in a context of weakening external demand growth. The possibility of changing rapidly towards a more domestic-demand-oriented growth strategy will depend largely on how closely the sectoral structure of domestic production is linked to the pattern of domestic demand. This linkage will be particularly weak in countries that export a large proportion of primary commodities. It therefore remains very important for these countries to use their resource-related revenues to diversify their sectoral structure of production by increasing the shares of manufactures and modern services, both public and private. By developing the linkages between the exporting sectors and the rest of the economy, this diversification would generate new employment and income opportunities, and strengthen the domestic market.

A strategy that places greater emphasis on domestic demand will need to aim at an appropriate balance between increases in household consumption, private investment and public expenditure. There is a strong interrelationship between these three components of domestic demand. Increased consumption of goods and services that can be produced domestically makes producers of those goods and services more willing to invest in their productive capacity. Higher investment is not only itself a source of domestic demand (even if a large share of the capital goods may have to be imported), but it is also a precondition for the creation of employment and for productivity gains that allow wages to grow along with the purchasing power of domestic consumers. Moreover, higher incomes of households and firms raise tax revenues, which can then be spent by the government for enhancing public services and infrastructure development, even at unchanged tax rates. Higher public spending, in turn, can create additional income for households and firms, and improve the conditions for private investment. Such investment is indispensable for increasing domestic supply capacity, and thus for reducing leakages of domestic demand growth through imports.

Increasing domestic consumption

Labour income is the most important source of household consumption, which generally accounts for between half and three quarters of aggregate demand, even in relatively poor countries and countries with a relatively large export sector. Thus fostering the purchasing power of the population in general, and of wage earners in particular, should be the main ingredient of a domestic-demand-driven growth strategy.

While export-led strategies focus on the cost aspect of wages, a domestic-demand-oriented strategy would focus primarily on the income aspect of wages, as it is based on household spending as the largest component of effective demand. If wage growth follows the path of productivity growth, it will create a sufficient amount of domestic demand to fully employ the growing productive capacities of the economy without having to rely on continued export growth.

In economies with fairly large formal sectors, the functioning of such an incomes policy could be enhanced by building institutions for collective bargaining and the introduction of legal minimum wages. In countries where informal employment and self-employment are widespread, targeted social transfers and public sector employment schemes can play an important complementary role. In countries with a large rural sector with many small producers, introducing mechanisms that ensure fair prices for agricultural producers – for instance by linking those prices to the overall productivity growth of the economy – would be another element of a strategy to increase domestic consumption, strengthen social cohesion and at the same time induce more productivity-enhancing investments. Moreover, the layers of the population that will primarily benefit from such an incomes policy would be likely to spend most of their income on locally produced goods and services. In addition, governments can take discretionary fiscal actions, such as providing tax rebates on certain consumer goods that are, or can be, produced domestically.

Spurring domestic demand by facilitating access to consumer credit for the acquisition of durable consumer goods tends to be risky, as amply demonstrated by recent experiences in a number of developed countries. The debt servicing burden of households may rapidly become excessive if interest rates rise, growth of household incomes stalls or the prices of assets used as collateral fall.

Increasing domestic investment

Domestic investment, both private and public, plays a crucial role in any growth strategy, regardless of whether it is oriented towards exports or domestic demand. The expectation that future demand will be high enough to fully utilize additional productive capacity is the main incentive for entrepreneurs to invest in expanding that capacity. Since exports are unlikely to grow at the same pace as in the past, given the current state of the world economy, domestic demand growth will become more important in forming the demand expectations of potential investors. A key determinant of their ability to strengthen productive capacity is the availability of long-term finance at an affordable cost and a competitive exchange rate. This in turn depends, to a large extent, on central bank policy and the structure and functioning of the domestic financial system.

Direct and indirect demand effects of public expenditure

The possibility of strengthening domestic demand by increasing public sector spending depends on the initial conditions of the public finances in each country, but also on the effects of increased public expenditure on public revenue. Public spending and taxation are potentially key instruments for shaping the distribution of purchasing power in an economy. Beyond its direct effects on aggregate demand, public investment in infrastructure and/or public services to specific industrial clusters are often a precondition for the viability of private investment, for enhancing the productivity of private capital, and for complementing the market mechanism by facilitating the creation of linkages between export industries and the rest of the economy. In addition, public expenditure on education and training can influence the potential of labour to contribute to productivity growth. Moreover, countercyclical fiscal policy can stabilize domestic demand during periods of slow growth or recession, and thus prevent a lowering of the demand expectations of domestic investors. This stabilization potential will be greater, the larger the share of the public sector in GDP.

Income redistribution through the taxation structure and transfers to households can strengthen the purchasing power of those income groups that spend a larger share of their income on consumption in general, and on domestically produced goods and services, in particular, than higher income groups.

Raising public revenues

The "fiscal space" for strengthening domestic demand, directly or indirectly, through increased public spending in developing countries, especially in low-income and least developed countries, tends to be more limited than in developed countries. This is not only because their tax base is smaller, but also their capacity to administer and enforce tax legislation is often weak. Moreover, in many of these countries public finances are strongly influenced by factors that are beyond the control of their governments, such as fluctuations in commodity prices and in interest rates on their external debt. But to a large extent fiscal space is also determined endogenously, since spending of public revenue creates income, and thus additional spending in the private sector, thereby enlarging the tax base. These income effects vary, depending on how the tax burden is distributed and public revenue is spent. Taking account of such compositional effects of both the revenue and the expenditure side implies that the scope for using taxation and government spending for strengthening domestic forces of growth may be greater than is often assumed.

In many developing and transition economies, there appears to be scope for more progressive taxation and for taxing wealth and inheritance, as well as for raising additional revenue by imposing higher taxes on multinational corporations. The latter would require that developing countries, in their efforts to attract foreign direct investment (FDI), avoid engaging in tax competition with each other. Such competition, like international wage competition, is at the expense of all the countries concerned. These considerations are of particular relevance for countries that are rich in mineral resources, where often only a very small share of the resource rents remains in the respective countries in the form of private income or public revenue.

In several low-income and least developed countries multilateral financial institutions and bilateral donors would need to help by providing additional resources for social spending, as well as support for improving the administrative capacities needed to strengthen the role of public finances in development strategies.

The rationale for debt-financed public spending

Rebalancing domestic and external forces of growth may also require a different approach to debt financing of public expenditure. It can be a strategic instrument not only in the context of a countercyclical fiscal policy, but also for stretching the fiscal burden of large public infrastructure projects. Such projects typically help to increase the productivity of the economy at large and generate benefits for households and firms in the future, by which time economic growth would help service the initially incurred debt.

While it may be preferable for governments to pay all public expenditure out of current revenue, a rational approach in a fast-growing developing economy could also be based on the principle that current expenditure, including social expenditure, should be financed by taxation and other current revenues, whereas public investment may be financed by borrowing, since such investment has a pay-off in the form of additional tax receipts from an enlarged tax base in the future. Governments should consider borrowing in foreign currency only to the extent that public investments or government support to private investments require importing capital goods, materials and know-how. Where there is a sufficient possibility for public sector borrowing for these purposes, an increase in credit-financed public expenditure may be considered a way to boost not only domestic demand but also domestic supply capacities.

Changing composition of consumption with rising personal incomes

Consumption patterns are changing with rising income levels. Once the income of individual consumers crosses a certain threshold, they will use a smaller share of that income for satisfying their basic or subsistence needs. The thresholds which trigger an acceleration of demand for other consumption items typically cluster at a level of per capita income at which an individual is considered to enter the "middle class" (i.e. those segments of the population in any society that have a certain amount of discretionary income at their disposal, which allows them to engage in consumption patterns beyond just the satisfaction of their basic needs). The future evolution of consumption patterns therefore depends on the number of people that are at around the entry level of the middle class, where the new spending patterns start emerging.

Based on a number of projections, it has been estimated that the proportion of the middle class in the total world population will increase from 26 per cent in 2009 to 41 per cent in 2020 and 58 per cent in 2030, and that this proportion will grow more than fourfold in developing countries. Asia will account for the bulk of this increase, with the number of people belonging to the middle class in this region estimated to grow sixfold; in Central and South America the number is expected to grow by a factor of 2.5, and in sub-Saharan Africa it should triple. A strategy that gives greater emphasis to domestic-demand-driven growth, if successful, might well accelerate these trends, as it would be associated with faster wage increases and a more equal income distribution than in the past. Therefore, many developing and transition economies could achieve a rapid acceleration of consumption of durable consumer goods in the medium term.

An enlarged middle class may be the most important source of buying power for domestic manufacturers, because it will eventually determine the extent of horizontal complementarities across all industries of the economy. And to the extent that the purchasing power of income groups below the level of the middle class also grows, there may be additional productivity gains in sectors and firms that produce primarily for the domestic market, as the lower income groups tend to spend their incomes on a greater share of locally produced or producible goods and services.

Domestic demand growth and its implications for the development of productive capacities

The import intensity of the three components of domestic demand (i.e. household consumption, government expenditure and investment) varies widely. Imports tend to be strongly correlated, on average, with investment and production for export, but less with consumption (especially consumption by households in the lower income brackets) and public expenditure. Still, if domestic productive capacity is not upgraded in accordance with the changing pattern of demand in a growing economy, the increase in domestic consumption expenditure will tend to induce higher imports. In order to prevent a deterioration in the trade balance as a result of both faster growth and the changing composition of domestic demand growth, coupled with lower export growth, it will be essential to strengthen domestic investment and innovation dynamics to bring about appropriate changes in the sectoral composition of domestic production.

Efforts to orient domestic production to respond to the changing level and composition of domestic demand will tend to be easier for those countries which in the past have relied significantly on exports of manufactures to developed countries, because they can build on their considerable existing productive capacity and experience in manufacturing activities. However, it will be more difficult if these activities have been geared mainly to the production of sophisticated goods for affluent consumers in developed countries, which few domestic consumers can afford. A rapid shift from an export-driven growth strategy to one that gives greater emphasis to an expansion of domestic demand to drive growth will be even more difficult in countries that have been relying on the production and export of primary commodities.

On the other hand, while developing countries should still seek to develop or adapt new technologies according to their specific needs, an advantage for producers in developing and transition economies that focus more on domestic than on global markets is that technological lagging tends to be less of a constraining factor.

Advantages of proximity to markets and regional integration

Another advantage for producers in developing countries is their proximity to their domestic market and, where applicable, their regional market. Changes in market conditions arising from the expansion and changing composition of domestic demand necessitate the identification of "latent demand" and the "steering" of firms to meet requirements specific to those new markets. In this regard, the local knowledge of domestic firms for the development of appropriate new products, distribution networks and marketing strategies may become a valuable asset in competing with foreign suppliers of similar goods. In addition, to the extent that developing and transition economies assume a greater weight in global consumption growth, the resulting changes in the pattern of global demand are likely to influence market opportunities for all these economies in areas of production that are more aligned than in the past to the patterns of demand prevailing in developing countries. This in turn will lead to changes in the sectoral allocation of investments in a way that better corresponds to the pattern of domestic demand in those countries.

Moreover, if many trade partners in the developing world were to expand their domestic demand simultaneously, they could become markets for each other's goods and services. The resulting increase in exports would help reduce the balance-of-payments constraints that arise from a slowdown of exports to developed countries. Consequently, strengthened regional integration and, more generally, intensified efforts to strengthen South-South trade, may be important complements to domestic-demand-led growth strategies.

Industrial policies in support of investment and structural change

Experience in developed and developing countries has shown that governments, in addition to market forces, can play an important role in support of industrialization. In the past, industrial policies have often focused on strengthening export capacities and establishing an export-investment nexus. However, a change in the respective weights of foreign and domestic demand may require an adaptation of industrial policy, with a greater emphasis on strengthening the competitiveness of domestic producers in domestic markets and gearing production structures to the changing composition of domestic demand as per capita income grows. Such adaptation may need to fully utilize the policy space still available to these countries following the Uruguay Round trade agreements and various regional and bilateral trade and investment agreements. Furthermore, some of these agreements may need to be revised to take better account of the interests of developing countries, for example by allowing them a greater degree of temporary protection of certain industries that are at an early stage of development.

 Capital formation that responds to changing demand patterns may be supported by helping private firms to identify the product groups that show the greatest dynamism as an increasing share of the population enters the middle class. Public support measures may also facilitate coordination of production along the value-added chain, including fiscal and financial support for new production activities that are considered strategically important for domestic production networks. A proactive industrial policy may be especially important − and have the greatest impact − in economies that are still dependent on natural resources and where there is an urgent need for diversification of production.

Challenges for financial policies in developing countries

The adjustment of productive capacities to changes in the composition of aggregate demand in developing and transition economies requires reliable and low-cost access of their producers to financial resources for productive investment. In the current global context, although there is ample liquidity in the banking systems of the major developed countries, uncertainty in financial markets is particularly high. This increases the risk of emerging markets being affected by disturbances emanating from the behaviour of international capital markets, since a volatile international financial environment, fragile national banking systems and weak domestic financial institutions have often hindered investment in many countries.

This presents a number of challenges for financial policy in developing and transition economies: first, they need to protect their national financial systems against the vagaries of international finance; second, policymakers should draw the right lessons from past financial crises, in particular, that an unregulated financial sector tends to generate economic instability and resource misallocation; and third, they should aim to make their domestic financial systems, especially their banking systems, more supportive of investment in real productive capacity.

Atypical behaviour of international capital flows since 2008

Over the past three decades emerging market economies experienced frequent waves of international capital flows. Such waves typically started when growth was slow, liquidity was abundant and interest rates were low in the developed countries. This made emerging markets seem attractive destinations for private international capital flows. However, those waves ebbed when interest rates rose in the developed countries or when financial market participants deemed external deficits or the foreign indebtedness of the destination countries to have become unsustainable.

At present, monetary and financial conditions in major developed countries resemble those that in the past proved to be conducive to surges of capital flows to emerging market economies. In developed countries, interest rates have fallen to almost zero in an effort to tackle both the protracted crisis and the difficulties in their financial sectors. Their central banks have also injected large amounts of liquidity into the financial system. However, these measures have not succeeded in inducing banks to increase their lending to the private sector. Moreover, there are fairly large interest rate differentials in favour of emerging markets. So far, these conditions have not resulted in strong and sustained capital outflows from developed to developing countries; rather, where such outflows have occurred, they have been very volatile.

Prior to the eruption of the financial crisis, there were large capital flows from developed countries to emerging market economies, which ended abruptly in 2008. But, distinct from past episodes, this "sudden stop" was not triggered either by an increase in interest rates in the developed countries, or by excessive current account deficits or debt servicing problems in the emerging market economies. Rather, they appear to have been motivated by uncertainty about the possible repercussions of the financial crisis on the latter economies, and attempts by international investors to minimize their overall risk exposure. When private capital flows to emerging market economies surged again in 2010 and 2011, this too was atypical, because sudden stops are usually followed by a prolonged period of stagnation of inflows or even outflows from these countries. Faced with low profit-making opportunities in the major financial centres, it may have been expected that investors would be encouraged by the rapid resumption of GDP growth in the emerging market economies and the perception that their financial systems were more stable than those of developed countries. However, newly worsening prospects in developed countries in the second half of 2011, including higher perceived risks related to the sovereign debt of some of them, again curtailed capital flows towards the emerging market economies as investors sought to reduce their overall portfolio risks.

The vagaries of international finance remain a threat

Emerging market economies have been relatively resilient in the face of the destabilizing effects of the latest waves of capital flows on their national financial systems. This observation does not mean, however, that they have become structurally less vulnerable. Rather, it shows the merits of their policy reorientation with respect to external finance since the turn of the millennium. An increasing number of developing-country governments have adopted a more cautious attitude towards large capital inflows. Some of them were able to prevent or at least mitigate currency appreciation through intervention in the foreign exchange market, along with associated reserve accumulation. Others also resorted to capital controls. Another factor explaining how several of them were able to cope with the adverse financial events was their lower levels of external debt and its more favourable currency composition compared with earlier episodes.

However, since global financial assets amount to more than three times the value of global output, even minor portfolio adjustments oriented towards developing countries can lead to an increase in such flows at a rate that has the potential to destabilize the economies of these countries in the future. In the current situation of high uncertainty, investor sentiment, rather than macroeconomic fundamentals, is tending to drive capital movements, as has frequently been the case in the past. But there is also uncertainty with regard to the fundamentals. On the one hand, an extended period of low interest rates in the developed countries, combined with stronger growth and a tendency towards higher interest rates in emerging market economies could lead to a new surge of capital flows to the latter. On the other hand, a tightening of monetary policy in the major reserve currency countries could cause a drastic reduction or reversal of net private capital flows from them.

Reducing exposure to international financial markets

As long as the international community fails to agree on fundamental reforms of the international financial and monetary system, developing and transition economies need to design national strategies and, where possible, regional strategies, aimed at reducing their vulnerability to global financial shocks. In the current situation, this means that these economies need to exercise extreme caution towards cross-border capital flows, bearing in mind that the seeds of a future crisis are sown in the phase of euphoria, when a wave of financial inflows is in the making.

For many years, the prevalent view considered almost any kind of foreign capital flows to developing countries as beneficial. This view was based on the assumption that "foreign savings" would complement the national savings of the recipient countries and lead to higher rates of investment there. However, both theoretical considerations and empirical evidence show that even huge capital inflows can be accompanied by stagnating investment rates, because the link between capital inflows and the financing of new fixed investment tends to be very weak. For the same reason, substantial increases in fixed investment can be accompanied by strong capital outflows.

External financing of developing and transition economies has repeatedly proved to be a double-edged sword. On the one hand, it can be a way of alleviating balance-of-payments constraints on growth and investment. On the other hand, a large proportion of foreign capital inflows has often been directed to private banks for financing consumption or speculative financial investments that have generated asset price bubbles. Moreover, when capital inflows are not used for financing imports of goods and services, they often lead to a strong currency appreciation that makes domestic industries less price competitive in international markets. Financial inflows and outflows, and their instability, have often led to lending booms and busts, inflationary pressures and the build-up of foreign liabilities without contributing to an economy's capacity to grow and service such obligations. A drying up or reversal of inflows exerts pressure on the balance of payments and on the financing of both the private and public sectors. A reliance on private capital inflows has therefore tended to increase macroeconomic and financial instability and hamper, rather than support, long-term growth. Moreover, private capital flows have been mostly procyclical. For both these reasons, they have played a major role in balance-of-payments and financial crises in the developing world over the last three decades.

Greater reliance on domestic capital markets for the financing of government expenditure helps reduce vulnerability to credit crunches and exchange-rate instability. Debt denominated in local currency also allows monetary authorities to counter external shocks or growing trade deficits with a devaluation of the nominal exchange rate without increasing the domestic currency value of that debt. Finally, debt denominated in local currency allows the government a last-resort option of using debt monetization in a time of crisis, thereby reducing the insolvency risk and lowering the risk premium on the debt. On the other hand, the amount and direction of foreign capital flows are largely determined by factors that are often unrelated to the investment and trade-financing needs of the receiving countries and are beyond the control of their authorities.

Protective measures against external disturbances

Pragmatic exchange-rate management aimed at preventing currency overvaluation can limit the destabilizing effects of speculative capital flows. In addition, interest rate differentials, which often attract carry-trade speculation, can be limited when inflation is kept under control. This can be done not primarily by means of a restrictive monetary policy and high policy interest rates, but with the help of other instruments, such as an incomes policy that aims at keeping average wage increases in line with, and not exceeding, productivity growth and the inflation target of the central bank.

Destabilizing effects of capital flows can also be prevented, or at least mitigated, by resorting to capital controls, which are permitted under the International Monetary Fund's (IMF) Articles of Agreement, and for which there is extensive experience in both developed and developing countries. While the IMF has recently recognized that capital controls are legitimate instruments, it recommends resorting to them only in situations when a balance-of-payments crisis is already evident, and after all other measures (e.g. monetary and fiscal adjustment) have failed. The problem with such an approach is that it does not recognize the macroprudential role that control of capital inflows can play in preventing such a crisis from occurring in the first place.

Reconsidering regulation of the financial system

The hypothesis that deregulated financial markets are efficient because actors in these markets possess all the information necessary to anticipate future outcomes, and will use this information rationally so that the financial system can regulate itself, has been refuted by the present crisis. This should prompt policymakers in developing and transition economies to draw their own lessons for shaping their countries' financial systems.

Certain regulatory measures that are now envisaged in developed countries may also be relevant and important to developing countries. Such measures include, in particular, those aimed at improving the governance of banks, reducing incentives for highly risky behaviour of market participants, and resolution mechanisms allowing authorities to wind down bad banks and recapitalize institutions through public ownership. The separation of commercial retail banking (receiving deposits, delivering loans and managing payments) from risky investment banking activities is a principle that should also guide bank regulations in developing countries. This would help prevent individual financial institutions from growing excessively large and assuming such a diversity of activities that their performance becomes systemically important. Such measures may be easier to implement in countries where financial systems are still in the process of taking shape, and where the financial sector is still relatively small but bound to expand as their economies grow.

International standards and rules relating to capital requirements and liquidity under the Basel accords, which aim at reducing the risk of bank failure and the need for public bailouts by containing excessive leveraging, may not always be suited to the specific circumstances and requirements of developing countries. Relatively small banks in developing countries may require different rules than large, internationally operating banks in developed countries. But it also needs to be recognized that in many of the developing countries which have experienced serious banking crises since the 1980s, capital and liquidity requirements were much higher than those prescribed by the Basel rules, and that the application of those rules led to a restriction of bank lending, especially to small and medium-sized enterprises (SMEs). These countries should therefore be allowed to adapt prudential rules to their specific situation and needs.

In any case, financial regulation should be conceived in such a way that it is not inimical to growth. In particular, it should encourage long-term bank lending to finance productive investment and discourage lending for unproductive and speculative purposes. This is important because of the interdependence between financial stability and growth: financial stability supports growth because it reduces the uncertainty that is inevitably involved in any financing operation, while stable growth supports financial stability because it reduces the risk of loans becoming non-performing.

Monetary versus financial stability

The current experience in major developed countries shows that massive money creation by central banks has had little, if any, effect on the expansion of credit to the private sector. This suggests that, contrary to the monetarist approach, policymakers should focus more on the volume of bank credit than on money creation for promoting financial stability. Moreover, the purposes for which bank credit is used have an impact on the level and composition of aggregate demand. In providing credit, banks can play a key role in ensuring financial stability. They have to discriminate between good and bad projects, and reliable and unreliable borrowers, instead of behaving like passive intermediaries, or losing interest in the economic performance of their borrowers after securitizing their debt and transferring the risk to another entity.

The experience of the developed countries in the past few years has shown that monetary stability, in the sense of consumer price stability, can coexist with considerable financial instability. In the euro zone, the elimination of exchange rate risk and low inflation even served to generate financial instability: it favoured large capital flows from banks in the core countries of the zone to countries in the periphery and the virtual elimination of interest rate differentials between these two sets of countries. However, those capital flows were not used for spurring competitiveness and production capacities, but rather for feeding bubbles and the financing of current account deficits. This amplified intraregional disparities, instead of reducing them, and generated the crisis in the deficit countries within the common currency area. This outcome is similar to that of many developing and transition economies in previous decades, particularly in Latin America and South-East Asia, where monetary stability based on a fixed nominal exchange rate led to financial crises.

Fostering the financing of domestic investment

The financial sector can play a key role in accelerating economic growth through the financing of fixed capital formation that boosts production and generates employment. Thus, in order to support development strategies that promote domestic demand as a driver of growth, it is essential for developing countries to strengthen their financial systems.

Retained profits constitute the most important source for the financing of investment in real productive capacity. At the same time, rising demand is decisive for helping to meet expectations of profitability of additional investment in productive capacity, and that profitability in turn finances private investment, resulting in a strong profit-investment nexus. In addition, bank credit is essential, although its relative importance depends on country-specific circumstances. Bank financing enables firms to accelerate their capital formation over and above what is possible from retained profits. Therefore, growth dynamics depend critically on the availability of sufficient amounts of bank credit at a cost that is commensurate with the expected profitability of investment projects. The banking system as a whole can provide investment credit without the prior existence of a corresponding amount of financial savings. The central bank can support the creation of such credit through the provision of adequate liquidity to the banking system and by keeping the policy interest rate as low as possible.

Beyond that, government intervention may facilitate access to credit, especially for sectors and firms engaged in activities that are of strategic importance for the structural transformation and growth of the economy. One possibility may be the provision of interest subsidies for the financing of investment in areas of activity that are considered to be of strategic importance; another is influencing the behaviour of the banking system in the way it allocates credit.

The banking system and credit orientation

Public intervention in the provision of bank credit will be especially important in developing countries that are aiming at strengthening domestic forces of growth, since long-term loans for investment and innovation, as well as loans to micro, small and medium-sized enterprises are extremely scarce even in good times. Commercial banks in developing countries often prefer to grant short-term personal loans or to buy government securities, because they consider the risks associated with maturity transformation (i.e. providing long-term credits matched by short-term deposits) to be too high.

A revised regulatory framework could include elements that favour a different allocation of bank assets and credit portfolios. Banks could be encouraged, or obliged, to undertake a more reasonable degree of maturity transformation than in the past. Public guarantees for commercial bank credit for the financing of private investment projects, may encourage private commercial banks to provide more lending for such purposes. Such arrangements would reduce the credit default risk, and hence also the risk premium on long-term investment loans. The resulting lower interest cost for investors would further reduce the probability of loan losses and thus the likelihood of requiring governments to cover such losses under a guarantee scheme.

Similarly, within the framework of a comprehensive industrial policy, co-financing by private banks, which take a microeconomic perspective, and public financial institutions that act in the interest of society as a whole, could help to ensure that investment projects are both commercially viable and support a strategy of structural change in the economy at large.

There are many examples where credit policy has been implemented with the help of various public, semi-public and cooperative specialized institutions which have financed agricultural and industrial investment by SMEs at preferential rates. National development banks may provide financial services that private financial institutions are unable or unwilling to provide to the extent desired. Such banks played an important countercyclical role during the current crisis when they increased lending just as many private banks were scaling back theirs. In addition, smaller, more specialized sources of finance also have an important role to play in the overall dynamics of the development process.

Changing views about the role of central banks

Strengthening the supportive role of the banking system may also require reviewing the mandate of central banks, and even reconsidering the principle of central bank independence. Indeed, the traditional role of central banks only as defenders of price stability may be too narrow when the requirements of development and the need to stabilize the financial sector are taken into account.

Their use of monetary policy as the sole instrument for fighting inflation has often led to high real interest rates that discouraged private domestic investment and attracted foreign capital inflows of a speculative nature. This tended to lead to currency overvaluation with a consequent decrease in exports, and thus a lowering of demand expectations of domestic producers. An incomes policy based on productivity-related wage growth would facilitate the conduct of monetary policy, because it would exclude, or at least significantly reduce, the risk of inflation generated by rising unit labour costs. This would facilitate the task of the central banks to gear their monetary policy more to the creation of favourable financing conditions for domestic investment.

The need for reconsidering the role of central banks has never been more evident than during the latest financial crisis. Central bank independence did not prevent this crisis, but when it erupted these banks had to take "unconventional" measures to stabilize financial markets in the interests of the economy as a whole, rather than simply maintaining price stability. The concerted action of central banks and governments was indispensable in tackling the effects of the crisis, including by bailing out institutions that were considered "too big to fail". This experience has led to a recognition that central banks can make a major contribution to the stability of financial markets and the banking system.

A further step would be to recognize that central banks can play an active role in the implementation of a growth and development strategy. Since financial stability depends on the performance of the real sector of the economy, bolstering economic growth should also be considered a major responsibility of these institutions. They can support maturity transformation in the banking system through their role as lenders of last resort and their provision of deposit insurance. The latter reduces the risk of a sudden withdrawal of deposits, which would cause liquidity constraints for banks, while the former could respond to liquidity shortages, should they occur. But there are also numerous examples from both developed and developing countries of central bank involvement in directing credit, through, for example, direct financing of non-financial firms, selective refinancing of commercial loans at preferential rates, or exempting certain types of bank lending from quantitative credit ceilings.

These schemes played a pivotal role in the rapid industrialization of many countries. However, they did not always deliver the expected outcomes. For example, in several countries where public banks sometimes provided credit to other public entities for purposes that were not related to productive investment, non-performing loans burdened their balance sheets and undermined their lending capacities. But it also needs to be recognized that it was the privatization of public banks and the deregulation of financial systems that paved the way to major financial crises in Latin America and in East and South-East Asia. In light of these different experiences, developing countries need to carefully weigh the pros and cons of government involvement in credit allocation when shaping or reforming their domestic financial sectors. They should also implement well-designed governance and control mechanisms for both public and private financial institutions in order to ensure that these institutions operate in the interests of the economy and society as a whole.

Supachai Panitchpakdi
Secretary-General of UNCTAD

CURRENT TRENDS AND CHALLENGES IN THE WORLD ECONOMY

A. Recent trends in the world economy

1. Global growth

The global economy is still struggling to return to a strong and sustained growth path. World output, which grew at a rate of 2.2 per cent in 2012, is forecast to grow at a similar rate in 2013. Developed countries will continue to lag behind the world average, with a likely 1 per cent increase in gross domestic product (GDP), due to a slight deceleration in the United States and a continuing recession in the euro area. Developing and transition economies should grow by about 4.7 per cent and 2.7 per cent respectively (table 1.1). Even though these growth rates are significantly higher than those of developed countries, they remain well below their pre-crisis levels. Furthermore, they confirm the pace of deceleration that started in 2012.

Economic activity in many developed countries and a number of emerging market economies is still suffering from the impacts of the financial and economic crisis that started in 2008 and the persistence of domestic and international imbalances that led to it. However, continuing weak growth in several countries may also be partly due to their current macroeconomic policy stance.

Among *developed economies*, growth in the European Union (EU) is expected to shrink for the second consecutive year, with a particularly severe economic contraction in the euro area. Private demand remains subdued, especially in the euro-zone periphery countries (Greece, Ireland, Italy, Portugal and Spain), due to high unemployment, wage compression, low consumer confidence and the still incomplete process of balance sheet consolidation. Given the ongoing process of deleveraging, expansionary monetary policies have failed to increase the supply of credit for productive activities. In this context, continued fiscal tightening makes a return to a higher growth trajectory highly unlikely, as it adds a deflationary impulse to already weak private demand. While foreign trade (mainly through the reduction of imports) contributed to growth in the euro area, this was more than offset by the negative effect of contracting domestic demand, which even the surplus countries have been reluctant to stimulate. This perpetuates disequilibrium within the euro zone and reduces the scope for an export-led recovery of other countries in the zone. Hence, despite the fact that the tensions in the financial markets of the euro area have receded following intervention by the European Central Bank (ECB), prospects for a resumption of growth

Table 1.1

WORLD OUTPUT GROWTH, 2005–2013

(Annual percentage change)

Region/country	2005	2006	2007	2008	2009	2010	2011	2012	2013[a]
World	**3.5**	**4.1**	**4.0**	**1.5**	**-2.2**	**4.1**	**2.8**	**2.2**	**2.1**
Developed countries	**2.4**	**2.8**	**2.6**	**0.0**	**-3.8**	**2.6**	**1.5**	**1.2**	**1.0**
of which:									
Japan	1.3	1.7	2.2	-1.0	-5.5	4.7	-0.6	1.9	1.9
United States	3.1	2.7	1.9	-0.3	-3.1	2.4	1.8	2.2	1.7
European Union (EU-27)	2.1	3.3	3.2	0.3	-4.3	2.1	1.6	-0.3	-0.2
of which:									
Euro area	1.7	3.3	3.0	0.4	-4.4	2.0	1.5	-0.6	-0.7
France	1.8	2.5	2.3	-0.1	-3.1	1.7	2.0	0.0	-0.2
Germany	0.7	3.7	3.3	1.1	-5.1	4.2	3.0	0.7	0.3
Italy	0.9	2.2	1.7	-1.2	-5.5	1.7	0.4	-2.4	-1.8
United Kingdom	2.8	2.6	3.6	-1.0	-4.0	1.8	0.9	0.2	1.1
South-East Europe and CIS	**6.5**	**8.3**	**8.6**	**5.2**	**-6.6**	**4.5**	**4.5**	**3.0**	**2.7**
South-East Europe[b]	4.7	4.8	5.5	3.7	-4.3	0.0	1.1	-1.4	0.3
CIS	6.7	8.7	8.9	5.3	-6.8	4.9	4.8	3.4	2.9
of which:									
Russian Federation	6.4	8.2	8.5	5.2	-7.8	4.5	4.3	3.4	2.5
Developing countries	**6.8**	**7.6**	**7.9**	**5.3**	**2.4**	**7.9**	**5.9**	**4.6**	**4.7**
Africa	5.8	5.9	6.2	5.2	2.8	4.9	1.0	5.4	4.0
North Africa, excl. Sudan	5.1	5.4	4.7	4.6	3.2	4.1	-6.1	7.8	3.6
Sub-Saharan Africa, excl. South Africa	6.7	6.5	7.7	6.6	4.9	6.4	4.8	5.3	5.4
South Africa	5.3	5.6	5.5	3.6	-1.5	3.1	3.5	2.5	1.7
Latin America and the Caribbean	4.5	5.6	5.6	4.0	-1.9	5.9	4.3	3.0	3.1
Caribbean	7.4	9.4	5.8	3.1	-0.1	2.6	2.4	2.5	2.7
Central America, excl. Mexico	4.8	6.4	7.0	4.1	-0.2	4.1	5.2	5.0	4.1
Mexico	3.2	5.2	3.3	1.2	-6.0	5.5	4.0	3.9	2.8
South America	5.0	5.5	6.6	5.5	-0.2	6.4	4.6	2.5	3.2
of which:									
Brazil	3.2	4.0	6.1	5.2	-0.3	7.5	2.7	0.9	2.5
Asia	7.8	8.6	9.0	5.8	3.9	8.9	7.1	5.0	5.2
East Asia	8.6	9.9	11.0	6.9	5.9	9.5	7.7	6.0	6.1
of which:									
China	11.3	12.7	14.2	9.6	9.2	10.4	9.3	7.8	7.6
South Asia	8.0	8.3	8.9	5.2	4.7	9.4	6.6	3.0	4.3
of which:									
India	9.0	9.4	10.1	6.2	5.0	11.2	7.7	3.8	5.2
South-East Asia	5.8	6.1	6.6	4.3	1.2	8.0	4.5	5.4	4.7
West Asia	6.8	7.0	4.6	3.8	-1.7	7.0	7.1	3.2	3.5
Oceania	3.4	2.9	3.5	2.7	2.3	3.6	4.3	4.1	2.7

Source: UNCTAD secretariat calculations, based on United Nations, Department of Economic and Social Affairs (UN-DESA), *National Accounts Main Aggregates* database, and *World Economic Situation and Prospects (WESP): Update as of mid-2013;* ECLAC, 2013; ESCAP, 2013; *OECD,* 2013; IMF, *World Economic Outlook,* April 2013; Economist Intelligence Unit, *EIU CountryData* database; JP Morgan, *Global Data Watch*; and national sources.

Note: Calculations for country aggregates are based on GDP at constant 2005 dollars. CIS includes Georgia.

   a Forecasts.

   b Albania, Bosnia and Herzegovina, Croatia, Montenegro, Serbia and the former Yugoslav Republic of Macedonia.

of consumption and investment in these countries remain grim.

Japan is bucking the current austerity trend of other developed economies by providing a strong fiscal stimulus in conjunction with monetary policy expansion with the aim of reviving economic growth and curbing deflationary trends. An increase of government spending on infrastructure and social services, including health care and education, has been announced, to be accompanied by efforts to boost demand and structural policies oriented towards innovation and investment. To complement these efforts, in April 2013 the Bank of Japan announced that it will increase its purchase of government bonds and other assets by 50 trillion yen per year (equivalent to 10 per cent of Japan's GDP) in order to achieve an inflation target of 2 per cent. Overall, these measures could help maintain Japan's GDP growth at close to 2 per cent in 2013.

The United States is expected to grow at 1.7 per cent, compared with 2.2 per cent in 2012, due to a new configuration of factors. Partly owing to significant progress made in the consolidation of its banking sector, private domestic demand has begun to recover. The pace of job creation in the private sector has enabled a gradual fall in the unemployment rate. On the other hand, cuts in federal government spending, enacted in March 2013, and budget constraints faced by several State and municipal governments are a strong drag on economic growth. Since the net outcome of these opposing tendencies is unclear, there is also considerable uncertainty about whether the expansionary monetary policy stance will be maintained.

By contrast, *developing countries* continue to be the main drivers of growth, contributing to about two thirds of global growth in 2013. In many of them, growth has been driven more by domestic demand than by exports, as external demand, particularly from developed economies, has remained weak. Developing countries are expected to grow at the rate of 4.5–5 per cent in 2013, similar to 2012. This would result from two distinctive patterns. On the one hand, growth in some large developing economies, such as Argentina, Brazil, India and Turkey, which was subdued in 2012, is forecast to accelerate. On the other hand, several other developing economies seem unlikely to be able to maintain their previous year's growth rates. Their expected growth deceleration

partly reflects the accumulated effect of continuing sluggishness in developed economies and lower prices for primary commodity exports, but also the decreasing policy stimuli which were relatively weak anyhow. The combination of these factors may also affect China's growth rate, which is expected to slow down moderately from 7.8 per cent in 2012 to about 7.6 in 2013. Even though this would be only a mild deceleration, it is likely to disappoint many of China's trading partners.

Among the developing regions, *East, South* and *South-East Asia* are expected to experience the highest growth rates in 2013, of 6.1 per cent, 4.3 per cent and 4.7 per cent, respectively. In most of these countries, growth is being driven essentially by domestic demand. In China, the contribution of net exports to GDP growth was negligible, while fixed investment and private consumption, as a result of faster wage growth, continued to drive output expansion. Encouraged by various incomes policy measures, domestic private demand is also support-ing output growth in a number of other countries in the region, such as India, Indonesia, the Philippines and Thailand (ESCAP, 2013). In addition, along with GDP growth, credit to the private sector has tended to rise, further supporting demand.

Economic growth in *West Asia* slowed down dramatically, from 7.1 per cent in 2011 to 3.2 per cent in 2012, a level that is expected to be main-tained in 2013. Weaker external demand, especially from Europe, affected the entire region, but most prominently Turkey, which saw its growth rate fall sharply from around 9 per cent in 2010 and 2011 to 2.2 per cent in 2012, but it is expected to accelerate towards 3.3 per cent in 2013. The Gulf Cooperation Council (GCC) countries maintained large public spending programmes to bolster domestic demand and growth, despite scaling back their oil production during the last quarter of 2012 to support oil prices. Finally, the civil war in the Syrian Arab Republic not only greatly affected that country but continued to heighten perceptions of risk with regard to neighbour-ing countries, which resulted in subdued investment, tourism and trade in Jordan and Lebanon.

Growth in *Africa* is expected to slow down in 2013, owing to weaker performance in North Africa, where political instability in some countries has been mirrored in recent years by strong fluctua-tions in growth. In sub-Saharan Africa (excluding

South Africa), GDP growth is expected to remain stable in 2013, at above 5 per cent. The main growth drivers include high earnings from exports of primary commodities and energy as well as tourism, and relatively strong growth of public and private investment in some countries. Angola, Côte d'Ivoire, the Democratic Republic of the Congo, Ethiopia, Gambia, Ghana, Liberia, Rwanda, Sierra Leone and the United Republic of Tanzania are likely to see rapid growth bolstered by strong investments, especially in infrastructure, telecommunications, energy and the extractive industries. On the other hand, growth in several middle-income countries of Africa is forecast to decelerate further in 2013, in particular in countries that have close trade ties with Europe, including South Africa. Moreover, several least developed countries (LDCs) of West Africa which depend on exports of single commodities remain vulnerable to drastic swings in demand for those commodities.

Growth is set to remain relatively stable in *Latin America and the Caribbean*, at around 3 per cent, on average, as a slowdown in some countries, including Mexico, is likely to be offset by faster growth in Argentina and Brazil. In 2012 and the first months of 2013, regional growth has been driven mostly by domestic demand based on moderate but consistent increases in public and private consumption and investment (ECLAC, 2013). Governments generally turned to more supportive fiscal and monetary policies in a context of low fiscal deficits and low inflation for the region as a whole. Growth of exports and imports fell sharply in 2012, which resulted in a slight increase in the region's current account deficit. Domestic demand will continue to support growth in 2013 based on rising real wages and employment, as well as an expansion of bank credit. In addition, a recovery of agriculture and investment should contribute to better economic performances in Argentina and Brazil after weak growth in 2012. On the other hand, owing to sluggish international demand and lower export prices of oil and mining products (although they remain at historically high levels) a slowdown is expected in the Bolivarian Republic of Venezuela, Chile, Ecuador, Mexico and Peru.

There has been a downward trend in the economic performance of the *transition economies* since 2012. The impact of the continuing crisis in much of Western Europe caused the economies of South-Eastern Europe to fall into recession in 2012, and they will barely remain afloat in 2013. The members of the Commonwealth of Independent State (CIS) maintained a growth rate of over 3 per cent in 2012 based on sustained domestic demand, but this is expected to slow down slightly in 2013. The region's economic prospects remain closely linked to the performance of the economy of the Russian Federation and to commodity price developments, particularly in oil and natural gas.

The continuing expansion of developing economies as a group (in particular the largest economy among them, China) has led to their gaining increasing weight in the world economy, which suggests the possible emergence of a new pattern of global growth. While developed countries remain the main export markets for developing countries as a group, the share of the latter's contribution to growth in the world economy has risen from 28 per cent in the 1990s to about 40 per cent in the period 2003–2007, and close to 75 per cent since 2008. However, more recently, growth in these economies has decelerated. They may continue to grow at a relatively fast pace if they are able to strengthen domestic demand and if they can rely more on each other for the expansion of aggregate demand through greater South-South trade. However, even if they achieve more rapid growth by adopting such a strategy, and increase their imports from developed countries, this will not be sufficient to lift developed countries out of their growth slump.

2.   *International trade*

(a)   *Goods*

International trade in goods has not returned to the rapid growth rate of the years preceding the crisis. On the contrary, it decelerated further in 2012, and while the outlook for world trade remains uncertain, the first signs in 2013 do not point to an expansion. After a sharp fall in 2008–2009 and a quick recovery in 2010, the volume of trade in goods grew by only 5.3 per cent in 2011 and by 1.7 per cent in 2012. This slower rate of expansion occurred in developed, developing and transition economies alike (table 1.2).

Sluggish economic activity in developed countries, particularly in Europe, accounted for most of this very significant slowdown. In 2012, EU imports

Table 1.2

EXPORT AND IMPORT VOLUMES OF GOODS, SELECTED REGIONS AND COUNTRIES, 2009–2012

(Annual percentage change)

Region/country	Volume of exports				Volume of imports			
	2009	2010	2011	2012	2009	2010	2011	2012
World	**-13.3**	**13.9**	**5.2**	**1.8**	**-13.6**	**13.8**	**5.3**	**1.6**
Developed countries	**-15.5**	**13.0**	**4.9**	**0.4**	**-14.6**	**10.8**	**3.4**	**-0.5**
of which:								
Japan	-24.8	27.5	-0.6	-1.0	-12.2	10.1	4.2	3.7
United States	-14.0	15.4	7.2	4.1	-16.4	14.8	3.8	2.8
European Union	-14.9	11.6	5.5	-0.2	-14.5	9.6	2.8	-2.8
Transition economies	**-14.4**	**11.3**	**4.2**	**1.0**	**-28.2**	**15.9**	**15.7**	**3.9**
of which:								
CIS	-13.9	11.4	4.2	1.3	-29.1	19.7	17.4	5.0
Developing countries	**-9.7**	**16.0**	**6.0**	**3.6**	**-10.2**	**18.8**	**7.4**	**4.5**
Africa	-9.5	8.8	-8.3	5.7	-6.2	8.4	2.8	8.0
Sub-Saharan Africa	-7.8	9.6	-0.7	0.1	-9.0	9.7	7.9	4.2
Latin America and the Caribbean	-7.4	8.3	4.6	2.2	-17.9	22.5	10.8	2.5
East Asia	-10.9	24.1	10.4	5.2	-5.3	22.7	7.4	4.3
of which:								
China	-14.1	29.1	13.0	7.2	-1.1	25.4	10.3	5.9
South Asia	-6.1	10.0	8.8	-10.2	-5.5	14.0	6.0	2.0
of which:								
India	-6.8	14.0	14.2	-2.5	-0.9	13.8	9.1	5.8
South-East Asia	-10.0	18.6	4.4	2.2	-15.8	22.0	6.7	6.0
West Asia	-4.8	5.7	6.5	6.9	-14.2	8.4	8.1	5.8

Source: UNCTAD secretariat calculations, based on *UNCTADstat*.

of goods shrank by 2.8 per cent in volume and by 5 per cent in value. Extremely weak intra-EU trade was responsible for almost 90 per cent of the decline in Europe's exports in 2012. However, trade performance was also weak in other developed countries. In Japan, exports have not yet recovered from their sharp fall caused by the earthquake of 2011,[1] while the volume of its imports has continued to grow at a moderate pace. Among the other major developed countries, only the United States maintained a positive growth rate of both exports and imports, although that of its exports appears to be decelerating further in 2013. This signals a mounting headwind for the world's largest economy, where exports initially appeared to spur a recovery.

Trade growth also decelerated considerably in developing and transition economies in 2012, though the figures remained positive for most countries. In the transition economies, the rate of growth of the volume of exports was 1 per cent in 2012, down from 4.2 per cent in 2011, and that of imports was

3.9 per cent in 2012, down from 15.7 per cent in 2011. Likewise, in developing countries the rate of growth of exports fell from 6 per cent in 2011 to 3.6 per cent in 2011, and that of imports from 7.4 per cent in 2011 to 4.5 per cent in 2012.

At the subregional level, two notable exceptions stand out from this general pattern of developing-country trade. The first is the recovery of trade in some North African economies from low levels in 2011, which contributed to higher trade growth in Africa as a whole. The second is the absolute decline in the volume of exports from South Asia, explained mainly by a reduction of oil exports from the Islamic Republic of Iran,[2] though India's export volumes also fell, by 2.5 per cent. This was largely due to the economic slowdown in Europe, which accounts for almost one fifth of India's total exports, as well as weak exports to China.

An examination of longer time periods puts into perspective the structural changes associated with the slowdown of trade. By the end of 2012, the volume of global trade was only 7.5 per cent above its 2007 level. The average annual growth rate during the period 2008–2012 was about 1.4 per cent – well below the 7.4 per cent registered during the period 2003–2007.

With regard to China, the powerhouse of global trade in recent years, the slowdown is even more striking. The world's largest exporter experienced a sharp deceleration of its exports as a consequence of the 2008–2009 economic crisis, largely due to its reliance on demand from developed countries. The rate of growth of China's exports (by volume) decelerated to 13 per cent in 2011 and to 7.2 per cent in 2012, in sharp contrast to their massive growth rate of 27 per cent during the period 2002–2007 following China's accession to the World Trade Organization (WTO). This was the first time since the East Asian crisis in the late 1990s that China's export growth was slower than that of its GDP. Concomitantly, in 2012, the growth of China's imports decelerated to 5.9 per cent by volume and to 4.3 per cent by value, from 19 per cent and 26 per cent, respectively, between 2002 and 2007. As a result, only regions exporting a large proportion of primary commodities (i.e. Africa, West Asia and, to a lesser extent, Latin America) saw a significant increase in their exports to China in 2012, both by volume and value.

Several exporters of manufactures in Asia registered a sizeable slowdown of growth in their external trade. For example, between 2002 and 2007, the volume of exports of the Republic of Korea, Thailand and Malaysia increased by an annual average of 14 per cent, 10 per cent and 9 per cent, respectively; in 2012, those rates fell to 1.5 per cent in the Republic of Korea, 2.5 per cent in Thailand and 0.5 per cent in Malaysia. This was the result not only of lower import demand from Europe, but also of slower growth in some developing regions, in particular East Asia.

The crisis of 2008–2009 altered trade patterns in both developed and developing countries. On the one hand, imports and exports (by volume) of developed regions have remained below their pre-crisis levels, with the exception of the United States where exports have exceeded their previous peak of August 2008. On the other hand, exports from the group of emerging market economies were 22 per cent above their pre-crisis peaks, while the corresponding figure for their imports was 26 per cent higher. However, the pace of growth of trade of these economies has

slowed down significantly: during the pre-crisis years, between 2002 and 2007, their export volume grew at an average annual rate of 11.3 per cent, but fell to only 3.5 per cent between January 2011 and April 2013. Growth in the volume of their imports also slowed down, from 12.4 per cent to 5.5 per cent over the same period (chart 1.1).

Available data for the first half of 2013 tend to confirm that the recent slowdown persists. Data from the CPB Netherlands Bureau for Economic Policy Analysis (CPB) show that the volume of international trade grew by a year-on-year average of less than 2 per cent in the first five months of 2013. Among the developed countries exports and imports virtually stagnated in the United States and fell in the EU and Japan. Exports from emerging economies decelerated during the same period, with the exception of those from the emerging Asian economies, which increased by 6.2 per cent in the first months of 2013.[3]

Overall, this general downward trend in international trade highlights the vulnerabilities developing countries continue to face at a time of lacklustre growth in developed countries. It is also indicative of a probably less favourable external trade environment over the next few years, which points to the need for a gradual shift from the reliance on external sources of growth towards a greater emphasis on domestic sources.

(b) Services

Similar to merchandise trade, world trade in commercial services grew by 1–2 per cent in 2012, according to preliminary estimates by UNCTAD/WTO. Within this broad category, international tourism grew by 4 per cent in 2012, both in terms of receipts in real terms (i.e. adjusting for exchange rate fluctuations and inflation) and the number of arrivals. Tourism roughly accounts for 30 per cent of world exports of services and for 6 per cent of overall exports of goods and services. It also ranks fifth as a worldwide export category after fuels, chemicals, food and automotive products, and even first in many developing countries. The Americas recorded the largest increase in receipts from tourism (7 per cent), followed by Asia and the Pacific (6 per cent), Africa (5 per cent) and Europe (2 per cent). By contrast, receipts in West Asia were again down by 2 per cent (World Tourism Organization, 2013). Tourist receipts

Chart 1.1

WORLD TRADE BY VOLUME, JANUARY 2004–APRIL 2013

(Index numbers, 2005 = 100)

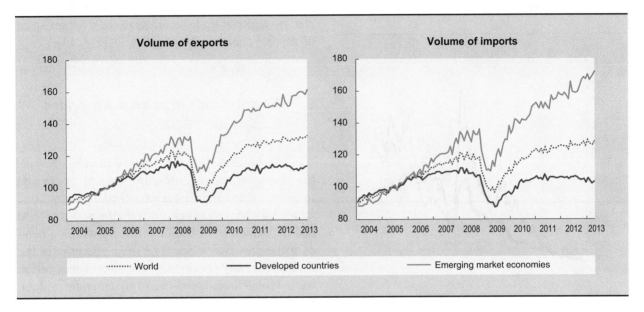

Source: UNCTAD secretariat calculations, based on CPB Netherlands Bureau of Economic Policy Analysis, *World Trade* database.
Note: Emerging market economies excludes Central and Eastern Europe.

of the top 10 destinations, which include 7 developed economies together with China, Hong Kong (China) and Macao (China), remained virtually unchanged in 2012, whereas several emerging market destinations, including India, South Africa, Thailand, Ukraine and Viet Nam registered double-digit growth figures.

The growth of international transport services – the second largest category of commercial services – while positive, was hindered by a number of downside factors, including the continued recession in the euro area, fragile recovery in the United States, and the relative deceleration and rebalancing of growth of the Chinese economy. Preliminary data indicate that world seaborne trade – a measure of demand for shipping, port and logistics services – climbed by 4.3 per cent in 2012.

In particular, dry bulk trade expanded by 6.7 per cent in 2012, in line with the long-term trend, driven mainly by two main commodities – iron ore and coal. Trade in iron ore rose by 5.4 per cent, though this was considered the slowest increase in more than a decade. A strong increase in China's demand was met by exports from Australia and, to a lesser extent, by long-haul shipments from Brazil. Meanwhile,

imports from India, previously China's third largest supplier, dropped by over 50 per cent as a result of rising export taxes on iron ore as well as mining and export bans. Coal shipments increased significantly (12.3 per cent) driven by strong demand for steam coal (14.2 per cent) stemming from the recovery in European imports and rapidly growing imports by China. In the United States, greater use of domestically produced shale gas resulted in an increase in its coal exports, which in turn lowered international coal prices and drove up global demand for coal.

Developments in tanker trade, which accounts for one third of global seaborne trade, mirrored the behaviour of global oil demand. In 2012, demand for crude oil increased marginally by 1.5 per cent in volume. Meanwhile, the growth of containerized trade decelerated to 3.2 per cent, from 7.1 per cent in 2011. The volumes of such trade continued to be affected by weak performance on the main-lane East-West routes linking Asia to Europe and North America. Growth was mainly driven by an increase in that trade on secondary routes, in particular, South-South, North-South and intraregional routes. Containerized trade accounts for about 16 per cent of global merchandise trade by volume and over 50 per

Chart 1.2

MONTHLY COMMODITY PRICE INDICES BY COMMODITY GROUP, JAN. 2002–MAY 2013

(Index numbers, 2002 = 100)

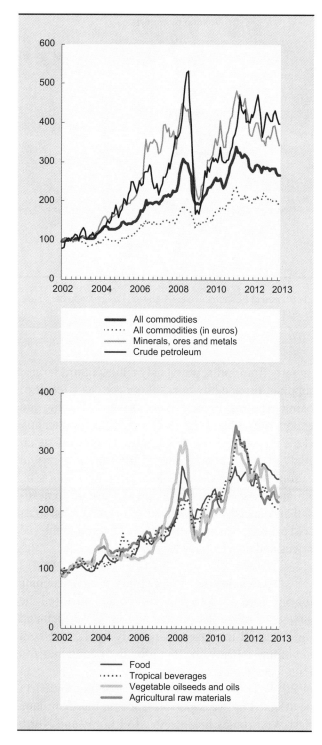

Source: UNCTAD secretariat calculations, based on UNCTAD, *Commodity Price Statistics Online* database.

Note: Crude petroleum price is the average of Dubai/Brent/ West Texas Intermediate, equally weighted. Index numbers are based on prices in current dollars, unless otherwise specified.

cent by value, but it remains under severe pressure. The industry continues to face the problem of how to absorb excess shipping supply capacity, as well as how to employ the rapidly growing capacity of very large ships when most of the growth is being generated by regional trade which requires medium-sized or smaller container ships (UNCTAD, 2013).

3. Recent trends in commodity prices

During 2012 and the first five months of 2013, the prices of most commodity groups continued to retreat from their peaks reached in early 2011 (chart 1.2). Major exceptions were the prices of food and oil, which have been fluctuating within a band over the past two years. The main reasons for the decline in many commodity prices over this period were weak demand growth and an uncertain outlook for global economic activity, together with improved supply prospects. However, most commodity prices still remain at substantially higher levels than the average prices recorded during the commodity price boom of 2003–2008 (table 1.3).

Prices of food and vegetable oilseeds and oils surged in mid-2012 as a result of reduced supplies caused by weather-related events, most notably the worst drought in the United States in half a century. Food crops were also adversely affected by unfavourable climatic conditions in the Black Sea area and in Australia. While the increase in the prices of food commodities such as corn, wheat and soybeans was alarming, a food crisis was avoided mainly because rice, which is critical for food security, was not affected, and countries refrained from imposing trade restrictions. Food prices fell in the second part of the year owing to better supply prospects. After the tight markets and high prices of 2012/2013, forecasts for 2013/14 point to a better world cereal supply and demand balance (FAO, 2013). With good prospects for production and replenishment of stocks, prices should ease. This is not the case, however, for soybeans, which, in mid-2013, recorded a rise in prices resulting from tight supplies and low inventories, particularly in the United States.

The price of oil has been high and relatively stable over the past year. Between July 2012 and June 2013 the average price for Brent/Dubai/West

Table 1.3

WORLD PRIMARY COMMODITY PRICES, 2007–2013

(Percentage change over previous year, unless otherwise indicated)

Commodity groups	2007	2008	2009	2010	2011	2012	2013[a]	2011–2013 versus 2003–2008[b]
All commodities[c]	13.0	24.0	-16.9	20.4	17.9	-8.4	-3.3	68.6
All commodities (in SDRs)[c]	8.6	19.5	-14.5	21.7	14.1	-5.5	-2.2	63.9
All food	13.3	39.2	-8.5	7.4	17.8	-1.4	-4.3	77.0
Food and tropical beverages	8.6	40.4	-5.4	5.6	16.5	-0.4	-3.3	78.1
Tropical beverages	10.4	20.2	1.9	17.5	26.8	-21.5	-13.5	77.9
Coffee	12.5	15.4	-6.9	27.3	42.9	-25.7	-16.2	96.9
Cocoa	22.6	32.2	11.9	8.5	-4.9	-19.7	-5.8	42.9
Tea	-12.3	27.2	16.5	-1.0	11.4	0.8	-14.2	52.8
Food	8.5	42.5	-6.0	4.4	15.4	2.0	-2.4	78.2
Sugar	-31.7	26.9	41.8	17.3	22.2	-17.1	-15.5	121.5
Beef	1.9	2.6	-1.2	27.5	20.0	2.6	1.4	63.4
Maize	38.2	34.0	-24.4	13.2	50.1	2.6	-0.5	112.5
Wheat	34.3	27.5	-31.4	3.3	35.1	-0.1	0.8	53.9
Rice	9.5	110.7	-15.8	-11.5	5.9	5.1	-2.9	64.0
Bananas	-0.9	24.6	0.7	3.7	10.8	0.9	-6.2	58.2
Vegetable oilseeds and oils	52.9	31.9	-28.4	22.7	27.2	-7.6	-11.4	69.5
Soybeans	43.0	36.1	-16.6	3.1	20.2	9.4	-6.4	67.4
Agricultural raw materials	12.0	20.5	-17.5	38.3	28.1	-23.0	-5.3	70.3
Hides and skins	4.5	-11.3	-30.0	60.5	14.0	1.4	3.4	22.8
Cotton	10.2	12.8	-12.2	65.3	47.5	-41.8	2.2	87.2
Tobacco	11.6	8.3	18.0	1.8	3.8	-3.9	2.0	45.9
Rubber	9.5	16.9	-27.0	90.3	32.0	-30.5	-8.4	119.4
Tropical logs	19.5	39.3	-20.6	1.8	13.8	-7.4	1.0	28.6
Minerals, ores and metals	12.8	6.2	-30.3	41.3	14.7	-14.1	-0.8	54.9
Aluminium	2.7	-2.5	-35.3	30.5	10.4	-15.8	-4.0	1.1
Phosphate rock	60.5	387.2	-64.8	1.1	50.3	0.5	-8.2	88.6
Iron ore	77.4	26.8	-48.7	82.4	15.0	-23.4	10.1	26.6
Tin	65.6	27.3	-26.7	50.4	28.0	-19.2	8.7	125.2
Copper	5.9	-2.3	-26.3	47.0	17.1	-9.9	-3.9	70.2
Nickel	53.5	-43.3	-30.6	48.9	5.0	-23.4	-5.9	-2.8
Lead	100.2	-19.0	-17.7	25.0	11.8	-14.2	6.3	60.1
Zinc	-1.0	-42.2	-11.7	30.5	1.5	-11.2	0.4	5.6
Gold	15.3	25.1	11.6	26.1	27.8	6.4	-6.6	184.6
Crude petroleum[d]	10.7	36.4	-36.3	28.0	31.4	1.0	-2.2	77.3
Memo item:								
Manufactures[e]	7.5	4.9	-5.6	1.9	10.3	-2.2	..	..

Source: UNCTAD secretariat calculations, based on UNCTAD, *Commodity Price Statistics Online*; and United Nations Statistics Division (UNSD), *Monthly Bulletin of Statistics*, various issues.
Note: In current dollars unless otherwise specified.
   a Percentage change between the average for the period January to May 2013 and the average for 2012.
   b Percentage change between the 2003–2008 average and the 2011–2013 average.
   c Excluding crude petroleum. SDRs = special drawing rights.
   d Average of Brent, Dubai and West Texas Intermediate, equally weighted.
   e Unit value of exports of manufactured goods of developed countries.

Texas Intermediate (WTI) was $105.5 per barrel, with prices fluctuating between $99 and $111 per barrel. Upward pressure on oil prices has been related to a decline in production by members of the Organization of the Petroleum Exporting Countries (OPEC) in the last quarter of 2012, and to geopolitical tensions in West Asia which affected oil supplies. By contrast, downside pressures on oil prices in 2013 have been mostly linked to increased production, mainly in North America, as well as sluggish global demand growth, particularly in members of the Organisation for Economic Co-operation and Development (OECD). Indeed, it is expected that all of the growth in demand for oil in 2013 will come from non-OECD countries, while demand may actually fall in OECD countries. Overall, it appears that new supplies will provide a buffer against supply shocks stemming from geopolitical tensions. However, some observers see a tighter market when the different oil grades are considered: there could be an abundant supply of light and sweet crude oil, but not of medium and sour crude. Prices of oil and metals also increased in early 2013 based on expectations of improved global economic conditions. However, subsequently, metal prices declined once more due to slow growth of demand and increasing supplies, as well as rising inventories.

Commodity prices also continue to be influenced by the activities of financial investors. The rebound in oil and metal prices observed in the second half of 2012 may have been partly related to the third round of quantitative easing in the United States, with some of the increased liquidity probably being used to invest in commodity futures markets. By mid-2013, indications that this monetary stimulus could be scaled back, together with a credit squeeze in China, fuelled a wave of sell-offs in commodity derivatives. Thus, in the same way as financial investors contributed to amplifying the increases in commodity prices by buying commodity derivatives over the past decade, the commodity sell-offs by financial investors may well have had some influence on the decline in commodity prices in 2013. For example, data from Barclays (2013) show that commodity assets under management fell by $27 billion in April 2013. Moreover, according to media reports, banks are expected to downsize or withdraw from their commodity investment business due to increased regulatory and capital costs.

The commodity price corrections in 2012 and 2013 might point to a reversal of the rising trend in prices witnessed during the first decade of the millennium. On the other hand, they could merely be a pause in that trend. Section B of chapter II provides a more detailed assessment of the likely evolution of commodity prices over a longer term.

B. The structural nature of the latest crisis

The recurrence of economic crises is one of the best established facts in economic history. However, not all crises are similar, nor do they require similar policy responses. An accurate assessment of a crisis must determine whether it is the result of temporary problems, which may be resolved mainly by self-correcting mechanisms, or more systemic problems. In the first case, the *status quo ante* can be expected to be restored after a certain period of time. In the case of a structural (or systemic) crisis, however, changes to the prevailing economic and social framework become necessary.

The analysis in the previous section has revealed that neither the developed economies, nor the developing and transition economies have been able to return to the rapid growth pace they experienced before the onset of the latest crisis. Many praised the "green shoots" of renascent growth in 2010, but, soon after, the prospect of a rapid return to a "normal" state faded. The notion of what is "normal" itself is changing, and several observers are speaking of a "new normal" with regard to economic performances that can be expected in different countries and regions. This refers, in general, to lower growth rates, but also, and more fundamentally, to the changing conditions and driving forces behind that growth. Since, as this *Report* argues, the factors that underpinned the pre-crisis economic expansion were unsustainable, endogenous adjustment mechanisms or automatic stabilizers are not likely to restore them. Moreover, relying on such a strategy will not succeed in returning economies to their previous growth pattern, nor is it desirable.

There is increasing recognition of the structural nature of the present crisis, as evidenced by the widespread calls for structural reforms. However, identifying the kinds of reforms needed depends critically on a correct diagnosis of the nature of the structural problems. Many proponents of structural reforms believe their main goals should be to improve competitiveness and restore the strength and confidence of financial markets. These goals are supposed to be achieved by short-term measures such as the compression of labour costs and fiscal austerity. However, so far, this approach has delivered disappointing results. Other proposals include radical measures, such as more flexible labour markets, lower social security coverage and a smaller economic role for the State. However, none of these proposed reforms are likely to solve the structural problems, and may even aggravate them, because they appear to be based on a flawed diagnosis.

1. An impossible return to the pre-crisis growth pattern

(a) Persistent employment problems

Five years after the onset of the global crisis, employment conditions remain precarious in most developed countries. Unemployment rates grew persistently in the EU, from 7.2 per cent in 2007 to 11 per cent in May 2013. In the United States, the open unemployment rate declined from its peak of 10 per cent in late 2009/early 2010 to 7.6 per cent in mid-2013, which is still historically high compared with less than 5 per cent in 2007. However, open unemployment rates, only partially depict the employment situation; if these rates are considered along with discouraged workers, those marginally attached to the labour force and those employed part time for economic reasons, the total rate of labour

underutilization was 14.3 per cent in June 2013.[4] In Japan, employment indicators have improved significantly: unemployment is down to 4.1 per cent in May 2013, after exceeding 5.5 per cent in mid-2009, and is thus heading towards its pre-crisis low of 3.5 per cent.[5]

In the developed countries as a whole, the total number of employed declined from 510 million in 2007 to 500 million in 2012; the employment rate (defined as a percentage of the working age population) in these countries fell from 68.8 per cent to 66.6 per cent.[6] Had that rate not fallen, total employment would have reached 517 million persons in 2012, which means that the employment deficit caused by the crisis (i.e. fewer employed people than expected based on pre-crisis trends) amounted to 17 million persons. This jobs gap or deficit resulting from the crisis has been larger and longer lasting than in any previous crisis affecting developed countries over the past three decades (chart 1.3).

Open unemployment in developing countries has been quite different since the onset of the crisis compared with the pre-crisis period. Among the largest developing and transition economies (those that are members of the G-20), only Mexico and South Africa had higher unemployment rates at the end of 2012 than before the crisis; all the other countries managed to reduce that rate. Between 2007 and 2012, 130 million jobs were created in the developing countries (excluding China and India), sufficient to prevent an increase in their jobs deficit (chart 1.3). Most developing countries, however, continue to face huge long-standing employment problems, including low participation rates in formal activities, particularly among women, high youth unemployment and a large proportion of low-quality jobs.

The discrepancies between developed and developing countries with regard to employment generation reflect their different growth performances. In developed countries, the strategy of creating jobs by reducing (or allowing a reduction of) real wages has not delivered the expected results in the presence of slow, or in some cases negative, output growth. Such wage policies have an adverse impact on aggregate demand, which makes private firms less willing to invest and to hire new workers. Reducing the price of labour does not lead to the expected outcome of equilibrating demand and supply on the labour market, because lowering the price of labour (the real wage) not only reduces the costs of producing

Chart 1.3

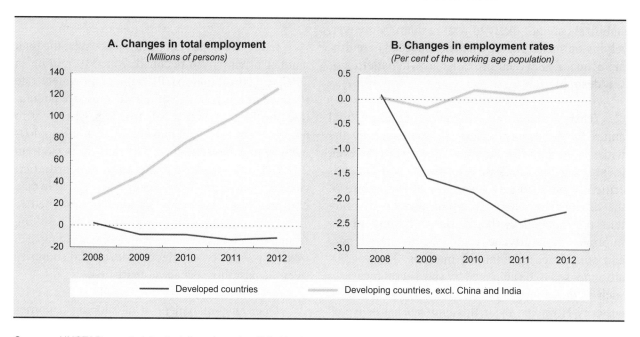

**CHANGES IN TOTAL EMPLOYMENT AND EMPLOYMENT RATES IN
DEVELOPED AND DEVELOPING COUNTRIES, 2008–2012**

Source: UNCTAD secretariat calculations, based on ILO, *Key Indicators of the Labour Market (KILM)* database; and UN-DESA, *World
Population Prospects: The 2012 Revision* database.
Note: China and India are excluded because small variations in their estimates would significantly alter global outcomes.

goods and services, but also the demand for those
goods and services. Attempts to overcome employment problems by lowering wages and introducing
greater flexibility to the labour market are bound to
fail because they ignore this macroeconomic interdependence of demand and supply that causes the
labour market to function differently from a typical
goods market. To the extent that lower unit labour
costs in one country give producers in that country a
competitive advantage on international markets, any
increase in employment as a result of higher exports
will be at the expense of production and employment
in the importing countries.

(b) Adjustments that do not adjust

In the current policy debate, there is broad
agreement about the goals but not about how best
to achieve them, and sometimes the means appear
to be confused with ends. Restoring growth and
employment levels, reducing public debt ratios,
repairing banking systems and re-establishing credit
flows are generally shared objectives. However,

disagreement on priorities, on the appropriate policy
tools, as well as on the timing and sequencing, leads
to quite different, and sometimes opposite, policy
recommendations. For instance, the dominant view in
most developed countries and in several international
organizations, at least since 2010, has been that fiscal
consolidation is a prerequisite for sustained growth
because it will bolster the confidence of financial
markets and prevent sovereign defaults. Indeed, this
was adopted as a major commitment at the G-20
summit in Toronto in June 2010. Those opposed to
this shift towards fiscal austerity see fiscal consolidation as a long-term goal which would be achieved
through sustained growth, and not as a precondition
for growth. In this view, premature fiscal tightening
will not only be very costly in economic and social
terms; it will also be counterproductive, because, with
slower growth, fiscal revenues will be lower, and the
public-debt-to-GDP ratio is unlikely to decline, or
may even rise further (see, for instance, *TDR 2011*,
chap. III; Krugman, 2012; Calcagno, 2012).

The impact of a change in public revenue and in
spending on GDP (i.e. the value of fiscal multipliers)

has been studied extensively. Many of these studies, including by the International Monetary Fund (IMF, 2010), suggest that fiscal multipliers are relatively low. For example, the ECB estimates short-term fiscal multipliers to be generally lower than 1, which means that the negative impact on GDP growth of a reduction of government spending or an increase of taxes over the first two years is smaller than the amount of that fiscal change. On the other hand, the long-term multiplier of a spending cut would be positive, meaning that the level of the GDP that would be obtained after a transitory period of more than 10 years following a fiscal tightening would be higher than the level expected without it. This would result from the reduction of labour taxes that would be made possible by an improved budget position resulting from fiscal austerity; gains would be larger if, in addition, fiscal consolidation also led to lower sovereign risk premiums (ECB, 2012).[7] However, a recent study by the IMF (2012) found that fiscal multipliers in times of economic depression were much higher than the values it had estimated in previous reports. The reason is that in an economy with a huge amount of idle resources, an increase in public spending does not involve any "crowding out" of private expenditure. This means that expansionary fiscal policies are an important instrument to spur growth and actually reduce the public-debt-to-GDP ratio. However, the IMF recommendation does not go so far as to recommend such policies; it merely recommends undertaking fiscal adjustment over a longer time span. It suggests that policymakers should determine the pace of fiscal adjustment taking into account not only the values of short-term fiscal multipliers and debt-to-GDP ratios, but also the strength of private demand and the credibility of fiscal consolidation plans (Blanchard and Leigh, 2013).

A set of estimates of fiscal multipliers are presented in table 1.4 based on the United Nations Global Policy Model. Even if only the effects of an increase in fiscal expenditure during the first year are considered, the results strongly support the hypothesis of high multipliers, which significantly exceed 1 in all the cases, and are frequently greater than 1.5. On the other hand, multipliers associated with changes in taxation are much lower, in all cases below 0.5 in absolute values.[8] This means that the composition of a fiscal package may be at least as important as its size. In particular, it would be possible to design fiscal packages comprising both higher taxes and expenditure, which would therefore have a neutral

Table 1.4

SHORT-TERM FISCAL MULTIPLIERS

	Government spending on goods and services	*Government taxes net of transfers and subsidies*
Argentina	1.66	-0.36
Brazil	1.84	-0.37
Canada	1.51	-0.27
China	1.76	-0.42
CIS	1.54	-0.33
France	1.48	-0.27
Germany	1.38	-0.29
India	1.65	-0.41
Indonesia	1.64	-0.41
Italy	1.48	-0.31
Japan	1.35	-0.29
Mexico	1.59	-0.36
South Africa	1.68	-0.31
Turkey	1.71	-0.39
United Kingdom	1.32	-0.26
United States	1.58	-0.36

Source: UNCTAD secretariat estimates, based on United Nations Global Policy Model (see the annex to this chapter).

Note: Multiplier values represent first-year impact on GDP of one-unit *ex-ante* increases in government spending or government revenues (i.e. taxes net of transfers and subsidies).

ex-ante effect on the fiscal balance, but still a positive impact on growth. This in turn would enlarge the tax base and would eventually deliver a positive *ex-post* effect on the fiscal balance and the public-debt-to-GDP ratio. But given the high values of government spending multipliers, it is likely that a debt-financed increase in fiscal expenditure would generate enough growth and supplementary fiscal revenues to reduce that ratio.[9] As shown in the annex to this chapter, this effect would be even stronger if several countries pursued expansionary policies simultaneously.

Despite growing evidence that fiscal austerity hampers GDP growth, many governments are unwilling to change this strategy as they believe they do not have enough policy space for reversing their fiscal policy stance;[10] instead, they are relying on monetary policy for supporting growth and employment. However, there is little scope for monetary policy to further reduce interest rates in developed economies, as these are already extremely low. In addition, so far, unconventional monetary policies (i.e. quantitative monetary expansion) have failed to revive credit to the private sector. Banks and other financial institutions that have access to liquidity will not automatically increase their supply of credit commensurately, as they may still have to consolidate their balance sheets. Moreover, even if they did expand their credit supply, many private firms would be unlikely to borrow more as long as they have to consolidate their own balance sheets without any prospect of expanding production when they face stagnant, or even falling, demand. This is why using monetary policy for pulling an economy out of a depression triggered by a financial crisis may be like "pushing into a string".

On the other hand, central bank interventions (or announcements of their intentions) have proved remarkably effective in lowering risk premiums on sovereign debt. Thus, monetary and fiscal policies may be used for different purposes for tackling the crisis. Fiscal policy, given its strong potential impact on aggregate demand, could be used to support growth and employment instead of trying to restore the confidence of financial markets through fiscal austerity. Meanwhile, central banks could enlarge their role as lenders of last resort (LLR) to generate that confidence and maintain interest rates at low levels. Moreover, these central bank actions to support credit and growth are more likely to succeed if they are accompanied by an expansionary fiscal policy.

2. Roots of the crisis: the build-up of structural problems

Since the late 1970s and early 1980s policies based on supply-side economics, neoliberalism and finance-led globalization have involved a redefinition of the role of the State in the economy and its regulatory tasks; an extraordinary expansion of the role of finance at the national and international levels; an opening up of economies, including a reduction of trade tariffs; and a general increase in inequality of income distribution. The resulting new roles of the public, private and external sectors, the expansion of finance and the increasing income concentration altered the structure and dynamics of global demand in a way that heightened vulnerabilities, eventually

leading to the crisis. In other words, the present crisis was not the unfortunate result of some misguided financial decisions; rather, it was the culmination of a number of structural problems that have been building up over the past three decades, which created the conditions for greater economic instability.

(a) Income inequality

In order to achieve sustained global growth and development, there has to be consistent growth of household income, the largest component of which is labour income obtained from the production of goods and services.[11] However, over the past three decades, labour income in the world economy has been growing at a slower pace than the growth of world output (chart 1.4), with some diverging trends over the past decade.[12]

The observed declining trends in the share of labour income – or wage share – have often been justified as being necessary in order to reduce costs and induce investment. However, wage income

Chart 1.4

SHARE OF WORLD LABOUR INCOME IN WORLD GROSS OUTPUT, 1980–2011

(Weighted averages, per cent)

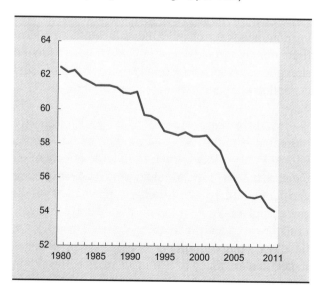

Source: UNCTAD secretariat calculations, using UN Global Policy Model, based on UN-DESA, *National Accounts Main Aggregates* database; and ILO, *Global Wage* database.
Note: Mixed income, typically from self-employment, is included in the labour share.

constitutes a large proportion of total income (about two thirds in developed countries), and is therefore the most important source of demand for goods and services. Thus, sizeable reductions of such income relative to productivity gains will have tangible negative effects on the rate of household consumption. And, to the extent that productive investment is driven by expectations of expanding demand, second-round effects of lower consumption on investment would seem unavoidable.

The decline in the share of labour income has led to a rising trend of profit mark-ups in the world as a whole. The tendency of companies to seek profit gains from exploiting wage differentials, rather than through innovation and investment, has produced limited dynamic benefits for the rest of society. In other words, the presumed transmission of higher profits to higher gross fixed capital formation has not materialized.[13]

In addition to these negative effects on long-term growth, greater income inequality also contributed to the financial crisis. The links between expanding finance and rising inequality operated in two ways. The larger size and role played by the financial sector led to a greater concentration of income in the hands of *rentiers* (both equity holders and interest earners) and a few high-wage earners, especially in the financial sector. Concomitantly, greater inequality led to rising demand for credit, both from households whose current income was insufficient to cover their consumption and housing needs and from firms that distributed a disproportionate share of their profits to their shareholders (*TDR 2012*, chap. II). This led to a financial bubble that eventually burst, leaving many households, firms and banks in financial distress.

(b) Smaller role for the State

Another long-running trend since the early 1980s has been the diminishing economic role of the State in many countries by way of privatization, deregulation and lower public expenditure (on the latter, see section C of this chapter and table 1.7). This served to increase economic fragility in different ways.

When the public sector's share of GDP shrinks, economic vulnerability increases because of that sector's diminished capacity to compensate for the usual fluctuations in the business cycle and to cope

with significant crises.[14] But even more relevant than governments' ability to intervene, is their willingness to conduct countercyclical policies at a time when the desirability for balanced fiscal budgets has become dogma (Galbraith, 2008).

Calls for balancing budgets frequently overlook the fact that one economic sector's deficit is necessarily another sector's surplus. Therefore, a reduction (or increase) in the public sector deficit shows up as either a reduction (or increase) in the private sector surplus, or a reduction (or increase) in the surplus of the rest of the world, or a combination of these two. For the world as a whole, where the external sector is, by definition, in balance, public and private sectors mirror each other. This can be illustrated by the evolution of public and private sector balances at the global level between 1971 and 2011 (chart 1.5). As this chart shows aggregate values, it mainly reflects what happened in the largest countries. It appears that between the mid-1970s and 1990, there was a persistent and rather stable public deficit (and private surplus) at around 3.5 per cent of global output. This in itself did not pose a problem: it is normal for the private sector to run surpluses, since its assumed objective is wealth accumulation. And that level of public deficit would not lead to any explosive accumulation of public debt stocks; on the contrary, it would be consistent with a stable debt-output ratio if, at the same time, nominal output were to grow sufficiently.[15]

This contrasts with the considerable instability observed since the beginning of the 1990s. It is noteworthy that periods of shrinking public deficits actually preceded major crises in 2001 and 2008. It was possible to cut public deficits because the private sector was reducing its savings and many private agents became highly indebted in the wake of unsustainable financial bubbles. Pressures to reduce fiscal deficits can be destabilizing to the extent that those deficits are mirrored by shrinking private sector surpluses. Indeed, they are partly responsible for the greater frequency of financial crises.

Another factor contributing to those crises since the 1980s has been widespread financial liberalization, which is another major aspect of the reduced economic role of the State. Financial deregulation, coupled with the extraordinary expansion of financial assets, allowed macroeconomic policies limited room for manoeuvre, and their effects came to be increasingly swayed by reactions on financial markets.

Chart 1.5

FINANCIAL POSITIONS OF PUBLIC AND PRIVATE SECTORS IN THE WORLD ECONOMY, 1971–2011

(Per cent of world domestic product)

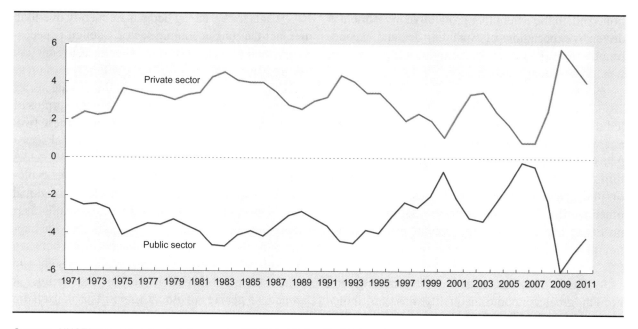

Source: UNCTAD secretariat calculations, using UN Global Policy Model, based on UN-DESA, *National Accounts Main Aggregates* database; IMF, *Government Financial Statistics*; Eurostat; and national sources.

Note: Figures above zero denote a surplus and below zero a deficit. Surpluses indicate additions to the net stock of financial wealth, and deficits indicate additions to the stock of debt. Except for small errors of measurement and aggregation of large numbers, the surpluses and deficits mirror each other.

Moreover, as the access of governments to central bank financing was limited, the financial sector gained greater influence over policymakers.

This interaction between developments in the financial sector, together with the weakening of government and central bank influence on the economy, generates a particular problem when a recession does not result from cycles in the real sector of the economy, but instead from overindebtedness of the private sector as a whole. Koo (2013a) describes this type of recession as follows: "When a debt-financed asset price bubble bursts, the private sector is left with a huge debt overhang, and to climb out of this state of negative equity it must pay down debt or increase savings, even if interest rates are zero. When the private sector as a whole is minimizing debt, the economy continuously loses aggregate demand equivalent to

the saved but unborrowed amount. This situation has come to be known as a balance sheet recession." In such a situation, the choice is between a prolonged recession and a public-deficit-financed recovery. As the private sector takes a long time to reduce its debt, additional borrowing by the public sector would be the only recourse. As noted by Koo (2013b), "the only way to keep both the GDP and money supply from shrinking is for the government – the last borrower standing – to step in and borrow the unborrowed savings and spend them in the private sector."[16]

At the same time, however, governments are reluctant to increase their debt for fear of negative reactions from the financial markets and from public opinion, much of which has been given to understand that financial markets "know better" than governments (Koo, 2013a).

(c) The prominent role of a poorly regulated financial sector

The value of global financial assets grew from $14 trillion in 1980 to $56 trillion in 1990 and $206 trillion in 2007; and in current GDP terms it tripled, from 120 per cent of GDP in 1980 to 365 per cent in 2007 (Lund et al., 2013: 14). This expansion was accompanied (and encouraged) by extensive deregulation of national financial markets and the progressive liberalization of international capital movements. As a result, cross-border capital flows jumped from $500 billion in 1980 to a peak of $12 trillion in 2007. This would explain why an increasing proportion of financial assets are owned by non-residents. Between 1980 and 1995, the stock of foreign-owned financial assets represented around 25 per cent of global financial assets. This share increased to 28 per cent in 2000, 38 per cent in 2005 and almost 50 per cent in 2007–2010, when foreign-owned assets exceeded $100 trillion, or 150 per cent of world output.

This more prominent role of financial markets carries the risk of greater economic instability, because these markets are intrinsically prone to boom-and-bust processes, especially if they are loosely regulated. A typical process begins with rising prices of financial and non-financial assets, which boost wealth temporarily and serve as collateral for new credits or equity withdrawals. This in turn finances private spending and also new asset acquisitions, which push up asset prices further. This process can continue for a relatively long time, which sustains economic growth and thus helps enhance investor confidence. However, eventually the asset price bubble that had sustained a credit-boom expansion will burst, leading to a drastic and long-lasting contraction of economic activity.

This portrays many historical episodes of "manias, panics and crashes" (Kindleberger, 1978), including the bubble that triggered the present crisis. It is indeed surprising that, as the bubble grew, some worrying signals were dismissed by policymakers as well as rating agencies and financial agents because, although household debt was rising, the value of household assets was also rising (Bernanke, 2005).[17] Due to an exclusive focus on monetary stability the early signals of financial instability went unheeded.

According to some observers, monetary policy that focuses exclusively on low inflation rates contributes to the credit cycle (Godley, 1999; Shin, 2010). Usually, low or falling interest rates reflect low current or expected inflation. This may allow the burden of the debt service to fall or remain low despite a rising stock of debt. But as soon as perceptions of risk change, interest rate premiums rise. The burden of servicing debts that were contracted at flexible interest rates or the costs of revolving debt that is reaching maturity rise, sometimes drastically. In addition, a drastic reversal of credit demand and, by implication, of spending, may trigger an economic downturn that would make debt repayments more difficult.

The extraordinary expansion of the financial sector over the years has also been accompanied by changes in its patterns of operation, which contributed to an increase in financial fragility. These included a high level of financial leveraging, an increasing reliance on short-term borrowing for bank funding, the extension of a poorly capitalized and unregulated shadow financial system, perverse incentives that encouraged excessive risk-taking by financial traders, a reliance on flawed pricing models and the "lend and distribute" behaviour that weakened the role of banks in discriminating between good and bad borrowers. The procyclical bias of bank credit was exacerbated by value-at-risk models and the Basel rules on bank capital, which allowed banks to expand credit during booms, when risks seemed low and the price of collaterals rose, and obliged them to cut lending during downturns. The vulnerability of the financial system also increased as a result of its growing concentration and loss of diversity. Much of its operations today are handled by "too-big-to-fail" institutions which tend to take on far greater risks than would be taken by smaller institutions. As the same type of business strategies tended to be replicated across the financial sector, the system became more vulnerable to macroeconomic shocks (such as the collapse of real estate markets) that affected all the agents at the same time (see *TDR 2011*, chap. IV).

The search for rapid gains led to large flows of credit – including loans that were insufficiently collateralized – that were used for consumption, rather than for financing productive investment and innovative enterprise. This kind of credit-fuelled spending by the private sector had the potential to offset the subdued demand that was caused by lagging wages and worsening income distribution. However, debt-driven consumption is not a viable option in the long run.

It is possible that some of the characteristics of the credit boom in developed countries are being replicated in developing countries, with some variations. Asset appreciations and private spending that exceeds income are often supported by capital inflows, usually channelled through domestic financial institutions. In such cases, currency mismatches between debt and revenue tend to generate or reinforce the credit boom-and-bust cycle.

Through these different channels, the growing size and role of the financial sector, together with its present structure and modes of functioning, have become a major source of economic instability and misallocation of resources in many countries. It has also facilitated the rise of international imbalances, another key structural problem that is examined in the next subsection.

(d) International imbalances with asymmetric adjustments and a recessionary bias

Increasing current account imbalances and the expansion of international finance are closely intertwined. In the immediate post-war era, there are unlikely to have been any countries that had large external deficits for extended periods of time. But such deficits have become more and more common in the era of financialization that started in the 1980s and deepened from the 1990s onwards.

Large surplus and deficit imbalances in the world economy from the mid-1970s to the early 1980s were mostly due to oil shocks (chart 1.6). These shocks contributed to the expansion of international financial markets through the recycling of petrodollars. However, the imbalances were considered temporary, as it was assumed that oil-deficit countries would devise strategies to reduce their oil-import bills. By contrast, in the middle of the 1980s the United States had an external deficit of about 3 per cent of GDP which was unrelated to oil. This was matched by surpluses in Japan and a few Western European countries, which took concerted corrective action in 1985. The smooth correction of external imbalances that followed could be considered the last time there was proactive international coordination in the management of trade and exchange rates. But it may also serve as a lesson about the limits of a framework for policy coordination that focuses

exclusively on exchange rates while disregarding the growing instability of the global financial system as a whole in view of subsequent developments.

By the end of the 1990s, a tendency towards rising global imbalances re-emerged, owing largely to current account deficits in a few developed countries where credit-driven expansion became prevalent, as described in the previous subsection. This tendency was reinforced by the adoption of export-led strategies by developed-country exporters of manufactures, such as Japan and a few North European countries, followed by Germany. During the 1990s, and more clearly after the Asian financial crisis, a number of developing countries that emerged as suppliers of low-cost manufactures generated growing external surpluses. Others that also sustained surpluses included net exporters of energy and raw materials, especially during the 2000s when commodity prices turned favourable. These factors together caused global current account imbalances to peak in 2006 at nearly 3 per cent of world income. The reversal that followed from 2007 onwards coincided with the first signs of financial turmoil in the major deficit country, the United States, and culminated with the financial and economic crisis in 2008–2009. This highlighted the limitations of the asset-appreciation, credit-driven model discussed above. Global imbalances have remained at about 2 per cent since 2009 – a level that is still historically high. Furthermore, global imbalances have been on the rise since 2009.

Export-led growth strategies, to the extent that they have frequently led to trade surpluses, are only sustainable if other countries maintain trade deficits over a long period. In short, the success of such strategies in some countries relies on external deficits in other countries, and the willingness and capacity of the deficit countries to pile up external debt. But since the crisis, developed countries with deficits seem to be less willing and able to play the role of global consumer of last resort due to their ever-increasing indebtedness. Despite this, policymakers in some countries are trying to respond to weaker domestic demand by gaining export market shares through improved international competitiveness. This is particularly the case with those crisis-hit countries that were running large current account deficits before the crisis and have undertaken recessionary adjustments programmes. The most common measure adopted, at least in the short run, has been internal devaluation, particularly through wage compression. However,

Chart 1.6

CONTRIBUTIONS TO GLOBAL IMBALANCES OF SELECTED GROUPS OF COUNTRIES, 1970–2011

(Current account balance as a percentage of world gross product)

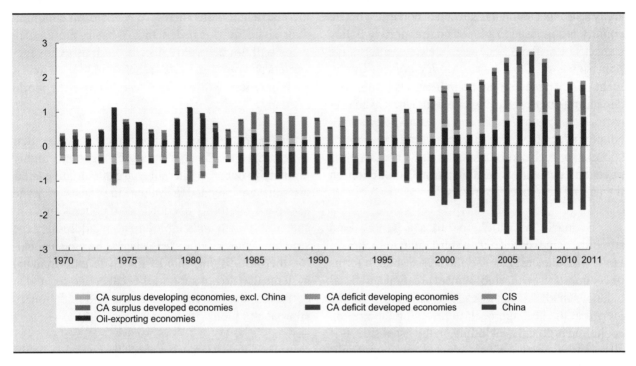

CA surplus developing economies, excl. China   CA deficit developing economies   CIS
CA surplus developed economies   CA deficit developed economies   China
Oil-exporting economies

Source: UNCTAD secretariat calculations, based on UN-DESA, *National Accounts Main Aggregates* database; IMF, *World Economic Outlook (WEO)* database.

Note: Deficit and surplus classification was based on the average current account (CA) position between 2004 and 2007. CIS includes Georgia.

this simultaneously action by several trade partners contributes to a global compression of income and reinforces a race to the bottom. This not only has negative effects on global aggregate demand, since a country's lower wage bill constitutes a demand constraint that affects other countries as well, but it also undermines their efforts to gain competitiveness (Capaldo and Izurieta, 2013).

A global mechanism to help rebalance external demand will not be effective if it places the entire or most of the burden of adjustment on deficit countries. Such an asymmetric adjustment is deflationary, since debtor countries are forced to cut spending while there is no obligation on the part of creditor countries to increase spending, which leads to a shortfall of demand at the global level. It would be preferable, from an economic and social point of view, if surplus countries assumed a greater role in the rebalancing process by expanding their domestic demand. Ideally, an asymmetric *expansionary* approach would be the

most effective way to restart global output growth on a sustainable basis. In such an approach, the adjustment burden would be taken on primarily by the surplus countries by way of stronger wage increases and fiscal expansion.

In order to explore the global consequences of these alternative approaches, the annex to this chapter presents three simulations showing the outcomes of alternative policy strategies. They are quantitative exercises based on the United Nations Global Policy Model. These exercises show the performance of the world economy divided into 25 countries or groups of countries at the horizon 2030 based on two alternative scenarios in addition to the baseline scenario. The baseline scenario is an economic projection assuming that there will be neither policy changes nor shocks ahead. Both alternative scenarios involve the following policy changes aimed at stimulating the economy: expansionary fiscal policies, with higher public consumption and investment spending;

progressive income redistribution through a wage policy, taxation and public transfers; and a supportive monetary policy in terms of low interest rates and greater access to credit, while avoiding the creation of financial bubbles. Surplus countries are assumed to apply a stronger stimulus than deficit countries, but no country is supposed to adopt a contractionary policy stance. The difference between these two alternative scenarios is that in scenario A, *all countries* implement policy changes that are more or less ambitious depending on their starting position, whereas in scenario B, *only developing and transition economies* adopt such policy changes. In addition, the policy stimulus in scenario B is smaller due to balance-of-payments constraints resulting from non-action on the part of developed countries.

Scenario A, which includes a generalized stimulus, achieves not only a substantial reduction of global imbalances, but also the best results in terms of economic growth, employment creation and fiscal balances in all the countries. This is in line with the view that the best approach to resolving the present economic problems, including on the fiscal side, is if all countries simultaneously adopt expansionary policies, taking into account their respective capacities, rather than adopting generalized austerity.

Scenario B, in which only developing and transition economies apply more expansionary policies, yields inferior economic results, though still clearly better results than those of the baseline. This is especially true for developing and transition economies. Expansionary policies pursued by them may compensate for protracted slow growth of exports to the developed countries. Also developed countries obtain some benefits in this scenario compared with the baseline scenario, even if these are minor. But these mostly stem from the fact that, instead of coordinating efforts towards a genuine global rebalancing and acceleration of growth, the developed countries will press ahead with individual policies towards achieving external competitiveness by squeezing labour income. Their gains therefore result from enlarging their share in global demand. What is more, such gains will not be evenly distributed between wage-earners and profit-earners in these countries. Finally, such practices will not help to rebalance the world economy.

These exercises are not forecasts, since their hypothesis of extensive policy changes are highly unlikely to occur. Rather, they are quantitative exercises that are intended to evaluate the consistency and economic feasibility of coordinated policies aimed at spurring growth and employment by addressing the structural causes of the crisis, such as income inequality, the diminishing role of the State and financial systems that do not support the real economy, and at correcting the present asymmetric and deflationary approach to global imbalances.

The simulations also show that a general shift towards expansionary policies is economically feasible, and would deliver better results in all respects than the baseline scenario. This supports the view that all countries should engage in a coordinated effort aimed at a sustained expansion of global demand. This exercise also shows that even if developed countries persevere with their current policies, there is, nevertheless, scope for developing and transition economies to improve their economic performances by providing a coordinated economic stimulus. Hence, encouraging regional cooperation and South-South trade would need to be an important component of their development strategies.

C. Developing and transition economies are continuing to grow, but remain vulnerable

The shape of the world economy has changed significantly over the past three decades. The share of developing countries in global GDP has increased, and several developing countries and regions have assumed a greater role as additional drivers of global economic growth. Other elements of this rise of the South include the growing importance of developing countries in international trade and capital flows. This section starts with an account of developing countries' growth record over the past three decades, and goes on to discuss some issues related to their increased trade and financial integration. It argues that, while greater integration supported their rapid growth when the general external economic environment was favourable, with that environment now turning less favourable, it has also increased their vulnerability.

1. Growth performance since the early 1990s

The 1990s and the beginning of the new millennium saw a series of payments and financial crises in developing countries, including in Mexico in 1994, in some parts of Asia in 1997–1998 – with spillovers to Brazil and the Russian Federation in 2008 – in Turkey in 2000–2001 and in Argentina in 2001–2002. In spite of these crises, developing countries registered an average annual GDP growth of 4.7 per cent during the period 1991–2002, exceeding that of developed countries by over two percentage points (table 1.5). Meanwhile, average annual GDP growth of the transition economies declined by 2.6 per cent, largely as a result of their economic collapse in the early 1990s. Developing countries' growth performance during the period 1991–2002 was superior to that of developed countries for a number of reasons. One was their rebound from economic downturns related to debt crises that many of them had experienced in the 1980s along with sharp declines in commodity prices. Another was the mixed performance of developed countries, with a protracted period of slow growth in Japan, uneven growth in Europe, and a sharp growth deceleration in the United States, which was associated with the bursting of the dot-com bubble in 2001.

During the period 2003–2007, output growth in developing and transition economies accelerated, even as developed countries continued to experience relatively slow growth, on average. The average annual GDP growth of both developing and transition economies exceeded that of developed countries by 4.5–5 percentage points (table 1.5). The onset of the global economic and financial crisis initially reinforced this trend, as the downturn in 2008–2009 was less dramatic and the subsequent recovery more rapid in developing than in developed countries. This growth differential in favour of developing countries was unprecedented (Akyüz, 2012), even though it subsequently shrank over the period 2010–2012.

Growth acceleration during 2003–2007 compared with the period 1991–2002 has diverged considerably across developing countries. It was particularly pronounced in some of the large developing and transition economies, such as Argentina, India, the Russian Federation, South Africa and Turkey, but much less so in Brazil, China and Mexico. The Republic of Korea even recorded lower average annual growth rates. The sharp increase in those rates in Argentina, the Russian Federation and Turkey was partly due to these countries' swift recovery from severe crises at the beginning of the

Table 1.5

COMPARATIVE OUTPUT GROWTH PERFORMANCE, SELECTED COUNTRIES AND COUNTRY GROUPS, 1991–2013

(Per cent)

	1991–2002		2003–2007		2008–2012		2010	2011	2012	2013
	Output growth (annual average)	Contribution to global growth	Output growth (annual average)	Contribution to global growth	Output growth (annual average)	Contribution to global growth		Output growth		
World	2.9	2.9	3.7	3.7	1.7	1.7	4.1	2.8	2.2	2.1
Developed economies	2.6	2.0	2.6	2.0	0.3	0.2	2.6	1.5	1.2	1.0
Transition economies	-2.6	-0.1	7.6	0.2	1.8	0.0	4.5	4.5	3.0	2.7
Developing economies	4.7	0.8	7.0	1.5	5.3	1.4	7.9	5.9	4.6	4.7
Africa	2.9	0.1	5.8	0.1	3.6	0.1	4.9	1.0	5.4	4.0
East, South-East and South Asia	6.5	0.5	8.3	0.9	6.8	1.0	9.3	7.0	5.3	5.5
West Asia	3.7	0.1	6.9	0.2	4.0	0.1	7.0	7.1	3.2	3.5
Latin America and the Caribbean	2.9	0.2	4.8	0.3	3.0	0.2	5.9	4.3	3.0	3.1
Oceania	2.2	0.0	3.1	0.0	3.4	0.0	3.6	4.3	4.1	2.7
Memo items:										
Argentina	2.6	0.0	8.9	0.0	5.8	0.0	9.2	8.9	1.9	4.8
Brazil	2.6	0.1	4.0	0.1	3.3	0.1	7.5	2.7	0.9	2.5
China	10.1	0.2	11.6	0.5	9.4	0.6	10.4	9.3	7.8	7.6
India	5.9	0.1	8.6	0.1	7.2	0.1	11.2	7.7	3.8	5.2
Indonesia	3.6	0.0	5.5	0.0	5.9	0.0	6.2	6.5	6.2	5.7
Mexico	3.1	0.1	3.6	0.1	1.6	0.0	5.5	4.0	3.9	2.8
Republic of Korea	6.1	0.1	4.4	0.1	3.1	0.1	6.3	3.7	2.0	1.6
Russian Federation	-2.7	-0.1	7.4	0.1	1.5	0.0	4.5	4.3	3.4	2.5
Saudi Arabia	2.0	0.0	4.7	0.0	4.4	0.0	5.1	7.1	5.9	4.0
South Africa	2.3	0.0	4.9	0.0	2.1	0.0	3.1	3.5	2.5	1.7
Turkey	3.3	0.0	7.3	0.1	3.5	0.0	9.2	8.8	2.2	3.3

Source: UNCTAD secretariat calculations, based on table 1.1.
Note: Data for 2013 are forecasts.

millennium, which had caused large output losses. In 2011–2012 growth performance gradually worsened in all developing regions, as well as in most countries individually (table 1.5), especially in Brazil, India and Turkey. Nevertheless, even in these latter countries, per capita income continues to exceed pre-crisis levels by a significant margin. This indicates that the adoption of countercyclical macroeconomic policies enabled many developing countries to mitigate the impact of the Great Recession on their economies for a certain period of time. However, the more recent worsening of their growth performance suggests that the growth stimulus effects of their expansionary policies may be petering out.

Despite the healthy growth in developing and transition economies, developed countries remained the main drivers of global growth until the onset of the current crisis. During the period 1990–2005, these latter countries accounted for about three quarters of global GDP (table 1.6), and the share of their contribution to global economic growth exceeded 50 per cent. By contrast, during the period 2008–2012, as a group they contributed very little to global growth (table 1.5). Since 2010, global growth has been driven mainly by developing countries, which have accounted for about two thirds of such growth, while the contribution of transition economies has been negligible.

Table 1.6

SHARES IN GLOBAL GDP, SELECTED COUNTRIES AND COUNTRY GROUPS, 1970–2012

	Market prices[a]									Purchasing power parity[b]						
	1970	*1980*	*1990*	*1995*	*2000*	*2005*	*2007*	*2010*	*2012*	*1990*	*1995*	*2000*	*2005*	*2007*	*2010*	*2012*
Developed economies	69.5	69.9	78.8	78.3	77.0	73.8	69.6	63.7	60.4	63.4	62.3	60.9	56.7	54.2	50.0	48.1
Transition economies	13.7	8.5	3.9	1.9	1.2	2.4	3.3	3.3	3.9	7.9	4.3	3.9	4.5	4.7	4.6	4.6
Developing economies	16.8	21.6	17.3	19.8	21.7	23.8	27.1	33.0	35.8	28.7	33.4	35.2	38.8	41.1	45.4	47.3
Africa	2.7	3.6	2.2	1.8	1.9	2.2	2.4	2.7	2.9	3.5	3.3	3.4	3.7	3.8	4.0	4.0
East, South-East and South Asia	7.5	8.3	8.1	10.1	11.0	12.8	14.8	18.9	21.3	13.6	17.8	19.7	23.2	25.3	29.0	30.7
West Asia	1.3	3.2	2.0	1.8	2.2	2.8	3.1	3.3	3.6	2.9	3.0	3.2	3.4	3.5	3.7	3.9
Latin America and the Caribbean	5.3	6.4	4.9	6.1	6.6	5.9	6.7	8.0	8.0	8.6	9.2	8.9	8.4	8.5	8.6	8.7
Oceania	0.1	0.1	0.1	0.1	0.0	0.0	0.0	0.1	0.1	0.0	0.0	0.0	0.0	0.0	0.0	0.0
Memo items:																
Argentina	1.0	0.6	0.6	0.9	0.9	0.4	0.5	0.6	0.7	0.7	0.8	0.8	0.7	0.8	0.9	0.9
Brazil	1.1	1.6	1.7	2.6	2.0	1.9	2.4	3.4	3.2	3.0	3.2	2.9	2.8	2.8	2.9	2.8
China	2.8	2.6	1.8	2.5	3.7	5.0	6.2	9.4	11.3	3.5	5.6	7.1	9.4	11.0	13.6	14.9
India	1.9	1.6	1.5	1.2	1.4	1.8	2.2	2.6	2.6	2.9	3.3	3.7	4.3	4.6	5.4	5.6
Indonesia	0.3	0.7	0.6	0.7	0.5	0.6	0.8	1.1	1.2	1.1	1.4	1.2	1.2	1.3	1.4	1.5
Mexico	1.3	1.9	1.3	1.0	2.0	1.8	1.8	1.6	1.6	2.4	2.3	2.5	2.3	2.2	2.1	2.1
Republic of Korea	0.3	0.5	1.2	1.8	1.6	1.8	1.9	1.6	1.6	1.3	1.7	1.8	1.9	1.9	2.0	1.9
Russian Federation	n.a.	n.a.	n.a.	1.3	0.8	1.7	2.3	2.3	2.8	5.3	2.9	2.6	3.0	3.2	3.0	3.0
Saudi Arabia	0.2	1.4	0.5	0.5	0.6	0.7	0.7	0.7	0.9	0.8	0.9	0.9	0.9	0.9	1.0	1.1
South Africa	0.5	0.7	0.5	0.5	0.4	0.5	0.5	0.6	0.5	0.8	0.7	0.7	0.7	0.7	0.7	0.7
Turkey	0.7	0.8	0.9	0.8	0.8	1.1	1.2	1.1	1.1	1.1	1.2	1.2	1.3	1.3	1.3	1.4

Source: UNCTAD secretariat calculations, based on IMF, *World Economic Outlook*, April 2013; Economist Intelligence Unit, *EIU CountryData* database; table 1.1; and *UNCTADstat*.

  a Calculated using dollars at current prices and current exchange rates.
  b Estimated on the basis of current GDP using 2005 PPP values.

The share of developed countries in the global economy was about 70 per cent in 1970 and reached almost 80 per cent during the 1990s, following a decline in the share of the transition economies during that decade (table 1.6). Since the beginning of the millennium, and especially as a result of the Great Recession, the share of developed countries in the global economy fell sharply to about 60 per cent in 2012. The share of developing countries increased by 7 percentage points between 1970 and 2005, and rapidly rose by another 12 percentage points during the subsequent seven years to reach over 35 per cent of global GDP in 2012.

Measured in terms of purchasing power parity (PPP), the share of developing countries in global output reached 47.3 per cent in 2012, and thus almost matched that of developed countries (table 1.6). This does not mean that developing countries have become as important as developed countries as drivers of global growth, because a country's contribution to global supply and demand, as well as the expansionary or deflationary impulses it transmits to the other countries, is determined by the market values of its goods and services, rather than by PPP equivalents. However, it is well known that economic development is associated with an increase in a country's price levels, as also reflected in an appreciation of its real exchange rate and an ensuing gradual closing of the gap in its PPP relative to developed countries.[18] This means that the increase in the weight of developing countries in the global economy to almost 50 per cent, as measured in PPP terms, could be taken to indicate the future evolution of their weight measured

Table 1.7

GDP BY TYPE OF EXPENDITURE, SELECTED COUNTRIES AND COUNTRY GROUPS, 1981–2011

Left panel

	Percentage of GDP				Average annual growth			
	1981–1990	1991–2002	2003–2007	2008–2011	1981–1990	1991–2002	2003–2007	2008–2011
Developed economies								
GDP	100.0	100.0	100.0	100.0	3.2	2.6	2.6	-0.1
HH	60.7	61.1	62.1	62.7	3.2	2.8	2.5	0.3
Gov	20.7	19.0	18.3	19.0	2.6	1.7	1.6	1.5
Inv	18.9	20.0	20.7	18.5	4.2	3.2	4.1	-4.0
Exp	13.3	19.3	24.3	26.5	4.9	6.5	6.5	0.8
Imp	13.2	19.2	25.5	26.8	5.7	6.9	6.6	0.1
Developing economies								
GDP	100.0	100.0	100.0	100.0	3.6	4.7	7.0	5.3
HH	58.3	57.3	54.6	52.9	3.7	4.4	5.9	4.5
Gov	16.1	14.4	13.5	13.6	3.7	3.6	5.9	5.7
Inv	24.3	25.7	27.5	30.8	1.6	4.8	10.4	7.4
Exp	22.2	30.3	40.4	42.0	3.5	8.2	12.0	5.9
Imp	19.6	27.2	35.9	39.6	3.2	7.7	13.1	7.0
Transition economies								
GDP	...	100.0	100.0	100.0	...	-3.0	7.6	1.2
HH	...	47.0	53.2	60.8	...	-1.3	10.7	3.3
Gov	...	20.2	16.7	15.2	...	-1.8	2.7	0.8
Inv	...	27.1	23.1	24.0	...	-12.2	14.9	-2.1
Exp	...	30.8	38.6	37.0	...	1.1	8.4	0.8
Imp	...	23.3	31.2	35.5	...	-2.7	15.5	0.9
United States								
GDP	100.0	100.0	100.0	100.0	3.6	3.5	2.8	0.0
HH	66.8	67.7	70.0	70.9	3.8	3.8	3.0	0.3
Gov	20.4	17.1	15.8	16.5	3.4	1.2	1.4	1.5
Inv	15.4	17.7	19.4	15.7	4.1	6.6	3.7	-5.1
Exp	6.5	10.0	11.1	13.1	6.0	6.0	7.2	2.6
Imp	7.9	12.2	16.3	16.2	7.9	8.9	6.4	-0.5
Europe								
GDP	100.0	100.0	100.0	100.0	2.5	2.3	2.6	-0.3
HH	57.7	57.8	57.6	57.5	2.5	2.3	2.2	0.0
Gov	22.4	21.2	20.4	21.1	1.9	1.6	1.9	1.3
Inv	18.9	19.7	20.8	19.6	3.4	2.8	4.7	-4.2
Exp	19.4	28.8	37.9	41.0	4.5	6.8	6.5	0.8
Imp	18.5	27.4	36.7	39.2	5.0	6.6	6.8	0.1
Japan								
GDP	100.0	100.0	100.0	100.0	4.6	0.9	1.8	-0.8
HH	58.1	57.8	57.6	58.6	4.0	1.3	1.1	0.4
Gov	15.4	16.4	18.3	19.0	3.6	3.0	1.0	1.7
Inv	27.0	26.6	22.5	19.8	6.1	-1.1	1.2	-4.7
Exp	8.1	9.8	14.5	15.7	4.9	3.9	9.6	-1.5
Imp	7.6	10.2	12.8	13.0	5.9	4.0	4.8	-0.7
China								
GDP	100.0	100.0	100.0	100.0	10.3	10.1	11.6	9.6
HH	53.5	45.2	38.9	35.9	11.8	8.7	8.0	8.8
Gov	14.5	14.7	14.0	13.2	11.8	10.0	9.8	7.9
Inv	38.0	38.3	41.7	46.4	7.9	10.6	13.4	13.4
Exp	9.7	20.3	36.0	39.9	13.6	18.3	20.0	13.7
Imp	9.4	17.5	30.4	35.3	14.3	17.1	18.6	18.0

Right panel

	Percentage of GDP				Average annual growth			
	1981–1990	1991–2002	2003–2007	2008–2011	1981–1990	1991–2002	2003–2007	2008–2011
Developing economies, excl.China								
GDP	100.0	100.0	100.0	100.0	3.1	3.8	5.9	3.8
HH	58.7	59.5	58.8	58.8	3.1	3.8	5.5	3.6
Gov	16.3	14.3	13.3	13.7	3.1	2.6	4.8	5.0
Inv	23.0	23.4	23.6	25.3	0.7	3.4	9.1	3.9
Exp	23.4	32.1	41.5	42.8	3.1	7.2	10.3	3.6
Imp	20.5	28.9	37.4	41.1	2.8	6.9	12.0	4.1
Latin America and the Caribbean								
GDP	100.0	100.0	100.0	100.0	1.7	2.9	4.9	2.8
HH	59.9	62.5	63.2	64.7	1.6	3.0	5.2	3.3
Gov	17.5	15.5	14.5	14.5	1.8	1.9	3.4	3.7
Inv	21.2	21.3	20.9	22.5	-2.1	3.9	7.7	2.3
Exp	11.9	18.8	24.5	23.9	4.7	7.6	7.8	1.7
Imp	10.3	18.1	23.2	26.7	0.1	8.4	11.2	4.4
Africa								
GDP	100.0	100.0	100.0	100.0	1.9	2.9	5.8	3.5
HH	61.7	62.4	62.1	62.8	1.9	3.2	5.1	4.3
Gov	16.0	15.6	14.7	16.0	2.7	1.6	6.5	5.9
Inv	21.4	18.0	19.6	22.3	-4.5	3.2	9.3	4.5
Exp	29.3	33.7	36.6	35.7	1.8	4.1	8.6	0.5
Imp	27.3	27.1	31.9	36.3	-2.4	4.7	10.6	4.1
West Asia								
GDP	100.0	100.0	100.0	100.0	1.4	3.7	6.9	3.7
HH	49.8	51.1	52.7	53.1	3.6	3.5	7.9	2.5
Gov	17.1	15.1	15.0	16.0	4.6	2.1	7.0	4.7
Inv	16.5	16.8	20.8	24.2	-0.2	3.9	15.1	4.1
Exp	42.5	40.5	45.6	44.7	-3.4	5.3	9.5	2.2
Imp	26.3	23.8	34.1	39.3	1.3	4.1	16.9	2.1
South Asia								
GDP	100.0	100.0	100.0	100.0	4.7	5.1	8.1	6.4
HH	65.5	61.2	58.3	57.3	4.1	4.7	7.2	5.6
Gov	13.6	12.2	10.9	11.3	3.0	4.7	5.9	9.0
Inv	30.3	26.8	32.1	35.8	2.7	4.1	14.2	7.4
Exp	11.3	15.9	21.1	23.0	6.0	7.0	13.6	8.6
Imp	15.9	16.0	22.5	27.1	0.9	6.0	17.1	9.0
South-East Asia								
GDP	100.0	100.0	100.0	100.0	5.1	4.6	6.2	4.5
HH	56.5	56.0	56.8	55.9	4.7	5.0	5.4	4.3
Gov	11.7	10.0	10.2	10.9	3.7	4.2	5.8	6.4
Inv	31.4	31.0	24.0	25.0	4.8	0.5	6.9	5.4
Exp	39.2	62.4	82.1	83.7	7.4	8.9	11.3	3.6
Imp	37.5	57.9	73.1	75.3	6.6	7.7	11.7	3.5
East Asia, excl.China								
GDP	100.0	100.0	100.0	100.0	8.7	5.4	4.9	3.3
HH	57.6	59.1	55.4	53.1	8.0	5.3	3.2	2.3
Gov	16.9	14.5	12.8	12.7	6.2	3.6	3.2	3.3
Inv	26.8	30.5	26.5	23.1	10.4	3.7	3.8	0.4
Exp	31.5	45.5	65.5	74.0	12.7	9.2	11.8	5.3
Imp	32.4	49.3	61.0	63.8	12.0	7.8	9.6	3.7

Source: UNCTAD secretariat calculations, based on *UNCTADstat*.

Note: Averages and growth rates based on constant 2005 prices and 2005 exchange rates. HH=household consumption expenditure; Gov=government consumption expenditure; Inv=gross capital formation; Exp=exports, Imp=imports. Numbers do not necessarily add up to 100 due to rounding.

in market values, provided that these countries continue their catch-up process.

These changes in the shares of different countries and country groups in global output and in their contributions to global growth have been accompanied by changes in the composition of aggregate demand in many of them. A comparison of the evolution of private consumption, public expenditure (more precisely, government consumption, since it excludes public investment), investment, exports and imports shows that between the 1980s and 2003–2007 government consumption as a share of GDP fell in the vast majority of regions (table 1.7). Government consumption in constant prices recovered in Africa, Latin America and West Asia during the period of the commodity price boom between 2003 and 2007, when many governments in these regions used windfall gains to boost social spending. Major exceptions to the general decline in the share of current government spending in aggregate demand were Japan, where spending increased with a view to compensating for the sharp decline in the share of private demand, and China, where it remained fairly stable, while the share of domestic consumption fell.

This comparison also shows a slight reversal of the widespread tendency of a declining share of government consumption in GDP during the period 2008–2011. This reversal resulted from a rapid expansion of countercyclical fiscal spending in all country groups (Griffith-Jones and Ocampo, 2009),[19] except in transition economies and China. This exception is partly due to the fact that most of the countercyclical fiscal stimulus in that country consisted of higher public investment rather than current expenditure. The share of investment (public and private) rose by 8 percentage points, averaging 46 per cent of GDP in the period 2008–2011. This was accompanied by a significant fall in the share of household consumption in GDP from an average of over 50 per cent in the 1980s to an average of about 36 per cent in the period 2008–2011.

The evolution of the composition of aggregate supply and demand over the three decades from 1981 to 2011 shows a very rapid growth of exports and imports, both in developed and developing countries (table 1.7). Their share in GDP, at constant prices, virtually doubled: from around 13 per cent to 27 per cent in developed countries, and from 20 per cent to close to 40 per cent in developing countries. At

current prices, this growth was somewhat slower in the latter group of countries (and has even slightly reversed since 2008) owing to a real appreciation of most developing-country currencies during the period, which resulted in their GDP at current prices growing faster than at constant prices. The increase was most notable in East and South-East Asia, where the share of exports in GDP rose by more than 30 percentage points between 1981–1990 and 2008–2011. Net exports in China (exports minus imports) amounted to 6 per cent of its GDP between 2003 and 2007.

To sum up, the larger role of international trade in the composition of aggregate demand in developing countries' growth was accompanied by a smaller role of government consumption in most of these economies. East Asia, especially China, also saw a significant decline in the share of household consumption in GDP. Until the early 2000s, increased participation in international trade had beneficial effects in a number of countries, especially in developing Asia, although much less so in Latin America and Africa. With the generally favourable external economic environment from 2003 until the onset of the latest crisis, their greater outward orientation contributed to an increase in the growth performance of all these developing regions. However, an export-oriented growth strategy also implies greater vulnerability to a deterioration of the external environment, as witnessed since 2008.

2. *Vulnerability to trade shocks*

The impact of an export-oriented strategy on a country's economic growth depends on the evolution of global demand for that country's exports and/or on price developments of those goods that constitute a large proportion of the country's export basket. Changing international prices have long been recognized as a major external source of a country's vulnerability. They have a particularly strong effect on countries that export mainly primary commodities, since prices of commodities have generally been more volatile than those of manufactures and services. In addition, the global financial crisis poses the risk of a severe slowdown of demand for manufactures exported by developing countries, and a further decline in the prices of such manufactures,

Chart 1.7

TRADE SHOCKS, BY DEVELOPING REGION AND EXPORT SPECIALIZATION, 2004–2012

(Change relative to GDP in previous year, per cent)

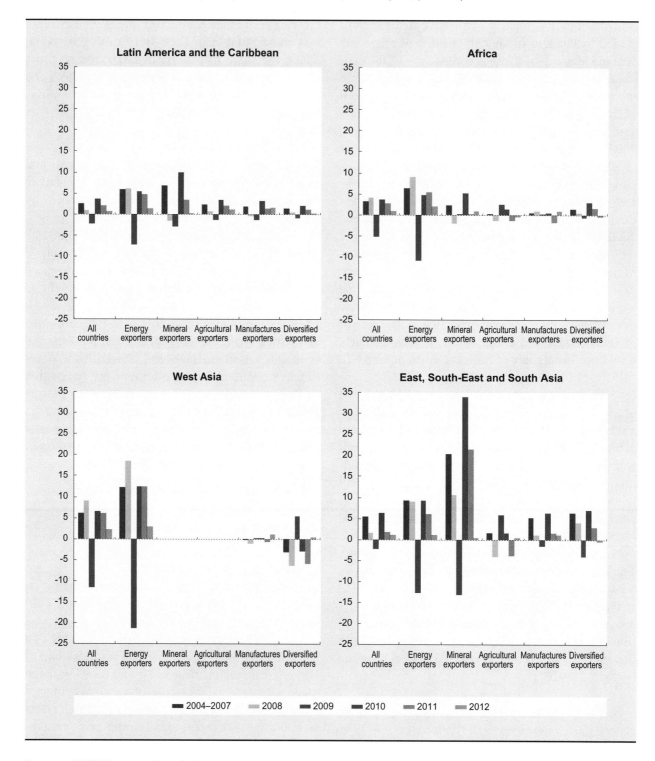

Source: UNCTAD secretariat calculations, based on *UN Comtrade*; *UNCTADstat*; United States Bureau of Labor Statistics (BLS);
            and CPB Netherlands Bureau for Economic Policy Analysis.
    Note: A trade shock is calculated as the gains and losses in national income (measured as a percentage of GDP) resulting from
            changes in export volumes and terms of trade. Within each region, countries are classified by export specialization where
            energy, minerals or agricultural products account for at least 40 per cent, or manufactures for at least 50 per cent, of a
            country's exports; all other countries are classified as diversified exporters.

Table 1.8

WORLD EXPORTS BY ORIGIN AND DESTINATION, SELECTED COUNTRY GROUPS, 1995–2012

(Per cent of world exports)

	Destination Origin	Developing economies	Transition economies	Developed economies	Total
1995	Developing economies	11.9	0.3	16.1	28.3
	Transition economies	0.3	0.6	1.1	2.1
	Developed economies	16.6	1.1	52.1	69.7
	Total	28.8	2.0	69.2	100.0
2000	Developing economies	13.1	0.2	18.8	32.1
	Transition economies	0.4	0.5	1.4	2.4
	Developed economies	15.0	0.8	49.8	65.5
	Total	28.5	1.5	70.1	100.0
2005	Developing economies	16.7	0.5	19.1	36.3
	Transition economies	0.6	0.7	2.1	3.5
	Developed economies	13.6	1.4	45.3	60.3
	Total	31.0	2.5	66.5	100.0
2008	Developing economies	19.8	0.8	18.3	38.9
	Transition economies	0.9	0.9	2.8	4.6
	Developed economies	13.6	1.9	40.9	56.5
	Total	34.3	3.7	62.0	100.0
2010	Developing economies	23.2	0.7	18.4	42.3
	Transition economies	0.9	0.7	2.1	3.7
	Developed economies	15.3	1.5	37.2	54.0
	Total	39.4	2.9	57.7	100.0
2012	Developing economies	25.3	0.8	18.5	44.7
	Transition economies	0.9	0.8	2.4	4.1
	Developed economies	15.0	1.7	34.6	51.2
	Total	41.2	3.3	55.5	100.0

Source: UNCTAD secretariat calculations, based on *UNCTADstat*.
Note: Numbers do not necessarily add up to 100 due to rounding.

especially low-skill-intensive products (see also chapter II of this *Report*).

To examine countries' vulnerability to international price and demand shocks, individual countries within each geographical region were classified according to their export specialization (chart 1.7). An analysis of this classification shows that both exporters of primary commodities and exporters of manufactures suffered severe trade shocks during the period 2008–2009. But it also shows that the beneficial impact of the subsequent rebound was both larger and more rapid for countries with a high share of primary commodities in their exports than for countries exporting mainly manufactures.

Some observers have interpreted developing countries' relatively rapid economic growth in recent years as a manifestation of their "decoupling" from

the economic performance of developed countries. This has led them to conclude that the widely expected protracted weakness of demand growth in developed countries may not cause a sizeable decline in developing countries' opportunities to export manufactures. Rather, developing countries could move to a new type of export-led growth, with South-South trade becoming the main driving force (Canuto, Haddad and Hanson, 2010). South-South trade has indeed gained in importance, with its share in total developing-country exports increasing from less than 30 per cent during the second half of the 1990s to almost 45 per cent in 2012. About half of this increase has occurred since 2008 (table 1.8).

However, as already mentioned, the rapid growth in developing countries in 2010 was mainly due to their adoption of countercyclical macroeconomic policies and their recovery from the slowdown

Table 1.9

SOUTH-SOUTH EXPORTS, BY REGION AND PRODUCT CATEGORY, 1995–2012

(Per cent of total South-South trade)

	Share in total South-South exports of the respective product category						Average annual percentage growth		
	1995	2000	2005	2007	2010	2012	1996–2002	2003–2007	2008–2012
Asia									
Asian exports to other developing countries									
Total merchandise	7.8	8.1	7.9	9.0	10.2	10.1	5.8	29.1	14.4
Manufactures	9.0	9.4	9.2	11.1	13.3	13.5	5.5	28.6	14.8
Primary commodities	5.2	5.4	5.4	5.6	5.4	5.5	7.2	30.7	12.6
Intraregional exports									
Total merchandise	76.5	76.7	77.1	75.3	73.7	74.4	5.4	23.5	12.1
Manufactures	80.8	81.7	82.3	80.5	78.9	78.8	5.4	21.3	10.6
Primary commodities	66.2	66.2	66.4	65.4	63.7	66.2	5.4	29.3	13.5
Intra- East and South-East Asian exports									
Total merchandise	58.7	55.9	53.3	49.4	46.5	45.8	4.5	20.6	11.2
Manufactures	68.8	70.0	68.0	64.2	60.9	60.3	5.4	20.0	9.9
Primary commodities	35.4	27.2	25.2	23.1	22.5	23.0	1.4	24.3	14.0
China's exports to other Asian developing countries									
Total merchandise	10.6	10.9	15.9	17.4	17.0	18.2	9.1	30.1	13.1
Manufactures	12.6	13.8	21.5	24.8	25.0	27.8	9.9	31.3	13.1
Primary commodities	5.9	4.9	5.0	4.4	4.0	4.5	5.0	20.8	13.8
Other Asian developing countries' exports to China									
Total merchandise	13.2	14.6	18.9	17.5	17.9	17.5	8.3	24.9	13.3
Manufactures	15.1	17.0	22.8	21.2	21.4	19.6	9.0	23.1	10.1
Primary commodities	9.2	10.0	11.6	11.1	12.5	12.9	5.6	32.3	17.9
Latin America and the Caribbean									
Intraregional exports									
Total merchandise	7.7	7.7	6.3	6.2	5.2	5.0	2.8	25.2	6.8
Manufactures	6.1	5.9	5.3	5.4	4.8	4.9	1.9	26.8	7.7
Primary commodities	11.6	11.7	8.7	7.9	6.1	5.6	4.0	23.2	5.7
Latin American and Caribbean exports to other developing countries									
Total merchandise	3.2	2.3	3.5	3.8	4.8	5.1	2.7	30.6	19.6
Manufactures	1.4	0.9	1.4	1.3	1.0	1.1	0.1	24.3	5.8
Primary commodities	7.3	5.3	8.0	8.7	11.7	11.7	3.9	32.7	22.4
Latin American and Caribbean exports to China									
Total merchandise	0.4	0.5	1.2	1.4	2.2	2.3	11.7	38.0	25.4
Manufactures	0.1	0.1	0.3	0.3	0.3	0.4	20.7	20.7	13.3
Primary commodities	1.3	1.2	3.0	3.6	5.6	5.5	9.8	42.7	26.8
Africa									
Intraregional exports									
Total merchandise	2.3	1.8	1.7	1.7	1.8	1.6	2.1	18.9	10.2
Manufactures	1.7	1.2	1.0	1.1	1.2	1.0	1.0	13.1	8.7
Primary commodities	3.7	3.0	2.9	2.7	2.6	2.5	3.0	22.7	10.7
African exports to other developing countries									
Total merchandise	2.4	3.2	3.4	3.9	4.3	3.8	7.9	32.3	12.6
Manufactures	0.9	0.8	0.8	0.6	0.8	0.8	1.8	18.0	12.3
Primary commodities	5.7	8.0	8.5	9.6	10.3	8.5	9.9	35.3	12.3
African exports to China									
Total merchandise	0.2	0.6	1.1	1.4	1.7	1.1	23.2	51.0	8.4
Manufactures	0.1	0.0	0.1	0.1	0.1	0.1	3.8	23.3	21.6
Primary commodities	0.5	1.6	3.3	3.9	4.6	2.6	27.4	53.3	7.8

Source: UNCTAD secretariat calculations, based on *UNCTADstat*.

Note: Shares of developing Oceania's exports are negligible and therefore not reported.

(or recession) of 2009, though their growth has been losing steam since then. Moreover, a disaggregation of developing countries' total exports by major product categories indicates little change in the two main characteristics of South-South trade, namely its narrow concentration in Asia, related to these countries' strong involvement in international production networks, with developed countries as final destination markets, and the major role of primary commodities in the expansion of South-South trade over the past two decades (see also *TDR 2005*, chap. IV). Three quarters of South-South trade takes place within Asia, and Asian exports to other developing countries account for another 10 per cent of such trade (table 1.9). China alone accounts for about 40 per cent of South-South trade, almost half of intra-Asian total merchandise trade and 60 per cent of intra-Asian trade in manufactures, as well as for about one third of all developing-country imports from Africa and Latin America. This implies that China has probably been the single most important country in stimulating South-South trade through its imports from other developing countries over the past two decades.

Moreover, the share of manufactured exports between countries in East and South-East Asia in total South-South trade in manufactures has declined significantly since 2000, and even more so since 2005 (table 1.9). This decline is mirrored by a decline in China's imports of manufactures from other developing Asian countries as a share of total South-South trade in manufactures. A contributory factor could be the decline in exports from Asian supply chains to their developed-country end markets.[20] But it could also be due to the rising share of primary exports from Latin America and Africa in South-South trade. However, on a cautionary note, it should be borne in mind that the large amount of trade between geographically close countries involved in international production chains results in considerable double-counting of South-South trade in manufactures, since the exports of countries participating in those chains generally have a high import content, and those chains play an important role in South-South trade.

The significant role of primary commodities in the dynamics of South-South exports reflects, *inter alia*, the rapid increase in the absolute value of South-South trade in mineral fuels and metals, which has grown much more rapidly than that of any other product category, especially since 2008 (chart 1.8).

On the other hand, while developing-country exports to developed countries have grown less rapidly, overall, low-, medium- and high-skill and technologically-intensive manufactures were the most dynamic product groups in South-North trade over the period 1995–2012, second only to mineral fuels.

Taken together, there is little evidence to support the view that South-South trade has become an autonomous engine of growth for developing countries. Rather, the close links between the dynamics of South-South trade, on the one hand, and trade in primary commodities and trade within international production networks whose final destination is developed-country markets, on the other, indicates that engaging in South-South trade has probably done little to reduce developing countries' vulnerability to external trade shocks. However, if developing countries could shift to a growth strategy that gives a greater role to domestic demand growth, a greater share of their manufactured imports would be destined for final use in their domestic markets rather than being re-exported to developed countries. Such a shift could well increase the contribution of South-South trade to output growth in developing countries.

This strengthens the argument for a renewed role for domestic demand as the motor for a sustained and balanced growth of the world economy. Another set of adverse conditions related to the relatively more subdued growth performance of developing countries arises from the heightened instability of capital flows. Indeed, emerging economies saw a sudden reversal of the large capital inflows they had received until early 2013, following the first signs of a probable withdrawal of quantitative easing by the Federal Reserve of the United States in June 2013, which exacerbated uncertainty in the financial markets, with possible repercussions for the macroeconomic policies of many developing countries.

3. Vulnerability to financial instability

The strong rise in cross-border capital movements since the mid-1970s has been accompanied by an increase in the share of developing countries as recipients of international capital flows. However, capital flows to developing countries have rarely exhibited a continuous and smooth tendency; rather,

Chart 1.8

EVOLUTION OF DEVELOPING-COUNTRY EXPORTS BY BROAD PRODUCT CATEGORY, 1995–2012

(Index numbers, 1995 = 100)

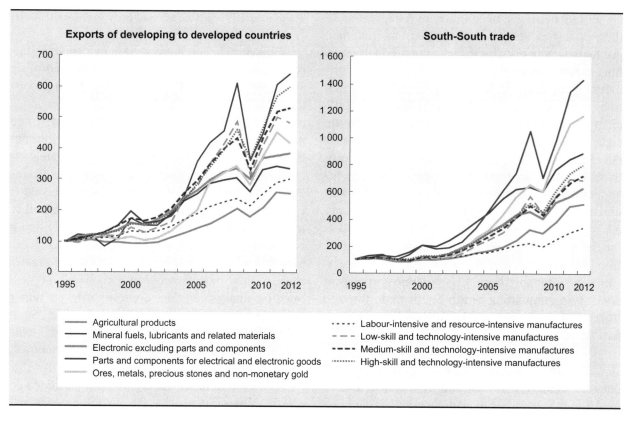

Source: UNCTAD secretariat calculations, based on *UNCTADstat*, Merchandise trade matrix.

they have frequently been punctuated by sudden reversals. The associated boom-bust cycles in domestic credit and asset prices have recurrently triggered severe crises in these countries. The sheer magnitude of capital outflows from developed to developing countries, driven by even minor adjustments in financial portfolios, tend to destabilize the economies of the latter countries, as discussed in chapter III of this *Report*.

Another important factor contributing to developing countries' financial vulnerability relates to the price formation mechanisms in markets, including exchange rates and commodity markets, which can have a strong impact on developing countries. The rapidly growing presence of financial traders on commodity markets has overridden market mechanisms, resulting in a looser link between the ultimate supply or demand of the commodity and the treatment of commodity futures as a financial asset. As traders

tend to make position changes based on information related to other asset markets, irrespective of prevailing conditions in specific commodity markets, they have tended to generate a positive correlation between the prices of different asset classes (equity shares, currencies usually used as targets in carry-trade operations and commodity prices) (*TDR 2009*, chap. II). Chart 1.9 shows how the prices of different kinds of assets, which were uncorrelated until the early 2000, have become highly correlated since 2002, and especially since 2008. The more synchronized price movements across those assets indicate a weaker operation of fundamentals in price formation in each of their markets. For instance, currency appreciation or depreciation generally did not reflect current account conditions in several developing economies: the Brazilean real appreciated, both in nominal and real terms, between 2006 and 2008, and again between 2009 and mid-2011, despite a persistent deterioration in its current account balance;

Chart 1.9

PRICE TRENDS IN GLOBAL ASSET MARKETS, 1980–2012

(Price index)

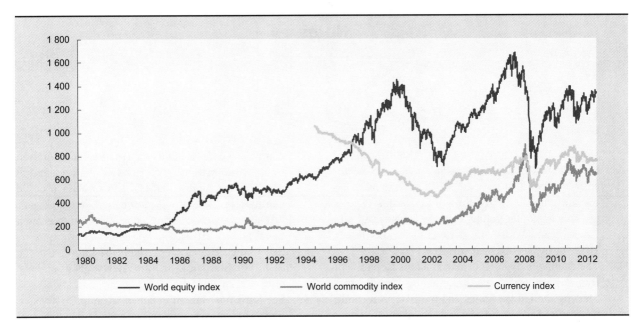

Source: UNCTAD secretariat calculations, based on Bloomberg.
Note: World equity index refers to the MSCI world index. World commodity index refers to the S&P GSCI index. Currency index refers to an equally weighted index, which includes the Australian dollar, the Brazilian real and the South African rand spot rates (average 1995 = 1,000).

similarly, between 2003 and mid-2008, Turkey's real effective exchange rate (REER)[21] appreciated by almost 50 per cent, in parallel with a gradual increase of its current account deficit.

This development has been exacerbated by the proliferation of information systems and models which are driven by the same data and trading principles (such as so-called "momentum trading", "risk-on/risk-off" behavioural responses or, generally, "algorithmic trading"). Trading based on these models is often done very rapidly (often referred to as high-frequency trading) and tends to result in herd behaviour, whereby market participants mimic each others' trading behaviour, follow the price trend for some time and try to disinvest just before the other market participants sell their assets (UNCTAD, 2011; Bicchetti and Maystre, 2012; and UNCTAD, 2012).

Taken together, the above evidence indicates that key prices for the economies of developing countries may move in ways unrelated to market fundamentals, and in tandem with those of other asset classes such as equities. The consequent high degree of cross-market correlation and herd behaviour risks making global financial markets "thinner", in the sense that virtually all market participants take bets on the same side of the market, which makes it more difficult to find a matching counterpart. The corollary to this is that relatively minor events can trigger a drastic change of direction in financial or financialized markets. In addition, such price changes may be more sensitive to changes in the monetary policies of developed countries, or in the general risk perception prevailing in those countries, than on supply and demand conditions in specific commodity markets and developing countries.

Notes

1 Despite the reconstruction and rehabilitation of machine production facilities in the areas of north-eastern Japan that were hit by the earthquake and tsunami and the robust growth of Japan's exports towards many developing countries in Africa, Latin America and West Asia, its overall exports fell in 2012 for the second year in a row.

2 The decline in exports from the Islamic Republic of Iran was primarily due to a tightening of trade sanctions by the United States and the EU. As a result, its exports of crude oil and lease condensate shrank by about 40 per cent, to approximately 1.5 million barrels per day (bbl/d) in 2012, compared with 2.5 million bbl/d in 2011.

3 At first sight, this evolution of exports of the group of emerging Asian economies slightly contrasts with the patterns of other developing regions. However, this relatively high figure of 6.2 per cent needs to be viewed with some caution. First, it results partly from relatively low levels in early 2012, which to some extent could reflect distortions associated with the Chinese New Year. Second, CPB robust trade data for January to April 2013 contrast with more negative signals emanating from China's customs figures for May and June 2013. According to the latter source, the value of China's exports shrank by 3.1 per cent in June year on year, down from a meagre 1 per cent in May. Meanwhile, imports fell by 0.7 per cent in June, year on year, having slipped by 0.3 per cent in May. Third, the year-on-year rise of 17.4 per cent of the value of exports for the January–April 2013 period presumably partly reflect overinvoicing practices by exporters speculating on the appreciation of the renminbi (*Financial Times*, "China to crack down on faked export deals", 6 May 2013). These practices would also affect CPB's data on trade volumes. For at least these reasons, it remains difficult to fully grasp the magnitude of the slowdown in this region. In addition, in all likelihood, the squeeze in the Chinese money market and an unexpected rise in inventories, which are extremely dependent on changes in the growth of the economy, also played a role in these recent low trade figures. Nevertheless,

recent anecdotal evidence of a marked deterioration in industrial activity, such as a fall in output and in new orders, suggest that China's slowdown could continue in the coming months (*Financial Times*, "Anaemic manufacturing data raise China growth fears", 1 July 2013).

4 See United States Department of Labor, Bureau of Labor Statistics, at: http://www.bls.gov/news.release/empsit.t15.htm.

5 See Statistics Bureau of Japan, at: http://www.stat.go.jp/english/data/roudou/lngindex.htm.

6 This decline in absolute terms was quite general: the EU lost 5 million jobs between the last quarter of 2007 and that of 2012; the United States lost 3.5 million jobs between December 2007 and December 2012; and in Japan employment fell by 1.5 million between December 2007 and May 2013, though this may be partly due to demographic trends, as the working age population diminished by 5.2 million persons between 1998 and 2012. See European Commission Eurostat, at: http://epp.eurostat.ec.europa.eu/portal/page/portal/employment_unemployment_lfs/data/database; United States Department of Labor, Bureau of Labor Statistics, at: http://www.bls.gov/news.release/empsit.t15.htm; and Statistics Bureau of Japan, at: http://www.stat.go.jp/english/data/roudou/lngindex.htm.

7 Multipliers differ, depending on which expenditure is reduced or which tax is raised, and the most costly are cuts in investment spending. Multipliers are much lower (generally below 0.6) if fiscal consolidation policies are credible (i.e. if markets are convinced that announced consolidation measures will be fully implemented and enduring). Based on these considerations, the ECB states that "While there may be a temporary deterioration in growth resulting from fiscal consolidation, well-designed fiscal adjustment leads to a permanent improvement in the structural balance and thus has a favourable impact on the path of the debt-to-GDP ratio. Consequently, postponing the necessary budgetary adjustment is not a credible alternative to a timely correction of fiscal imbalances" (ECB, 2012: 81).

8   Additional modelling exercises also show that the fiscal multipliers can have a greater impact on GDP depending mostly on: (i) the composition of the initial policy shock, and (ii) whether the expansionary shock is accompanied by income redistribution policies. Essentially, if progressive income distribution effects are included in the design of fiscal measures, the positive response to larger government spending is higher. Meanwhile, the negative effect on GDP of increased taxation, net of transfers and subsidies, is smaller if it consists of higher direct taxation, and larger if it consists of lower social transfers.

9   Arithmetically, the overall effect on the public-debt-to-GDP ratio of a debt-financed increase in public spending depends on the values of the fiscal multiplier, the public revenues as a percentage of GDP and the initial debt stock as a percentage of GDP. For instance, assuming a multiplier of 1.3, an initial debt-to-GDP ratio of 60 per cent and public revenues-to-GDP ratio of 35 per cent, an increase of 5 per cent of GDP in public spending would reduce the debt-to-GDP ratio to 59 per cent. The empirical debate, however, is basically economic, and revolves around the "crowding-out" debate. As stated in *TDR 2011*: "for those who believe in crowding out effects, increases in government spending reduce private expenditure. In this case, either supplementary spending is financed with borrowing and leads to a higher interest rate, which lowers investment and consumption, or the government opts to raise taxes to bridge the fiscal gap, which reduces private disposable income and demand. Hence, public stimulus will be irrelevant at best, and may even be counterproductive if it raises concerns among private investors. Theoretical models supporting this view have been criticized for their unrealistic assumptions – such as perfect foresight, infinite planning horizons, perfect capital markets, and an absence of distribution effects through taxation – which make them unsuitable for policy decisions in the real world. In particular, their starting point usually assumes full employment, when the discussion is precisely how to recover from an economic slump. Even in more normal times, however, the empirical evidence for crowding out is weak at best."

10   "Fiscal space" may have different meanings. The most comprehensive and useful from an economics point of view is the capability of generating a fiscal stimulus that would improve economic and fiscal conditions in the medium to long term. Hence, even if a country has high fiscal deficits and a high public-debt-to-GDP ratio, a government has fiscal space, from a dynamic perspective, if it can access low-cost financing and profit from the very high fiscal multipliers that exist during economic recessions. A static view of fiscal space only compares the current level of public debt or deficit with a given target (which may be self-imposed or agreed with the IMF or the European Commission).

11   This primary income is supplemented by income redistribution (or secondary income) implemented by the State through direct taxation and personal transfers.

12   The falling trends in the share of labour income are evident in both absolute and relative terms. In absolute terms, the growth of real wages of the population in the lower segments of income distribution has remained subdued, or even negative, in several developed countries over the past few decades (see, for example, *TDR 2010*). In developing countries, there was significant wage growth between 2000 and 2007, but this has slowed down, and in many cases halted, since the start of the recent financial crisis (Ashenfelter, 2012). In relative terms, available empirical analyses of the functional distribution of income, which cover various countries, also point to growing inequality in the distribution of value added. Labour income as a share of total income has been falling in almost all developed countries (Storm and Naastepad, 2012; *TDR 2012*). In developing countries, even though empirical evidence is scarcer and more heterogeneous, these shares have also declined, on average, although a reversal has taken place in the 2000s in a number of Latin American and South-East Asian countries (Stockhammer, 2012; *TDR 2012*).

13   Looking at the world economy as a whole, Onaran and Galanis (2012) show that a simultaneous and continuing decline in the wage share leads to a slowdown of global growth. Furthermore, in a more detailed investigation of 16 individual country members of the G-20, the authors find that 9 of these countries show a positive correlation between wage growth and GDP growth. Of the remaining 7 economies which show negative correlations between wage growth and GDP growth when considered individually, 4 of them effectively register lower growth when facing a simultaneous reduction in the wage share. Moreover, they find that when the wage shares of all economies fall simultaneously, these four economies contract as well. Galbraith (2012) reaches a similar conclusion based on a large empirical investigation across many countries and over time. In this case, however, a negative impact on growth from more unequal distribution is shown to be strongly influenced by the nature of the changes in income distribution, as well as by the socio-economic context and the level of development. For example, the effect of changes in income distribution on consumption in the United States over the past three decades is shaped by developments in the financial sector. On the one hand, the growth of the financial sector is a key determinant of the rapid deterioration of income distribution. (The vast data sample confirms that countries and cities that

predominantly host financial activities also display a high degree of inequality of income distribution.) On the other hand, the impact on household spending is mediated by the ability of the financial sector to extend credit to enable consumption, which can last until a crisis emerges. In developing countries, Galbraith (2012) confirms a pattern of inequality over the long run similar to what Kuznets posited, namely that rising inequality in early stages of development is followed by improvements in income distribution as development progresses. However, at some stages and in specific ways, developments in the financial sector also exert an influence on how rising inequality is transmitted to spending. Evidence from China, for example, shows that a greater share of the rising national income is contributing to financial speculation and real estate bubbles, and thus household consumption is not rising as fast as national income.

14   According to Minsky (1982), one of the reasons why recovery from the Great Depression of the 1930s was so difficult was the small amount of public expenditure around 1930, which was only 10 per cent of GDP in the United States.

15   For instance, a deficit of 3.6 per cent of GDP is consistent with a debt ratio that is stabilized at 60 per cent of GDP, with an annual real GDP growth of 3 per cent and an increase in the GDP deflator of 3 per cent.

16   These considerations mainly concern the degree of effectiveness of the multiplier, depending on the level, or lack, of aggregate demand and to what extent private agents are preoccupied with their own balance sheets. Another consideration in assessing the government's effectiveness in sustaining demand and employment relates to the degree of confidence of private agents in government actions (Berglund and Vernengo, 2004). With a similar consideration in mind, based on an empirical study of 140 countries over the period 1972–2005, Carrère and de Melo (2012), suggest that fiscal stimulus is effective provided the rest of the economy is stable and the fiscal deficit is contained. In sum, the effectiveness

of public spending to generate demand and employment depends not only on economic processes, but also on political ones (Kalecki, 1943).

17   As stated by Bernanke, "Some observers have expressed concern about rising levels of household debt, and we at the Federal Reserve follow these developments closely. However, concerns about debt growth should be allayed by the fact that household assets (particularly housing wealth) have risen even more quickly than household liabilities." Similar remarks were made by his predecessor as Chairman of the Federal Reserve Board, Alan Greenspan, in his testimony before the Committee on Banking, Housing, and Urban Affairs of the United States Senate in February 2005 (available at: http://www. federalreserve.gov/boarddocs/hh/2005/february/ testimony.htm).

18   This is explained by the so-called Balassa-Samuelson effect (i.e. price levels in wealthier countries are systematically higher than in poorer ones).

19   The United Nations (2010: table I.4) recorded the fiscal measures made public by many governments at the time of the crisis. Of the 55 countries covered, the 10 countries that applied the strongest stimulus measures, all but one were developing and transition economies. In eight of these countries, the measures amounted to more than 10 per cent of GDP spread over two to three years. However, following the implementation of such high levels of stimulus since 2012, there may have been a turnaround in the pace of government spending. Ortiz and Cummins (2013), on reviewing government projections up to 2016, as recorded by the IMF, note that there has been a shift towards fiscal austerity by 119 countries in 2013, and this is likely to increase to 132 countries by 2015.

20   *TDR 2002* (Part 2, chap. III) provides an early discussion of the role of international production networks in the export dynamism and industrialization of developing countries.

21   The REER corresponds to the nominal exchange rate of a currency vis-à-vis the currencies of all trading partners, adjusted for the inflation differentials.

References

Akyüz Y (2012). The staggering rise of the South? Research Paper No. 44, South Centre, Geneva.

Ashenfelter OC (2012). Comparing real wages. NBER Working Paper No. 18006, National Bureau of Economic Research, Cambridge, MA.

Barclays (2013). The Commodity Investor. 7 June.

Berglund PG and Vernengo M (2004). A debate on the deficit. *Challenge*, 47(6): 5–45.

Bernanke B (2005). Remarks at the Finance Committee Luncheon of the Executives' Club of Chicago, Chicago, 8 March.

Bicchetti D and Maystre N (2012). The Synchronized and long-lasting structural change on commodity markets: Evidence from high frequency data. UNCTAD Discussion Paper No. 208, Geneva.

Blanchard O and Leigh L (2013). Growth forecast errors and fiscal multipliers. IMF Working Paper No 13/1, International Monetary Fund, Washington, DC.

Calcagno, AF (2012). Can austerity work? Review of Keynesian Economics, 0(1): 24–36.

Canuto O, Haddad M and Hanson G (2010). Export-led growth v2.0. Economic Premise No. 3, Poverty Reduction and Economic Management Network, World Bank, Washington, DC.

Capaldo J and Izurieta A (2013). The imprudence of labour market flexibilization in a fiscally austere world. *International Labour Review*, 152(3): 1–26.

Carrère C and de Melo J (2012). Fiscal spending and economic growth: Some stylized facts. *World Development*, 40(9): 1750–1761.

ECB (2012). *Monthly Bulletin*, December. Frankfurt, European Central Bank.

ECLAC (2013). Economic Survey of Latin America and the Caribbean 2013: Three Decades of Uneven and Unstable Growth. Santiago, Chile.

ESCAP (2013). Economic and Social Survey of Asia and the Pacific 2013: Forward-Looking Macroeconomic Policies for Inclusive and Sustainable Development. United Nations publication, Sales No. E.13.II.F.2, Bangkok.

FAO (2013). *Food Outlook: Biannual Report on Global Food Markets*. Rome, June.

Galbraith JK (2008). *The Predator State: How Conservatives Abandoned the Free Market and Why Liberals Should Too*. New York, NY, Free Press.

Galbraith JK (2012*). Inequality and Instability: A Study of the World Economy Just Before the Great Crisis*. New York, NY, Oxford University Press.

Godley W (1999). Seven unsustainable processes: Medium-term prospects and policies for the United States and the world. Annandale-on-Hudson, NY, Levy Economics Institute of Bard College. (Revised in October 2000.)

Griffith Jones S and Ocampo JA (2009). The financial crisis and its impact on developing countries. Working Paper No 53, International Policy Centre for Inclusive Growth, United Nations Development Programme (UNDP), Brasilia.

IMF (2010). *World Economic Outlook*, Washington, DC. October.

IMF (2012). *World Economic Outlook*. Washington, DC. October.

Kalecki M (1943). Political aspects of full unemployment. *Political Quarterly*, 5(14): 322–331.

Kindleberger CP (1978). *Manias, panics and crashes: A history of financial crises*. London and Basingstoke, Macmillan.

Koo R (2013a). The world in balance sheet recession. In: Flassbeck H, Davidson P, Galbraith JK, Koo R and Ghosh J eds. *Economic Reform Now*. New York, Palgrave Macmillan, forthcoming.

Koo R (2013b). Monetary easing alone will not fix Japan. *Financial Times*, 18 March.

Krugman P (2012). *End This Depression Now!* New York, NY, WW Norton and Co.

Lund S, Daruvala T, Dobbs R, Härle P, Hwek J-H and Falcón R (2013). Financial globalization: Retreat or reset? *Global Economic Watch*, McKinsey Global Institute, McKinsey & Company.

Minsky HP (1982). Can "it" Happen Again? Essays on Instability and Finance. Armonk, NY, ME Sharpe.

Onaran O and Galanis G (2012). Is aggregate demand wage-led or profit-led? National and global effects. Conditions of Work and Employment Series No. 40. Geneva, International Labour Office.

Ortiz I and Cummins M (2013). The age of austerity: A review of public expenditures and adjustment measures in 181 countries. Working Paper, Initiative for Policy Dialogue and the South Centre, New York and Geneva.

Shin HS (2010). *Risk and Liquidity*, New York, NY, Oxford University Press.

Stockhammer E (2012). Why have wage shares fallen? A panel analysis of the determinants of functional income distribution. Conditions of Work and Employment Series No. 35. Geneva, International Labour Office.

Storm S and Naastepad CWM (2012). *Macroeconomics Beyond the NAIRU*. Cambridge, MA, Harvard University Press.

UNCTAD (*TDR 2002*). *Trade and Development Report, 2002: Developing Countries in World Trade*. United Nations publication, Sales No. E.02.II.D.2, New York and Geneva.

UNCTAD (*TDR 2005*). *Trade and Development Report, 2005: New Features of Global Interdependence*. United Nations publication, Sales No. E.05.II.D.13, New York and Geneva.

UNCTAD (*TDR 2009*). *Trade and Development Report, 2009: Responding to the Global Crisis: Climate Change Mitigation and Development*. United Nations publication, Sales No. E. 09.II.D.16, New York and Geneva.

UNCTAD (*TDR 2010*). *Trade and Development Report, 2010: Employment, Globalization and Development*. United Nations publication, Sales No. E.10.II.D.3, New York and Geneva.

UNCTAD (*TDR 2011*). *Trade and Development Report, 2011: Post-crisis Policy Challenges in the World Economy*. United Nations publication, Sales No. E.11.II.D.3, New York and Geneva.

UNCTAD (*TDR 2012*). *Trade and Development Report, 2012: Policies for Inclusive and Balanced Growth*. United Nations publication, Sales No. E.12.II.D.6, New York and Geneva.

UNCTAD (2011). Price formation in financialized commodity markets: The role of information. New York and Geneva, United Nations.

UNCTAD (2012). Don't blame the physical markets: Financialization is the root cause of oil and commodity price volatility. UNCTAD Policy Brief No. 25, Geneva.

UNCTAD (2013). *Review of Maritime Transport 2013*. Geneva (forthcoming).

UN-DESA (2010). *World Economic Situation and Prospects 2010*. United Nations publication, Sales No. E.10.II.C.2, New York.

World Tourism Organization (2013). *UNWTO World Tourism Barometer*, volume 11. Madrid, April.

ALTERNATIVE SCENARIOS FOR THE WORLD ECONOMY

This annex presents a quantification of global economic scenarios through 2030. It is intended to illustrate alternative scenarios for a balanced and sustained pro-growth global outcome based on the United Nations Global Policy Model.[1]

Three simulations are presented: a *baseline* and *two alternative scenarios*. The baseline is a projection assuming that there will be neither policy changes nor shocks ahead.[2] In the two *alternative scenarios*, a reorientation of macroeconomic policy towards the adoption of measures that provide stronger support for an expansion of aggregate domestic demand is assumed. These *alternative scenarios* assume a continuing path of economic convergence between countries, and incorporate the current macroeconomic constraints and potential of each economy or group of economies. In other words, they take into account their particular structural conditions, as well as the interactions between countries through trade and finance. The main distinction between the two alternative scenarios is that in one scenario all countries would be involved in a demand-driven policy effort (scenario A), while in the other scenario, only developing and emerging market economies would embark on this alternative macroeconomic policy stance (scenario B).

The alternative scenarios are grounded in macroeconomic reasoning, not political feasibility. Therefore, they do not discuss the policy coordination processes that would be needed at the regional or global levels, nor do they attach any probability to the occurrence of such processes. However, even though the political processes are not discussed, these simulations serve to illustrate the advantages that would result from a coordinated effort aimed at a sustained expansion of global demand. Left to the operation of markets alone, there would be no self-adjusting mechanisms for the world as a whole to ensure coherence between the policies of individual countries and avoid negative trade-offs and welfare losses. The quantifications shown here may provide policymakers with a concrete template to debate policy choices.

The policy assumptions in the alternative scenarios

The nature of the assumed policy changes is the same in both scenarios A and B, but in scenario A *all* countries, developed, developing and transition economies alike, are assumed to pursue more expansionary macroeconomic policies to the extent needed to ensure a growth-enhancing environment for each country. The main areas of assumed policy changes are listed below:

- A stronger role of the public sector, both in terms of spending and decisions on taxation. The proactive fiscal stance would aim at contributing to a stable growth of demand and at strengthening productive capacity through physical and social infrastructure, the provision of incentives to private investment and appropriate industrial and structural policies.

- Measures aimed at a more equal distribution of income through setting a minimum wage, direct taxation and welfare-enhancing programmes. These measures, which will effectively lead to wage increases closer to average productivity gains, will play a dual role: they will help sustain the expansion of aggregate demand, and, by virtue of such expansion, they will trigger improvements in productivity through demand-driven technical progress mechanisms.

- Supportive monetary and credit policies and improved financial regulations. Interest rates and credit availability are assumed to support private and public sector activity, and at the same time avoid excessive asset appreciations or financial fragility of private and public institutions.

- Tax and spending policies are assumed to be made consistent with an improvement in the financial positions of the public sectors in countries where they have been strained in the recent past. In such cases, government spending will increase at a slower rate than GDP growth, but will nevertheless provide a sizeable economic stimulus through spending fiscal multipliers that are significantly greater than 1 (as explained in section B of this chapter). Likewise, it will be assumed that fiscal positions will improve with the help of higher taxes imposed on sectors that are not employment-intensive.

- On the external front, it would involve reforms of the international monetary and financial systems. In these scenarios it is assumed that progressive adjustments of nominal and real exchange rates will be conducive to reducing global imbalances and fostering economic development. To narrow both trade and financial imbalances without deflationary adjustments in deficit countries, it is assumed that surplus countries will make a greater contribution than deficit countries through measures aimed at bolstering domestic demand. To enable industrialization and export diversification in developing countries, it is also assumed that there will be non-discriminatory market access for these countries and mechanisms to promote South-South cooperation, including in the area of environment-friendly technologies, as discussed below. Better regulation of commodity markets is assumed to reduce the adverse influence of their "financialization" on primary and energy prices.

- It is further assumed that measures, including incentives to private investment, government spending and taxation, will address environmental challenges by helping to mitigate carbon emissions and environmental degradation.[3] Investments in technological innovations for the more efficient production and use of energy and primary inputs are assumed to take priority. In addition, industrial policies in energy and primary commodity exporters will aim at greater economic diversification. New technologies will become more advanced and made available at the same pace as that of other technological developments in recent history.

In scenario B, it is assumed that the developed countries will maintain their currently dominant policy stances, and will therefore remain on a subpar growth trajectory driven by fiscal austerity and pressures to compress labour income. The latter may contribute to competitiveness gains in external markets, but also to reduced or slow growth of consumption. By contrast, developing and transition economies are assumed to press ahead with the set of policies described above, but since they would be facing a more adverse external environment, they would face harsher constraints.

In addition, it is assumed that the major developed countries will continue with their recent choices of monetary policy and financial regulation, which showed little concern for potential spillover effects on developing countries. Developing countries are assumed to implement some level of capital controls, but, in the absence of international cooperation, these measures will be only partially effective. Likewise, reducing external imbalances and promoting economic development will become more challenging if, as assumed, developed countries do not depart from their current policy stances. For example, facing harsher wage competition from the latter group, developing countries may not be able to improve on functional distribution of income to the extent they could in scenario A. Similarly, the greater market access assumed in scenario A to enhance export diversification of developing countries will be applied only by and among developing countries. Overall, these conditions will shake the confidence and expectations that generally influence portfolio and fixed capital investment, as well as financial costs. But even considering these limitations, there remains considerable scope for coordination among developing and emerging economies with regard to the aforementioned policy alternatives.

Outcomes of the scenarios

An illustrative set of outcomes resulting from the combination of assumptions in the two alternative scenarios is presented below for the major regions and for the world as a whole.[4] Chart 1.A.1 shows that GDP growth is significantly higher in scenario A than in both scenario B and the baseline scenario for all regions. It needs to be borne in mind that the current global conditions are particularly adverse, as both developed and developing countries still face huge challenges and bottlenecks resulting from the financial crisis.

The growth trajectory outcomes from the policy assumptions in scenario A are consistent with the obtained patterns of improved functional distribution of income, shown in chart 1.A.2. The recent past was marked by an unequivocal deterioration of income distribution between labour and profits in practically all regions, with partial exceptions in Latin America and some Asian countries. A catch-up of functional distribution is economically desirable and feasible, but might proceed at a relatively moderate pace. Such an improvement is a major factor for the growth of internal demand in each country as well as for the growth of global trade activity. In turn, economies of scale resulting from larger domestic and foreign markets induce technical progress. But these processes would take time and need to be jointly managed, since

Trade and Development Report, 2013

Chart 1.A.1

GDP GROWTH: HISTORICAL AND ESTIMATED UNDER THE TWO SCENARIOS, BY REGION/GROUP, CHINA AND INDIA, 1995–2030

(Per cent)

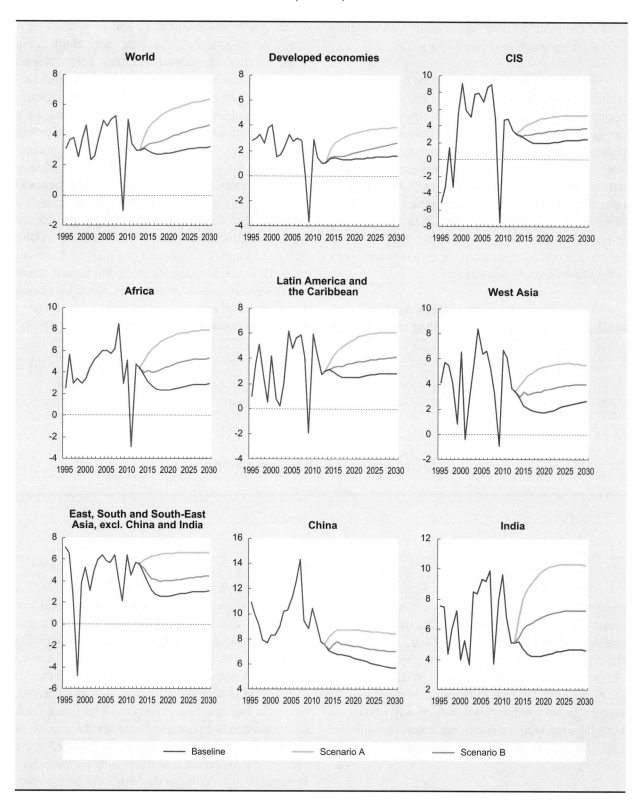

Source: UNCTAD secretariat calculations, based on United Nations Global Policy Model.
Note: Growth refers to GDP at constant 2005 PPP dollars. CIS includes Georgia.

Chart 1.A.2

LABOUR-INCOME SHARE: HISTORICAL AND ESTIMATED UNDER THE TWO SCENARIOS, BY REGION/GROUP, CHINA AND INDIA, 1995–2030

(Per cent of GDP)

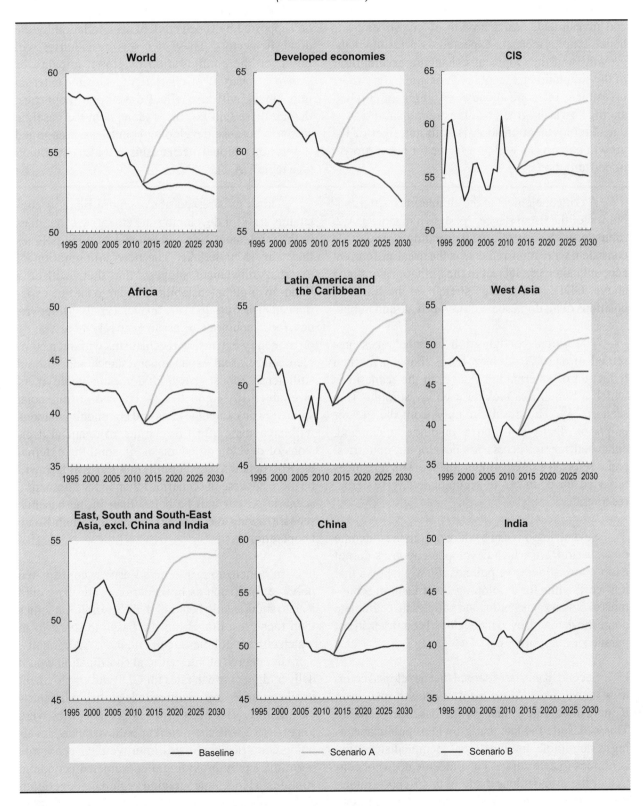

Source: UNCTAD secretariat calculations, based on United Nations Global Policy Model.
Note: CIS includes Georgia.

very rapid changes in income distribution and the consequent expansion of GDP growth may generate unsustainable trade deficits.

Employment growth is captured in table 1.A.1, together with the growth of private consumption and investment. Faster growth of investment, and hence employment, is expected as a result of the growth- and development-enhancing assumptions of the simulations, except in China and India, where investment rates are already very high and a rebalancing towards greater domestic consumption is due. Employment creation is both an effect of the growth patterns as well as a factor for faster growth of consumption.

A critical element in the simulations is the calibration of the fiscal stance. As shown in table 1.A.2, robust growth of government spending can be made consistent with improvements in the fiscal and current account balances. Subject to the limitations outlined above, GDP growth helps strengthen the financial positions of all domestic sectors – private and public.

The global configuration of imbalances presented in chart A of chart 1.A.3 shows a marked reduction of external imbalances in the scenario in which all countries provide a policy stimulus (i.e. scenario A). This results mainly from the greater emphasis of surplus countries on domestic demand, enhanced market access for developing countries, and a reform of international finance which reduces the need for countries to accumulate large external reserves.

Several lessons can be drawn from the outcome of scenario B, in which developed countries do not adopt more supportive policies. First, it shows that it is worthwhile for developing and transition economies to embark on coordinated policies that stimulate domestic demand, even if developed countries do not pursue similar policies.

Second, it can be observed that developed countries manage to achieve a faster growth rate, even if more moderately, than in the baseline scenario. This is despite the fact that growth of public spending is negligible and functional income distribution continues to deteriorate. The outcome does not contradict the propositions made in this Report; rather, it corroborates the proposition that such a strategy could yield some partial gains for some, though not all, countries at the same time. There will be two distinctive approaches, depending on the prevailing institutional structures. Some developed countries will continue to adopt an export-led strategy by stressing wage compression measures. In deficit developed countries, some degree of growth could be supported by renewed debt accumulation by the domestic sectors. These two sets of countries will influence the configuration of global imbalances shown in chart B of chart 1.A.3. Greater external imbalances will also affect developing countries, though these will not be as large as in the baseline scenario because developing countries are assumed to agree on regional mechanisms of trade cooperation (see table 1.A.2).

Third, as stressed above, more binding constraints arise for developing and emerging economies in the implementation and outcomes of the policies they aim to undertake. The new configuration of external imbalances suggests that there will be a build-up of global instability similar to the one experienced in the run-up to the financial crisis. Moreover, developed countries are assumed to rely more heavily on monetary expansion mechanisms without a complementary fiscal expansionary stance and without sufficiently robust growth of domestic employment (see tables 1.A.1 and 1.A.2). The risks of financial spillovers on exchange rates and commodity markets will have some effect on the macro-financial decisions of developing countries. In sum, the external environment that developing countries will face will be more adverse in scenario B than in the alternative scenario A, but will be better than in the baseline scenario owing to enhanced regional and South-South cooperation.

In conclusion, a demand-driven coordinated policy effort (such as in scenarios A and B) would lead to significantly better global economic outcomes than those resulting from the baseline scenario in which current policies are maintained. Additionally, a greater degree of international coordination would deliver higher growth rates for GDP and employment in all countries and would reduce global imbalances (scenario A). But even if developed countries were to persevere with their current policy stance, developing countries could still improve their economic performance by providing a coordinated economic stimulus. Hence, encouraging regional cooperation and South-South trade would need to be an important component of their development strategies. ■

Table 1.A.1

**PRIVATE CONSUMPTION, PRIVATE INVESTMENT AND EMPLOYMENT GAINS
UNDER THE TWO SCENARIOS, BY REGION/GROUP,
CHINA AND INDIA, 2007–2030**

		Average annual growth of private consumption (Per cent)				*Average annual growth of private investment (Per cent)*				*Employment gains (Millions of jobs created relative to the baseline scenario)*		
		2007– 2012	*2013– 2018*	*2019– 2024*	*2025– 2030*	*2007– 2012*	*2013– 2018*	*2019– 2024*	*2025– 2030*	*2013– 2018*	*2019– 2024*	*2025– 2030*
World	Baseline	2.9	3.1	2.9	3.0	3.7	2.6	3.1	3.8	.	.	.
	Scenario A	.	4.7	5.8	6.2	.	3.5	5.8	6.4	36.6	85.9	101.8
	Scenario B	.	3.6	4.1	4.4	.	2.7	4.0	4.9	17.6	42.2	52.5
Developed economies	Baseline	1.0	1.7	1.6	1.6	-2.2	1.9	2.4	2.8	.	.	.
	Scenario A	.	2.7	3.3	3.6	.	3.2	4.9	4.9	7.2	18.5	19.8
	Scenario B	.	1.7	2.0	2.3	.	2.1	3.3	4.2	0.5	2.5	3.9
CIS	Baseline	4.4	1.8	2.3	2.7	7.4	1.5	1.0	2.6	.	.	.
	Scenario A	.	3.8	5.1	5.3	.	2.9	5.5	5.7	0.7	2.2	2.8
	Scenario B	.	2.5	3.5	3.8	.	2.0	3.1	4.0	0.3	1.0	1.4
Africa	Baseline	5.2	3.5	3.0	3.0	7.0	4.4	2.9	3.3	.	.	.
	Scenario A	.	6.2	7.1	7.6	.	6.4	7.9	8.0	4.5	14.7	22.5
	Scenario B	.	4.5	4.8	5.2	.	5.1	5.5	5.9	2.5	8.5	13.2
Latin America and the Caribbean	Baseline	4.0	3.0	2.7	2.7	5.0	1.7	2.2	3.2	.	.	.
	Scenario A	.	4.1	5.4	5.9	.	2.1	5.5	6.2	3.4	6.5	6.9
	Scenario B	.	3.3	3.7	3.9	.	1.5	3.3	4.2	1.9	3.6	3.4
West Asia	Baseline	4.3	3.2	2.6	2.6	6.6	3.0	0.7	2.0	.	.	.
	Scenario A	.	5.6	6.1	5.9	.	3.9	5.9	6.3	1.5	4.8	6.3
	Scenario B	.	4.4	4.3	4.2	.	3.1	3.2	4.2	0.8	2.6	3.5
East, South and South-East Asia, excl. China and India	Baseline	5.1	3.9	3.0	2.9	6.5	5.4	1.6	2.4	.	.	.
	Scenario A	.	5.3	6.2	6.5	.	4.8	6.8	6.9	6.2	15.4	19.3
	Scenario B	.	4.3	4.1	4.2	.	5.2	3.5	4.1	3.8	9.7	12.0
China	Baseline	8.8	8.9	7.1	6.1	11.8	3.4	5.1	5.3	.	.	.
	Scenario A	.	12.3	11.1	9.5	.	3.5	5.7	6.5	8.0	12.1	9.1
	Scenario B	.	10.8	9.3	7.8	.	3.1	4.9	5.5	4.7	7.3	6.3
India	Baseline	7.8	5.2	4.8	4.7	8.4	2.2	2.2	3.7	.	.	.
	Scenario A	.	8.1	9.9	10.3	.	4.7	8.9	10.0	5.0	11.8	15.2
	Scenario B	.	6.5	7.2	7.3	.	2.9	5.1	6.5	3.0	7.2	8.8

Source: UNCTAD secretariat calculations, based on United Nations Global Policy Model.
Note: CIS includes Georgia.

Table 1.A.2

PUBLIC SPENDING, NET PUBLIC LENDING AND CURRENT ACCOUNT BALANCE UNDER THE TWO SCENARIOS, BY REGION/GROUP, CHINA AND INDIA, 2007–2030

		Average annual growth of public spending (Per cent)				Average annual net public lending (Per cent of GDP)				Current account balance (Per cent of GDP)			
		2007– 2012	2013– 2018	2019– 2024	2025– 2030	2007– 2012	2013– 2018	2019– 2024	2025– 2030	2007– 2012	2013– 2018	2019– 2024	2025– 2030
World	Baseline	3.6	2.1	2.3	2.8	-3.7	-3.6	-3.2	-3.0	-	-	-	-
	Scenario A	.	4.0	5.7	6.2	.	-2.7	-1.7	-1.7	-	-	-	-
	Scenario B	.	3.1	3.7	4.3	.	-3.5	-2.7	-2.4	-	-	-	-
Developed economies	Baseline	1.6	0.5	0.7	0.8	-5.6	-4.9	-3.7	-3.0	-0.5	-0.4	-1.3	-2.4
	Scenario A	.	1.2	3.0	3.5	.	-3.7	-2.5	-2.5	.	-0.4	-0.5	-0.8
	Scenario B	.	0.6	0.9	1.3	.	-4.8	-3.2	-1.9	.	-0.3	-0.5	-0.9
CIS	Baseline	3.1	2.0	1.6	1.7	1.2	0.6	0.4	0.9	2.5	0.2	0.7	1.4
	Scenario A	.	3.0	4.9	5.4	.	1.1	0.9	0.2	.	0.7	0.6	0.5
	Scenario B	.	2.5	3.5	3.8	.	0.7	0.2	-0.1	.	0.3	0.3	0.5
Africa	Baseline	7.2	1.6	1.2	2.2	-2.7	-4.3	-2.5	-1.1	-1.6	-4.3	-6.4	-5.8
	Scenario A	.	2.9	6.8	7.6	.	-2.8	-1.0	-1.1	.	-2.3	-1.5	-0.2
	Scenario B	.	2.2	4.2	5.0	.	-3.7	-2.4	-2.0	.	-3.6	-4.6	-4.0
Latin America and the Caribbean	Baseline	5.8	2.2	1.8	2.3	-2.4	-3.6	-3.2	-2.6	-2.7	-3.5	-3.8	-3.4
	Scenario A	.	4.1	5.5	6.0	.	-3.0	-2.4	-2.5	.	-2.5	-0.7	0.1
	Scenario B	.	3.1	3.7	4.0	.	-3.5	-3.4	-3.4	.	-3.1	-2.6	-2.0
West Asia	Baseline	5.0	3.0	1.8	2.8	4.7	0.5	-0.7	-0.1	7.9	2.4	0.8	2.0
	Scenario A	.	3.8	5.5	5.9	.	0.9	-0.7	-0.7	.	4.3	1.5	0.8
	Scenario B	.	3.3	3.9	4.5	.	0.5	-1.0	-1.0	.	3.3	0.8	0.8
East, South and South-East Asia, excl. China and India	Baseline	5.5	3.3	2.4	2.8	-2.8	-2.9	-3.2	-3.0	-1.6	-4.2	-4.5	-3.3
	Scenario A	.	8.5	7.1	6.8	.	-2.8	-2.8	-2.9	.	-2.2	-0.5	0.0
	Scenario B	.	6.2	4.8	4.7	.	-3.0	-3.6	-3.8	.	-3.7	-3.6	-2.9
China	Baseline	9.0	7.1	7.3	6.6	-1.0	-0.2	-1.3	-2.5	4.8	6.8	8.4	8.3
	Scenario A	.	12.2	9.9	8.7	.	-0.1	-0.0	-0.0	.	3.3	1.6	1.5
	Scenario B	.	10.4	8.8	7.8	.	-0.3	-1.0	-1.5	.	4.6	3.9	3.6
India	Baseline	9.7	4.9	4.7	4.9	-8.3	-9.6	-10.0	-10.1	-6.0	-4.8	-2.7	-1.9
	Scenario A	.	9.4	10.2	10.3	.	-6.2	-3.1	-3.0	.	-4.5	-1.8	-1.1
	Scenario B	.	7.4	7.6	7.7	.	-7.9	-6.7	-6.9	.	-4.7	-2.7	-2.2

Source: UNCTAD secretariat calculations, based on United Nations Global Policy Model.
Note: CIS includes Georgia.

Chart 1.A.3

GLOBAL IMBALANCES UNDER TWO SCENARIOS, 1980–2030
(Per cent of world output)

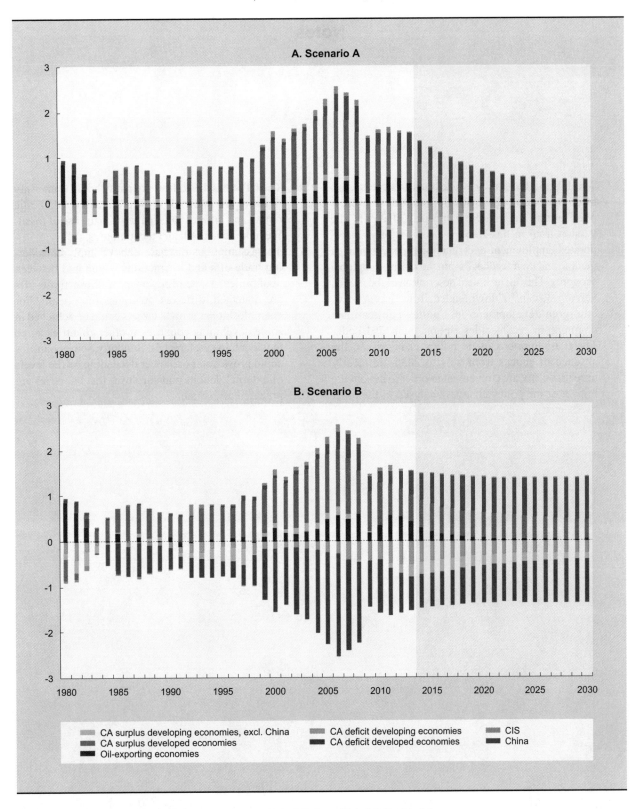

Source: UNCTAD secretariat calculations, based on United Nations Global Policy Model.
Note: The shaded area shows the simulation period. Deficit and surplus classification was based on the average current account (CA) position between 2004 and 2007. CIS includes Georgia.

Notes

1   The UN Global Policy Model can be accessed at: http://www.un.org/en/development/desa/policy/publications/ungpm/gpm_concepts_2010.pdf. The version used in this Report – number 5b – incorporates employment and functional distribution of income and their feedbacks into the macro and global economy. The full technical description of the model, version 3, can be downloaded from: http://www.un.org/en/development/desa/policy/publications/ungpm/gpm_technicaldescription_main_2010.pdf.

2   These assumptions of no policy changes and the absence of shocks from now to 2030 are clearly unrealistic, but are convenient in order to net out the impact of the policy changes analysed in the other two scenarios.

3   The GPM has the ability to quantify both the intensity of use of raw materials in the production of domestic output and differentiated patterns in the use of fossil-fuel and non-fossil-fuel technologies.

4   The assumptions discussed above imply considering trade-offs and interactions within and between economies. Depending on how these trade-offs are managed, different outcomes may result. For example, higher growth targets could be achieved in some developing countries if other countries agree to wider trade preferences. Similarly, some countries could grow faster or slower depending on the levels of external deficits and surpluses that countries are prepared to tolerate.

Chapter II

TOWARDS MORE BALANCED GROWTH: A GREATER ROLE FOR DOMESTIC DEMAND IN DEVELOPMENT STRATEGIES

A. Introduction

The global economy is still struggling to recover from the Great Recession of 2008–2009 resulting from busts in the housing and financial markets of the major developed countries. The examination of the current challenges for the global economy in chapter I of this *Report* indicates that these countries may have a long way to go to achieve a self-sustaining recovery. Meanwhile, a prolonged period of slow growth in these countries will mean continued sluggish demand and thus slower growth in their imports from developing and transition economies beyond the short term. Countercyclical macroeconomic policies might be able to compensate for resulting growth shortfalls for some time, but will eventually result in fiscal or balance-of-payments constraints unless they are followed by policies that adopt a more comprehensive and longer term perspective. This chapter discusses possible longer term policy options to support rapid and sustained economic growth in developing and transition economies, with a focus on the complementarity of external and domestic demand.

Prior to the onset of the economic and financial crisis, buoyant consumer demand in some developed economies, especially the United States, enabled the rapid growth of manufactured exports from industrializing developing economies. The consequent boost to these countries' industrial development and urbanization, in turn, provided opportunities for primary commodity exports from other developing countries. The overall expansionary – though eventually unsustainable – nature of these developments contributed to a prolonged period of output growth of the world economy, and seemed to vindicate many developing and transition economies in their decision to adopt an export-oriented growth model. However, their continued reliance on such a growth model does not seem viable in the current context of slow growth in developed economies. Accordingly, those developing and transition economies, and especially the larger ones among them, may need to consider a policy shift to a more domestic-demand-oriented growth model.

This chapter examines two main questions: (i) What determines whether developing and transition economies should shift emphasis from an export-oriented to a more domestic-demand-oriented growth strategy? (ii) What policy measures could help smooth such a transition in growth strategy?

The chapter first discusses, in section B, determinants of countries' vulnerability to external trade shocks. It emphasizes that the decline in real final expenditure was the main reason for the collapse of international trade in 2008–2009. Combined with the recognition that growth in developed countries' final expenditure may remain below pre-crisis rates for a protracted period of time, it argues that: (i) the effects of the trade collapse on manufactured exports from developing and transition economies may be indicative of a less favourable external trade environment for these countries for a number of years to come; and (ii) possible ensuing slower demand growth in the developing and transition economies that have a large proportion of manufactures in their exports, combined with weak growth in developed countries, may also reduce the export earnings of economies that rely mainly on exports of primary commodities. In evaluating possible future developments in the latter countries' export earnings, this section further suggests that this could depend to a large extent on whether commodity prices are in a so-called "super-cycle", and if so, at what point in the cycle they are currently situated. While economic activity in developed countries clearly has a direct impact on primary commodity price developments, its largest impact may be indirect and linked to its effect on the pace of industrialization and urbanization in developing and transition economies whose growth trajectories have been supported by exports of manufactures to developed-country markets. Section C focuses on manufactures, and examines which categories may be particularly affected by weak demand growth in developed countries.

Section D considers economic growth from a demand-side perspective. It begins from the main conclusion of the previous section, that the scope for a switch towards a more balanced growth strategy is greatest for those countries which have relied significantly on exports of manufactures to developed countries. It then builds on an examination (presented in the annex to this chapter) of what such a switch from an export-oriented to a more domestic-demand-oriented growth strategy would entail in economic terms. It discusses the possible implications for countries' balance of payments and for product-specific demand patterns resulting from an acceleration of expenditure in the different components of domestic demand (i.e. household consumption, investment and government spending). Particular attention is given to household consumption expenditure, which is by far the largest component of domestic demand, generally accounting for between half and three

quarters of aggregate demand. Therefore, an increase in this component would appear to be indispensable for sustained growth based on a strategy that places greater emphasis on domestic demand. The section also underlines the importance of both government spending and, especially, investment for boosting demand growth. This is particularly true for many countries in Latin America, where, despite a more rapid pace of gross fixed capital formation starting in the early 2000s, the share of investment in gross domestic product (GDP) has remained relatively low and constrains their potential growth. But it is also true for other developing countries, especially in East Asia, where investment is required in order to switch domestic supply capacities to meet changing demand patterns that are driven by rising household consumption expenditure.

The following are the main findings of this section. First, a more balanced growth strategy with a larger role for domestic demand needs to be based on the creation of domestic purchasing power through additional employment and wage-earning opportunities. Second, it is necessary to manage domestic demand expansion to prevent an excessive increase in demand for imports arising from a switch in growth strategy, which, coupled with lower export growth, might cause a deterioration in the trade balance. Third, nurturing the interrelationship between household consumption and investment will be of crucial importance in a shift towards a more balanced growth strategy. Investment needs to be increased, not only to create the jobs and incomes necessary for sustained growth of household consumption expenditure, but also to enable changes in the sectoral composition of domestic production so that it responds to sales opportunities arising from new demands by domestic consumers. The latter is true especially for large countries, while for small countries an increase in regional and South-South trade is likely to be of particular importance.

Section E discusses the policy implications of these findings at both the national and international levels to help smoothen the transition from one growth strategy to another. It emphasizes that the major policy challenges facing developing and transition economies differ significantly from those facing the developed economies. The latter still need to focus on consolidating their weakened financial systems and on demand management in an effort to return to a path of sustained economic growth, high levels of employment and socially acceptable distributional outcomes. Succeeding in this task would also have global benefits. It would maintain, and even enlarge, the kind of export opportunities that underpinned much of the successful growth of developing and transition economies during the pre-crisis period. However, such an outcome is unlikely to occur for several years to come because, to a large extent, exports of developing and transition economies to developed-country markets during the decade before the onset of the Great Recession relied on unsustainable policy stances in the developed countries.

It is clear that developing and transition economies should not neglect demand management; rather, they should maintain policies aimed at both strengthening growth and employment creation and at reducing domestic and external vulnerabilities. Nevertheless, the policy stance of developing countries needs to adapt to an external economic environment characterized by slow recovery and weak growth in developed economies. Such adaptation implies the need for a gradual shift in the relative importance of external sources of growth towards a greater emphasis on domestic sources.

B. Global trade shocks and long-term trends: terms-of-trade and volume effects

Countries exporting primary commodities are generally believed to be particularly sensitive to changes in the global economic environment for two reasons. One reason relates to commodity prices, which experience frequent and often sharp fluctuations. Another concerns volumes, and the fact that the income elasticity of demand for primary commodities is lower than that for manufactures. This means that demand prospects for exporters of manufactures tend to be more favourable than those for exporters of primary commodities as world income rises. This section examines the price and volume effects of the collapse of global trade in 2008–2009 and prospects for the future growth of demand for primary commodities and manufactures respectively.

1. Volume and price components of external trade shocks

Greater trade openness has helped promote economic growth in a number of countries, but, increasingly, it has also become a primary channel for the transmission of external shocks. Economic

downturns in developed countries cause sharp contractions in global demand and reduce the export opportunities of developing countries. This can result in an external trade shock for developing countries, reflected in a decline in their export volumes and changes in their terms of trade (i.e. the change in a country's average export price relative to its import price). The impact of such external trade shocks varies considerably across regions and individual countries, depending on their pattern of export specialization.

The collapse of world trade in 2008–2009 caused a deterioration in the terms of trade of countries whose exports are heavily concentrated in energy, and countries that export mainly manufactured goods experienced negative volume effects (chart 2.1).[1] Terms of trade and volume changes were equally important in countries which export predominantly minerals and metals, as in countries whose exports are either diversified or concentrated in agricultural products.

The remainder of this section examines issues related to changes in the prices of primary commodities before turning to demand prospects for manufactured exports from developing countries.

Chart 2.1

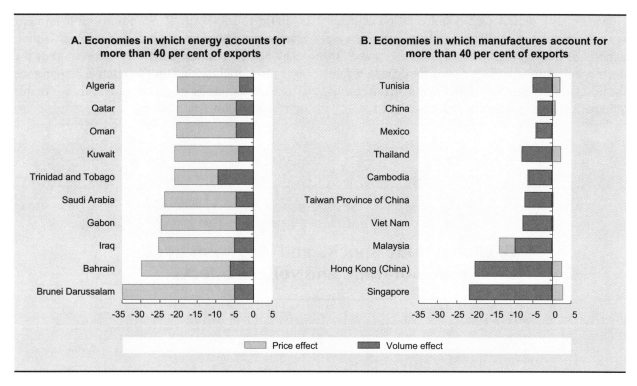

THE GLOBAL TRADE COLLAPSE OF 2008–2009:
MOST AFFECTED ECONOMIES, BY EXPORT SPECIALIZATION

(Trade shocks as a percentage of GDP)

A. Economies in which energy accounts for more than 40 per cent of exports

Algeria
Qatar
Oman
Kuwait
Trinidad and Tobago
Saudi Arabia
Gabon
Iraq
Bahrain
Brunei Darussalam

-35 -30 -25 -20 -15 -10 -5 0 5

B. Economies in which manufactures account for more than 40 per cent of exports

Tunisia
China
Mexico
Thailand
Cambodia
Taiwan Province of China
Viet Nam
Malaysia
Hong Kong (China)
Singapore

-35 -30 -25 -20 -15 -10 -5 0 5

☐ Price effect   ■ Volume effect

Source: UN-DESA, 2009.

2. Recent movements in the terms of trade

Price movements of internationally traded goods affect an individual country's gains from international trade, or its terms of trade. The extent of gains or losses resulting from changes in the terms of trade depends on the composition of the country's trade basket and the relative importance of foreign trade in its gross domestic product (GDP). Primary commodity production and exports are generally believed to offer limited opportunities for economic growth and development mainly because of a long-running deterioration in the terms of trade of primary commodities versus manufactures (i.e. a declining trend in the prices of primary commodities vis-à-vis those of manufactures) (chart 2.2). Other dimensions of the "commodity problem" relate to high price volatility and the concentration of market structures

that limits the share of the final price accruing to producers.

Since the turn of the millennium there has been a significant improvement in the terms of trade for commodity exporters vis-à-vis exporters of manufactures, which has also contributed to faster economic growth in commodity-exporting countries. The commodity price boom over the period 2002–2008 and another rapid rebound following a sharp price decline in 2008–2009 (see chart 1.2 and table 1.3 in chapter I) reflect a change in the commodity price trend, at least temporarily, from declining towards rising prices; but they also reflect a decline in world prices of certain, especially labour-intensive, manufactures. This turnaround is related to two structural changes in international trade in which developing countries have played a major role: first, a number of developing countries, notably China, have emerged as major consumers and importers of commodities;

Chart 2.2

TRENDS IN THE TERMS OF TRADE, SELECTED PRIMARY COMMODITY GROUPS VERSUS MANUFACTURES, 1865–2009

(Index numbers, 1970–1979 = 100)

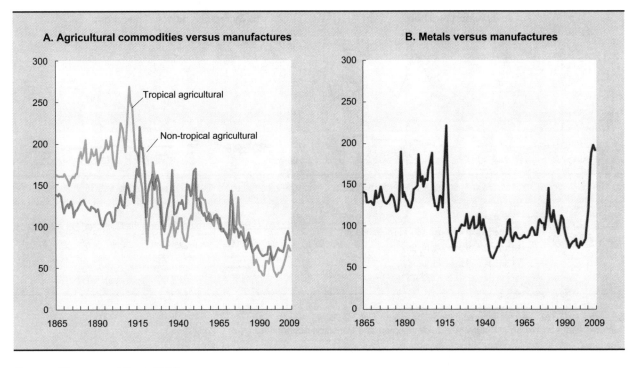

Source: Ocampo and Parra, 2010.

and second, manufactures now account for a sizeable share of some developing countries' export baskets.

Terms-of-trade trends for different groups of developing countries have tended to diverge (chart 2.3), depending on the composition of their respective exports and imports. Those developing countries whose oil and mineral and mining products account for a sizeable share of total exports experienced the largest gains from higher commodity prices vis-à-vis manufactures since the early 2000s. Oil exporters saw their terms of trade more than double in the past decade, implying that the prices of their exports grew more than twice as fast as the prices of their imports. Mirroring these trends by geographical area, the country groups that saw the largest terms-of-trade gains were the transition economies, Africa and West Asia. Similarly, Latin America registered significant terms-of-trade gains, although more moderate because of a relatively more diversified trade structure. The terms of trade

of exporters of agricultural commodities showed a slightly rising trend, reflecting both dissimilar price developments for different agricultural products (i.e. tropical beverages, food and agricultural raw materials) and the different weights of food and fuel imports in their import baskets. On the other hand, developing countries that are major exporters of manufactures, mainly those in East and South Asia, have experienced terms-of-trade losses since 2000.[2]

In 2010 and 2011, the terms of trade of commodity exporters recovered from the commodity price slump of 2009 in what appeared to be a continuation of the rising trend since the early 2000s (chart 2.3A). However, in 2012 their terms of trade stalled as a result of a decline of commodity prices from their peaks in 2011 (see discussion about recent commodity price developments in chapter I). Whether this represents just a pause or a reversal of the rising trend in their terms of trade during the 2000s is the focus of the next section.

Chart 2.3

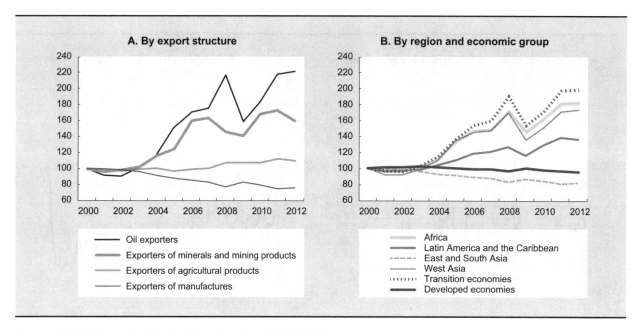

NET BARTER TERMS OF TRADE, 2000–2012

(Index numbers, 2000 = 100)

Source: UNCTAD secretariat calculations, based on *UNCTADstat*.
  Note: Data for export structure refer to developing and transition economies.

3. Factors affecting commodity prices: is a supercycle petering out?

Commodity prices are influenced by a complex interaction of multiple factors, which can span different time periods and can affect the volatility and/or the trend level of those prices. Commodity price developments are determined by the fundamentals of physical supply and demand of commodities, as well as by the greater participation of financial investors in primary commodity markets, because commodities are increasingly considered a financial asset. Another factor influencing commodity prices, which are normally denominated in United States dollars, is the evolution of the exchange rate of the dollar. There are also some factors specific to a particular commodity market, while others affect all primary commodities. Furthermore, it is not only market-related factors, but also economic policy and political aspects that matter. For example, geopolitics can have a very significant influence on the evolution of oil prices. While a precise measurement of the influence of each individual factor on the dynamics of commodity

prices is fraught with difficulties, especially for price forecasting, the objective of this section is to provide a broad assessment of the likely trend of commodity prices over the next one or two decades.

During the past decade, commodity markets have experienced substantial structural changes. One such change is the increasing presence of financial investors in commodity markets (see also *TDR 2009*, chap. II; *TDR 2011*, chap. V). Financial investments have a significant impact on price volatility and may cause extreme price changes in the short term; for instance, the commodity price surges in 2007 and the first half of 2008 were most probably linked to a speculative bubble, which burst with the collapse of prices in the second half of 2008 following the onset of the global financial crisis. A second major structural change, associated with the underlying physical market fundamentals, is the increasing demand for commodities in rapidly growing developing countries, notably China.

The latter factor, which is the main focus of this section, has more of an influence on the longer term trend of commodity prices. On the demand side, it has underpinned the sustained increase in commodity prices since 2003 that was interrupted only in 2008–2009 by a sharp fall in prices following the eruption of the global financial crisis. On the supply side, the historically low price levels of the 1990s led to a long period of underinvestment in production capacity. As a result, and due to increasing production constraints, supply was slow to react to rising demand. Consequently, with stocks generally declining, the trend was for prices to significantly increase. The tight structural supply and demand balances of many commodities also paved the way for other factors from the financial sector and policy side to lead to excessive price volatility.

Some observers have identified the commodity price surge between 2002 and 2011–2012 as the expansionary phase of a commodity "supercycle" – i.e. a trend rise in the prices of a broad range of commodities which may last two decades or more. It is associated with rising demand in a major country or groups of countries resulting from their process of industrialization and urbanization (Heap, 2005; Standard Chartered, 2010; Erten and Ocampo, 2012; Farooki and Kaplinsky, 2012).[3] The current supercycle has been characterized by rapid economic growth, industrialization and urbanization in a range of developing countries, among which China has played a particularly strong role because of the large size of its economy. Economic growth in China has been extremely natural-resource-intensive, partly driven by high levels of investment, especially in infrastructure and construction, and by the rapid growth of manufacturing, which generally demands more raw materials and energy than growth in the services and agricultural sectors. Consequently, China has become the world's leading consumer of many primary commodities, accounting for more than 40 per cent of global consumption of several commodities (table 2.1). At the same time, it is also a major producer of a number of commodities. But while Chinese commodity production increased during the first decade of the 2000s, this was not always sufficient to meet the rising demand. As a result, China has become a major importer of some commodities (ECLAC, 2012: box II.3), notably iron ore and soybeans. Indeed, it accounts for about 60 per cent of total world imports of both these commodities. China is also a major importer of other metals such as copper and nickel, and of agricultural raw materials such as cotton and natural rubber. Demand

for commodities strongly increased in other rapidly growing developing countries as well, but to a much lesser extent (table 2.1). And in developed countries, demand for some commodities declined between 2002 and 2012.

The increasing role of China on global commodity markets is due not only to the large size of its economy but also to the nature of its growth. It is for this reason that the recent slowdown in Chinese growth as well as its process of growth rebalancing, involving less reliance on exports and investment and greater efforts to promote domestic consumption, have reignited the debate on whether the expansionary phase of the commodity supercycle might be coming to an end. The lower average annual commodity prices of 2012 compared with those of 2011 could be considered an indication of such a possibility. Certainly, prices will stop rising at some point as supply and demand adjust; eventually they will reach an upper limit whereupon there will be demand destruction, substitution and technological advances in search of greater efficiency of use, and/or increases in supply as a response to high prices. However, the question that remains unresolved is whether such a turning point has been reached or whether the expansionary phase of the supercycle still has a number of years to run. If indeed the turning point has been reached, an additional question is whether commodity prices will plunge in a descendent phase of the supercycle, or whether they will remain at relatively high levels. In the latter scenario, the rise in commodity prices should be seen more as an upward shift than as the expansionary phase of the cycle.

Historical evidence shows that price trends have been closely related to the evolution of global economic activity and aggregate demand, particularly for metals (Erten and Ocampo, 2012). Episodes of rising prices have normally ended in price collapses when demand has fallen as a result of a deceleration of global growth or a recession. A similar outcome could be expected in the current context if global economic growth remains weak due to slow growth or stagnation in developed economies. However, the analysis of commodity consumption in table 2.1 clearly shows that the rise in commodity prices in the 2000s was strongly determined by developments in developing countries. It is therefore the growth outlook for these countries that matters most for future commodity demand trends. In particular, this implies that if China were to continue to depend on its exports

Table 2.1

CONSUMPTION OF SELECTED COMMODITIES, BY REGION AND ECONOMIC GROUP, 2002–2012

(Per cent)

A. Consumption growth between 2002 and 2012

	China	Other Asia and Oceania, developing	Africa	Latin America and the Caribbean	Transition economies	Developed economies	World total
Aluminium	392.7	105.2	101.8	54.6	-13.0	-4.4	78.5
Copper	223.0	12.6	70.2	32.4	88.3	-23.4	35.8
Nickel	894.1	-2.5	-9.1	-14.6	-4.8	-22.0	48.0
Cotton	24.4	31.4	-21.4	3.1	-13.6	-67.6	9.6
Corn	66.4	40.8	50.4	42.7	48.2	24.5	39.6
Meat, swine	26.6	31.3	99.2	38.7	34.4	-0.5	17.8
Rice	6.1	18.0	61.2	9.1	14.2	5.3	15.0
Wheat	16.9	19.4	42.6	14.9	-2.4	4.2	13.0
Soybeans	117.7	60.8	109.8	37.8	272.6	-12.7	36.5
Oil	95.4	33.9	36.3	25.2	18.8	-8.1	13.5

B. Contribution to global consumption growth between 2002 and 2012

	China	Other Asia and Oceania, developing	Africa	Latin America and the Caribbean	Transition economies	Developed economies	World total
Aluminium	81.1	18.4	1.8	2.8	-0.7	-3.4	100
Copper	113.4	6.9	1.9	4.8	7.4	-34.5	100
Nickel	132.3	-1.0	-0.6	-0.7	-0.3	-29.7	100
Cotton	74.9	135.4	-6.5	2.5	-5.0	-101.2	100
Corn	33.7	10.4	10.0	14.2	3.2	28.5	100
Meat, swine	69.8	10.3	1.5	11.2	8.3	-1.0	100
Rice	13.6	64.6	17.6	2.5	0.3	1.4	100
Wheat	22.6	40.9	23.4	6.0	-2.4	9.5	100
Soybeans	59.6	13.3	2.3	34.3	4.2	-13.6	100
Oil	48.2	53.1	9.1	16.2	6.9	-33.4	100

C. Share in global consumption

	China		Other Asia and Oceania, developing		Africa		Latin America and the Caribbean		Transition economies		Developed economies	
	2002	2012	2002	2012	2002	2012	2002	2012	2002	2012	2002	2012
Aluminium	16.2	44.8	13.7	15.8	1.4	1.6	4.0	3.5	4.4	2.2	60.2	32.3
Copper	18.2	43.3	19.8	16.4	1.0	1.2	5.2	5.1	3.0	4.2	52.7	29.8
Nickel	7.1	47.7	19.8	13.1	3.1	1.9	2.3	1.3	3.0	1.9	64.7	34.1
Cotton	29.7	33.6	41.6	49.8	2.9	2.1	7.8	7.4	3.6	2.8	14.4	4.3
Corn	20.1	23.9	10.1	10.2	7.9	8.5	13.2	13.5	2.6	2.8	46.1	41.1
Meat, swine	46.5	50.0	5.8	6.5	0.3	0.5	5.1	6.0	4.3	4.9	37.9	32.0
Rice	33.4	30.8	53.9	55.3	4.3	6.1	4.2	3.9	0.3	0.3	3.9	3.5
Wheat	17.5	18.0	27.5	29.1	7.2	9.1	5.2	5.3	12.9	11.1	29.7	27.4
Soybeans	18.5	29.5	8.0	9.4	0.7	1.2	33.1	33.4	0.6	1.5	39.1	25.0
Oil	6.8	11.7	21.1	24.9	3.4	4.0	8.7	9.6	4.9	5.1	55.2	44.7

Source: UNCTAD secretariat calculations, based on *World Bureau of Metal Statistics Yearbook 2013*; *BP Statistical Review of World Energy 2013*; and United States Department of Agriculture (USDA), *Production, Supply and Distribution* online database.

for growth, it is very likely to experience a further deceleration of growth as a result of lower exports to developed countries. This could in turn have a strong negative impact on commodity prices. However, if China succeeds in rebalancing its growth through an increase in domestic consumption, prospects for commodity demand and prices will be better.

Favourable demand conditions would also depend on the capacity of other highly populated and rapidly growing developing countries to move to a more commodity-intensive phase of economic growth and industrialization. This again should be based on the development of domestic markets in large developing countries such as India and Indonesia. Indeed, the share of the economies that are at the commodity-intensive stage of development doubled during the first decade of the 2000s, and now represents about 44 per cent of total GDP (Bloxham, Keen and Hartigan, 2012). The following subsection takes a closer look at the main drivers of demand in rapidly growing developing countries, the potential supply response and the prospects for commodity prices.

(a) Forces driving demand for commodities in rapidly growing developing countries

(i) Population and income growth and rising demand for food

Demand for food depends on population and income growth. The world's population increased by about one billion between 1999 and 2012, to reach a total of more than 7 billion people. Developing countries accounted for 95 per cent of this population increase, of which China and India alone contributed about one third. Although population growth is expected to slow down over the next decade, globally it is projected to increase by about 600 million up to 2020. Developing countries will continue to account for the bulk of the increase in the global population, though this will vary by region. The contribution of developing countries in Asia to population growth is expected to decrease from 58.6 per cent in 1999–2012 to 51.2 per cent in 2012–2020. China's contribution is set to fall from 11.5 per cent to 5.7 per cent, while that of India should remain stable at about 22 per cent. Africa's contribution is expected to increase from 27.6 per cent to 34.4 per cent over the same period, while that of Latin America is likely to remain stable at around 8 per cent (UNCTADstat).[4] The growing

population implies a greater demand for food, especially because the share of food in total household expenditures is higher in developing countries than in developed countries. This will require an increase in food production.

Demand for specific food items is strongly determined by the evolution of incomes and living standards. At low levels of per capita income, income growth mainly translates into increased calorie intake, and it is primarily the consumption of staple foods such as rice and wheat that will rise. Further income growth is typically associated with a shift in dietary consumption patterns. Consumers demand food with higher nutrient and protein content, including meat and dairy products and fruit and vegetables (*TDR 2005*, chap. II). According to the Food and Agriculture Organization of the United Nations (FAO, 2012a: 17), between the early 1990s and the end of the past decade, the shares of cereals, roots and tubers declined significantly worldwide, whereas the shares of fruit and vegetables and animal products, including fish, increased. However, the evolution of dietary changes diverged among regions. The share of cereals increased in Africa while it declined in Asia. By contrast the share of meat was significantly higher in Asia and Latin America. In China, during the period 2000–2010, total expenditure on food items continued to increase but its share in total living expenditure continued to decline. Per capita consumption of staple foods, mainly rice and wheat, followed a declining trend, while that of higher value foods, especially foods of animal origin, increased (Zhou et al., 2012).

Unlike for other commodities, the direct impact of demand for cereals in China on global demand and imports of cereals is likely to have been modest, particularly for rice (table 2.1). Apart from the decline in per capita cereal consumption, China and India have been pursuing a policy of self-sufficiency. Therefore their influence on global markets has been limited. However, the increase in Chinese grain imports since 2010, as reported in UN Comtrade statistics, may indicate that the country's self-sufficiency policy is reaching its limits.[5] The most significant impact of China on global food demand is in soybeans, as both Chinese consumption and imports of this commodity have increased significantly over the past decade. Demand for soybeans used as animal feed increased as a result of higher meat consumption. Demand for meat in China increased by 27.3 per cent between 2002 and 2010, so that twice as much meat is consumed in China as in the United States. Over the same period, the consumption of milk in India increased by 43.7 per cent (Brown, 2012). Higher demand for animal products exerts increased pressure on the production of feedstock. While the amount of grain fed to animals depends on farming techniques and the efficiency with which various animals convert grain into protein, which varies widely, it takes several kilos of grain to produce one kilo of meat. Generally, these trends are likely to continue over the next decade. Furthermore, the United States Department of Agriculture (USDA, 2013) projects a steady rise in China's imports of corn.

(ii) Intensity of commodity use in the industrialization process

China's growth process during the past decade has been characterized by a high and increasing intensity of use of commodities, particularly metals (i.e. a growing volume of metals consumed per unit of output). This is typical of a stage of rapid industrialization, wherein metals are increasingly required as input for growing manufacturing activities, including the production of consumer durables to meet rising demand, and for the construction of housing and physical infrastructure. At a certain point, this intensity of use should start to decelerate as the services sector grows in importance and contributes to an increasing share of the economy. Thus, intensity of use tends to follow an inverted U-shaped pattern as per capita income rises: it first rises as the economy moves from agricultural to manufacturing activities and then falls with an increased participation of services (*TDR 2005*, chap. II).

It may well be that the intensity of use of some metals in China is close to reaching, or has already reached, its peak, and therefore should be expected to slow down in the next few years, as argued by some observers (e.g. Nomura, 2012). However, China's per capita consumption of metals is relatively low (Farooki and Kaplinsky, 2012). This implies that metal consumption could remain robust, although it might grow at a slower pace. Moreover, although China's GDP growth is expected to slow down, it could continue to have a considerable impact on global markets, given the size of this economy. Given its high rates of growth over the past decade, the size of the Chinese economy in 2012 was much larger than it was in the early years of the commodity

boom. Therefore, even at a GDP growth rate of 7 or 8 per cent, China might have a similar impact on commodity markets as it did in previous years when it grew at around 10 per cent (see also CBA, 2012).

A major reason for the increasing intensity of metal use in China is that its rapid industrialization and growth, along with urbanization, have been supported by rising rates of investment in fixed capital, particularly in infrastructure and construction. These high rates have given rise to some concerns about the possibility of reaching overcapacity and the emergence of bubbles, for example in the real estate sector. However, it is worth noting that it is not only the rate of investment, but also the stock of fixed capital per capita, that counts in assessing whether investment may be excessive. Some observers argue that the stock of capital in China is still relatively small (Aglietta, 2012). Thus, the intensity of metal use is likely to remain high, even though the growth rebalancing process may result in an adjustment of the investment rate. Moreover, as the rebalancing process will not be accomplished overnight, eventual changes in commodity demand are likely to be gradual.

In addition, on balance, any potential negative impact of the growth rebalancing process in China on global commodity demand will largely depend on the extent to which demand from other rapidly growing developing countries rises. A number of countries which so far have exhibited a lower intensity of use of metals than China could move to a growth phase involving their more intensive use. If large and highly populated countries, such as India and Indonesia, were to follow China's industrialization path of the last decade, prospects for the demand for metals could remain robust. As it is unlikely that this demand will be based on exports to developed countries to the same extent as has been the case in China over the past two decades, much will depend again on the expansion of domestic demand in developing countries. Overall, infrastructure needs remain high in China as well as in other rapidly growing developing countries, a point that is briefly discussed in the next subsection.

(iii) Urbanization and infrastructure needs

Structural change and industrialization processes run parallel to that of urbanization, as the labour force moves from the agricultural to the manufacturing sector and thus from rural areas to cities. According to estimates by the United Nations (UN-DESA, 2012), the share of the urban population in the total population in China rose from 35.9 per cent in 2000 to 49.2 per cent in 2010, and it is expected to reach 55.6 per cent in 2015 and 61 per cent in 2020. This is still far below the urbanization rates in developed countries, which are projected to increase from about 75 per cent in the period 2001–2010 to around 80 per cent in 2020. According to Aglietta (2012), 400 million people living in the rural areas in China are expected to move to the cities between 2012 and 2030. Furthermore, 200 new cities of between 1 and 5 million inhabitants are expected to be built to develop the central and western areas of the country. However, this process will need strategic planning to be sustainable. The announced speeding up of reform of the *hukou* (household registration) system should help advance the urbanization process.[6] In addition to the construction of housing and other buildings, it involves the development of transport infrastructure, not only within the cities but also to link different cities, as well as other types of services infrastructure needed for the provision of energy and communications. Berkelmans and Wang (2012) expect Chinese residential construction to remain robust for the next couple of decades. Infrastructure needs are also likely to remain high, extending beyond the projects launched with the fiscal stimulus of September 2012.

In other developing countries the process of urbanization can also be expected to continue rapidly. The rate of urbanization in developing countries in Asia grew from 35.5 per cent in 2000 to 42.6 per cent in 2010, and is projected to reach 49.1 in 2020. In Africa, the respective rates of urbanization for these years are 35.5, 39.1 and 43.1 per cent. Urbanization rates in Latin America are much higher, at levels close to those of developed countries. Thus there is strong potential for an increase in demand for commodities by many developing countries in order to meet the development needs associated with urbanization, particularly for infrastructure development (Lawson and Dragusanu, 2008).

(iv) Increasing demand for energy and the fuel-food linkage

As noted above, economic growth and industrialization in rapidly growing developing countries are energy intensive. Increasing energy use is also associated with rising living standards. China, for instance, became the biggest energy consumer in the world in 2010, with its share in global primary energy consumption rising from 8 per cent in 1990 to 20 per cent in 2010 (Coates and Luu, 2012). Coal is its main energy source, but the share of coal in China's total energy consumption is expected to decline with a shift to cleaner energy sources. In the medium term, oil is likely to remain the main energy source for transportation. Indeed, demand for oil for transportation will continue to increase in parallel with rising demand for automobiles in China and other developing countries. While the share of China in global oil consumption and imports is not as high as for other commodities, it accounts for a large share in the growth of global demand for oil (table 2.1). Demand from developing countries, led by China and India, has driven global energy markets over the last decade. For example, between 2002 and 2012, demand for oil increased by 44.4 per cent in non-OECD countries, while it declined by 6.4 per cent in OECD countries. As a result, the share of non-OECD countries in global oil consumption increased from 39.1 per cent to 49.8 per cent (BP, 2013). Although improvements in energy efficiency are expected to contribute to a continued decline in energy use per unit of GDP, the rising demand for energy in rapidly growing developing countries will persist over the next few decades, though at slower rates than in the past decade (BP, 2011).

Surging demand for energy, high oil prices and the search for alternative sources of energy to tackle climate change have boosted demand for biofuels. These include ethanol, which is produced mainly from maize and sugar, and biodiesel, derived from oilseeds. Indeed, an increasing proportion of food crops are now grown for biofuels, leading to increasing competition for different land uses: for food, feedstock for animals and fuel, and for agricultural raw materials such as cotton. The rapid expansion of biofuel production is concentrated in a few areas. According to the FAO (2012b), by 2012 ethanol production absorbed over 50 per cent of the sugar cane crop in Brazil and 37 per cent of the coarse grain crop in the United States. Biodiesel production accounted for almost 80 per cent of the crops grown for vegetable oil production in the European Union (EU). Corn used for ethanol production in the United States reached 44.3 per cent of total corn use, up from only 12.6 per cent in 2002.[7] Government policies, such as mandates and subsidies or other kinds of support, have played a very important role in pushing this expansion of biofuel production. Without such support, it is doubtful whether such production would be profitable in some areas like the European Union and the United States. It is expected that demand for feedstock for biofuel production will continue to grow over the next decade (OECD-FAO, 2013; USDA, 2013).

(b) Supply response

The rapidly growing demand for commodities starting from the early 2000s pushed up prices, because, during the first years of the boom, supply was slow to respond. The extractive industries, in particular, which had experienced a long period of underinvestment, were taken by surprise. The mining and oil industries are capital-intensive, and it is only after several years that returns on investments are realized, as it takes a long time from the initial exploration until a mine or an oil deposit actually becomes productive. Moreover, increasingly, this sector is facing supply constraints because the more easily accessible deposits are becoming mature or exhausted. Consequently, exploration is forced to move to more remote areas or dig deeper to find and extract the resource. Mineral ore grades have been decreasing and it is more difficult to process more complex ores. In addition, there has been a shortage of supply of specialized labour in this sector. Added to this, production costs have risen as a result of the need to comply with increasingly stringent environmental requirements.

Overall, these constraints on supply and the rising production costs have contributed to reducing the efficiency of investment in the extractive industries. Nevertheless, investments in exploration have been rising significantly over the past decade, although there was a setback in 2010–2011 that reflected difficulties related to the global financial crisis. According to the Metals Economics Group (MEG, 2013), global exploration budgets increased from about $2 billion in 2002 to $21.5 billion in 2012. This investment allowed supply to increase and even led to surpluses in some metals markets (Smale, 2013). Even the copper market, which has been particularly tight over the past decade, is moving into surplus. However, in the current uncertain macroeconomic environment, it is unclear whether further financing for exploration will be forthcoming. This may delay projects, leading to lower production over the next few years.

Overcoming supply constraints in the energy and mining sectors depends strongly on technological innovations. One such innovation is the development of horizontal drilling and hydraulic fracturing techniques (known as fracking) in the oil and gas sector. Such technological advances, achieved mainly in the United States, have the potential to significantly change the global energy landscape. They have enabled that country to substantially increase its production of oil and gas, and could result in it becoming the world's leading oil producer by 2020 (IEA, 2012a). This would also reduce the United States' dependence on energy imports, which currently meet around 20 per cent of its total energy needs. Consequently, it would provide an additional push to the ongoing eastward shift in the international oil trade. It would also contribute to reducing global imbalances, as energy imports have been a major factor contributing to the United States trade deficit over the past few years (*TDR 2010*: chart 2.5). There are indications that these new developments are already affecting the oil exports to the United States of some major African oil-producing countries, such as Algeria, Angola and Nigeria.[8] It is still unclear whether the so-called "US shale gas revolution" can be replicated in some other countries. Moreover, the application of the new technologies remains controversial on environmental grounds, mainly with regard to water pollution.[9]

Agriculture also faces significant supply constraints. The two main ways to increase agricultural production are by expanding the cultivated area and increasing crop yields. However, the potential to increase arable land is limited (FAO, 2011) as is the availability of water for agriculture. And these resources are particularly scarce in those countries that are most in need of increasing their food production. Therefore, the other option is to improve agricultural yields. However, the pace of growth of agricultural productivity has been slowing in recent decades. The average annual rate of growth of grain yields declined from 2.2 per cent during the period 1950–1990 to 1.3 per cent during the period 1990–2011 (Brown, 2012). This decline partly reflects the failure of development policy reforms adopted during the 1990s, which led to a neglect of the agricultural sector such as expressed by reduced official development assistance (ODA) to this sector and less government involvement in developing countries, following structural adjustment programmes agreed with the international financial institutions. A major area of neglect related to investment in research and development. Indeed, agricultural productivity could be increased by reducing productivity gaps in developing countries (OECD-FAO, 2013) through greater investment in agriculture. In addition, higher prices of energy and other input costs, such as fertilizers and pesticides, have acted as additional constraints on agricultural production.

The supply of food and other agricultural products is also highly dependent on weather conditions, which contribute to short-term price volatility. For example, a severe drought in the United States in the summer of 2012 adversely affected the production of grains and soybeans leading to a third price spike since the global food crisis in 2008. There are also increasing concerns about the impact of climate change on agricultural production. Some of the weather-related disruptions in food supply, their higher frequency, and the slower growth of agricultural yields might partly be associated with climate change. Indeed, some observers suggest that climate change may pose the greatest threat to agricultural production and food prices in the future (Oxfam, 2012).[10]

4. Commodity prices: prospects

Projections about the evolution of commodity prices are particularly challenging given the high level of uncertainty in the current global economic environment. The minerals and metals sector faces the greatest downside risks due to new supply coming onstream just when demand growth from China appears to be decelerating. However, a supply crunch may reappear in a few years time. Regarding the oil sector, specialized energy agencies such as the International Energy Agency (IEA) and the Energy Information Administration of the United States see oil prices falling to slightly lower levels than those of 2011–2012, but nevertheless remaining historically high. In spite of still rising demand from some of the rapidly growing developing countries (although at a slower pace), market conditions should ease somewhat due to rising supplies of non-conventional oil. However, the production costs of these new supplies make them profitable only at relatively high price levels. In addition, the Organization of the Petroleum

Exporting Countries (OPEC) will likely continue to be a key force in influencing oil prices. Non-OECD countries are expected to remain the major sources of any increase in oil demand. Indeed, oil demand from these countries is expected to overtake that of OECD countries by 2014 (IEA, 2012b).

The outlook for the agricultural sector points to elevated prices. According to OECD-FAO (2013), agricultural commodity prices have become structurally higher, and are projected to remain firm over the next decade. This would be due to a combination of slower production growth and stronger demand, including for biofuels, as well as a supportive macroeconomic environment. Ethanol production is expected to increase by 67 per cent and biodiesel production by even more, but from a lower base. By 2022, biofuels will account for a growing share of the global production of sugar cane (28 per cent), vegetable oils (15 per cent), and coarse grains (12 per cent). On the supply side, growth of agricultural production is expected to slow down from an average rate of 2.1 per cent in 2003–2012 to 1.5 per cent in 2013–2022. Global projections by USDA (2013) similarly suggest that, following near-term declines, prices for corn, wheat, oilseeds and many other crops are set to remain at historically high levels.

Bearing in mind that forecasting commodity prices is a difficult task, particularly in the current global economic context, a possible scenario that can be derived from the above discussion is that, owing to slowing growth which could somewhat dampen the strong demand in China, commodity prices may not rise as fast as they have done in the past decade. Allowing for some downward adjustments in the short term, commodity prices should stabilize at a high plateau in comparison with the prices of the early 2000s.

There are three main viewpoints about the prospects for the commodity supercycle:

- The most optimistic observers hold that the expansionary phase of the supercycle still has many years to run, as China will continue along an intensive growth trajectory (Farooki and Kaplinsky, 2012; Coates and Luu, 2012). This will cause commodity prices to remain firm.

- Others argue that commodity prices have entered a calmer and more stable phase of growth, but will nevertheless remain at relatively high levels or a "new normal" (Bloxham, Keen and Hartigan, 2012; Goldman Sachs, 2012).

- Yet others believe that the expansionary phase of the supercycle has come to an end (Credit Suisse, 2013; Citi, 2013).

However, there seems to be overall agreement that there will not be a permanent collapse of commodity prices or a quick return to a long-running deteriorating trend over the next few years. Thus, exporters of primary commodities may be less adversely affected by systemic changes in the world economy than exporters of manufactures. As long as commodity prices remain at relatively high levels and commodity producers are able to appropriate a fair share of the resource rents, the main challenge for policymakers will be to ensure that revenues accruing from natural resource exploitation spur production and export diversification.

C. Volume effects on exporters of manufactures

Several studies have examined product-specific patterns relating to the sharp fall in world trade that occurred between the third quarter of 2008 and the first quarter of 2009 (e.g. Bems, Johnson and Yi, 2010; Levchenko, Lewis and Tesar, 2010; Gopinath, Itskhoki and Neiman, 2012). These studies indicate that: (i) trade in goods fell more than trade in services and that trade in durable goods (such as automotive products and industrial supplies) fell more than trade in non-durable goods; (ii) the sharp fall in consumer durables and other differentiated goods (branded manufactures) was entirely in terms of volume, with no price reductions; and (iii) declines in real final expenditure were responsible for most of the collapse of international trade in 2008–2009 (e.g. Bems, Johnson and Yi, 2013). The latter finding suggests that changes in the pattern of international trade of manufactures in 2008–2009 may be more than a short-term phenomenon. The high probability of continued slow growth in developed countries' final expenditure in the coming years, due to a prolonged slowdown in their growth rates, is likely to have a negative impact on the export opportunities of developing countries.[11]

These potential adverse effects may be assessed by examining the impact of declining imports by the United States. This is because the sizeable contribution to global growth of rapidly rising consumer demand in the United States was a main feature of the pre-crisis global economy. As discussed in some detail in *TDR 2010*, chap. II, prior to the onset of the current economic and financial crisis, United States personal consumption, amounting to about $10 trillion, represented around 70 per cent of that country's GDP and about 16 per cent of global GDP; consumer spending also accounted for over 70 per cent of United States GDP growth during the period 2000–2007. Most importantly, imports of consumer goods, including automobiles, accounted for about 85 per cent of the increase in the United States' non-energy trade deficit between 1997 and 2007. Over the same period, imports of non-food consumer goods, excluding automobiles, increased by about 150 per cent, boosting aggregate demand in the rest of the world by almost $300 billion in absolute terms.

United States imports of consumer goods, especially the non-food categories (excluding automobiles), became sluggish in 2008 (chart 2.4). Between the first quarter of 1999 and the third quarter of 2008, these imports grew, on average, by almost 2 per cent per quarter, before declining sharply. They then experienced a rebound, starting in the first quarter of 2009, but have stagnated at their pre-crisis level over the past two years.

If imports of non-food consumer goods by the United States are disaggregated into durable (excluding automobiles), semi-durable and non-durable goods,[12] there is a clear indication that the loss of import dynamism in the United States matters

Box 2.1

A SHIFT IN DEVELOPMENT STRATEGIES: LESSONS FROM THE LATIN AMERICAN EXPERIENCE AFTER THE CRISIS OF THE 1930s[a]

With the changing patterns of international demand, developing countries today are faced with the issue of whether to shift their development strategies by giving greater emphasis to domestic demand to drive economic growth. But it is not the first time in economic history that this impulse to shift to domestic-demand-oriented growth has arisen: the Great Depression in the 1930s evoked a similar response from Latin American countries, which advanced the process of industrialization.

Beginning in the 1870s, after a long period of political instability following their independence, most Latin American countries began a process of rapid integration into the global economy as exporters of primary commodities and importers of manufactures and foreign capital. They also attracted labour migration, which contributed to diversifying the pattern of domestic consumption. The expansion of exports spurred economic growth, which in turn generated new resources for their governments, consolidated national States and contributed to greater political stability. However, this development path depended heavily on a continuous expansion of demand for primary commodities from developed countries. It also contributed to worsening living conditions of the often landless rural populations and favoured the rise of a proletariat and urban middle class that claimed better social conditions and greater political participation in what were oligarchic social and political structures.

The vulnerability of such a development path became evident, initially with the First World War which disrupted trade and capital inflows. Thereafter, the Great Depression that began in 1929 led to a collapse of primary commodity exports and, as a consequence, to a severe contraction of imports and fiscal revenues, as well as sovereign debt defaults by most countries in the region. In these circumstances, which in some countries were further complicated by political crises, governments set aside their former liberal credo and adopted more pragmatic and interventionist policies. They abandoned the gold standard and established foreign exchange controls, and introduced quotas on imports and raised import tariffs. Currency devaluations and import restrictions improved relative prices of manufactures at a time when the capacity to import such goods had diminished significantly. The newly created central banks, which supported the domestic banking system, covered the financial needs of the private and the public sectors. These measures enabled the rapid expansion of domestic production of manufactures, which progressively replaced imports, setting in motion a process that came to be known as import substituting industrialization (ISI). Industrial production grew most notably in countries that already had manufacturing capabilities and whose governments supported domestic demand. Between 1929 and 1947, the share of manufacturing in GDP increased from 22.8 to 31.1 per cent in Argentina, from 11.7 to 17.3 per cent in Brazil, from 7.9 to 17.3 per cent in Chile, from 6.2 to 11.5 per cent in Colombia and from 14.2 to 19.8 per cent in Mexico (Furtado, 1976: 137).

After the Second World War, the ISI period came to an end: industrialization continued to rely primarily on domestic markets, but increases in domestic production of manufactured goods were no longer based on the substitution of previously imported goods, which had been reduced considerably by that time. Instead, a rapid expansion of domestic demand became the driving force behind output growth and domestic investment. Industrialization and, concomitantly, urbanization increased the influence of the local bourgeoisie, the middle class and industrial workers in the economy and in national politics. The resulting political change brought with it a deliberate reorientation of development strategy, which, by introducing long-term development projects, aimed at modernizing the productive apparatus and strengthening economic and social integration. Domestic demand was nurtured both by urbanization and the process of industrialization itself, which expanded employment in the modern sectors. In several countries more equal income distribution also boosted demand. Hence, the key elements of that strategy (industrialization and the expansion of domestic markets) supported each other in a virtuous circle (Sainz and Faletto, 1985).

Chart 2.4

UNITED STATES IMPORTS, SELECTED CONSUMER GOODS CATEGORIES, 1st QUARTER 1999–4th QUARTER 2012

(Billions of dollars)

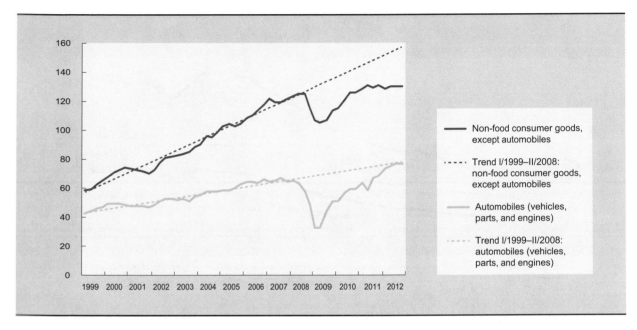

Source: UNCTAD secretariat calculations, based on United States Bureau of Economic Analysis, *International Data*, table 2a.
Note: Data for 2012 fourth quarter are preliminary estimates. The trend growth rate for imports of automobiles is 0.6 per cent per quarter, while that of non-food consumer goods is 1.8 per cent per quarter.

for developing countries' export opportunities (chart 2.5). The durable consumer goods category, was the most dynamic of the three product groups, with United States imports tripling between 1997 and 2007. Given that China and Mexico combined accounted for 60 per cent of United States imports of such goods in 2012, a stagnation of demand in the United States at below pre-crisis levels could have a major impact on these two exporting countries. China accounts for more than half of United States imports of semi-durable consumer goods, which continues to be the largest among the three product categories in spite of the decline of its share from over 60 per cent in 1995 to about 45 per cent in 2012. Non-durable consumer goods (a major component of which is pharmaceuticals) is the only category that has moved rapidly back to its pre-crisis dynamism. However, developing countries account for only a small share of United States imports of this product category.[13] Taken together, this evidence suggests that transmission of the economic slowdown through the trade channel has adversely affected developing countries' exports of products such as apparel

and household equipment to developed countries. Those exports had boosted growth in developing countries prior to the crisis and supported productive transformation.

An examination of data from the euro zone supports this finding. Following a decline in 2008–2009, euro-zone imports (excluding intra-euro-zone trade) of durable (excluding automobiles), semi-durable and non-durable consumer goods rebounded rapidly, and by 2010–2011 they had begun to exceed pre-2008 levels. However, the growth rate of these imports remains considerably lower than in the pre-crisis period: imports of semi-durable consumer goods, which represent more than two thirds of the euro zone's total imports of all these product groups, recorded an average annual growth rate of 12 per cent (and a growth rate of 23 per cent from China, which is by far the most important developing-country source, accounting for almost half of the euro zone's total imports of this product category) during the period 2002–2007, but only 10 per cent (8 per cent from China) during the period 2009–2011.

Chart 2.5

UNITED STATES IMPORTS OF CONSUMER GOODS (EXCL. FOOD AND AUTOMOBILES), BY CATEGORY AND SELECTED SOURCE COUNTRIES, 1995–2012

(Billions of dollars)

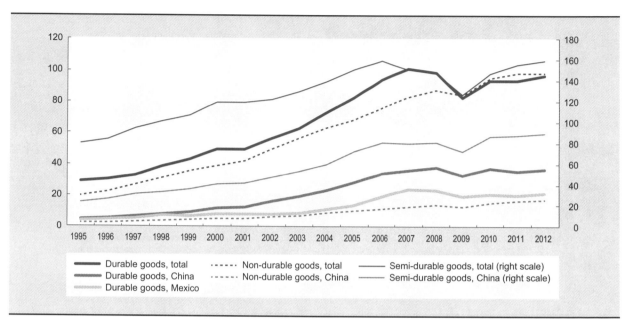

Source: UNCTAD secretariat calculations, based on *UN Comtrade*.

D. Towards more domestic-demand-oriented growth strategies

The possibility of changing rapidly from an export-oriented growth strategy towards a more domestic-demand-oriented one depends largely on what extent the sectoral structure of domestic production is delinked from that of domestic demand. Such a dissociation will be particularly strong in countries that export a large proportion of primary commodities. However, it will also be substantial for other countries that produce sophisticated goods for exports destined for affluent consumers in developed countries, but which few domestic consumers can afford.

Natural-resource-rich economies have long attempted to weaken this dissociation by diversifying

their sectoral structure of production through an increase in manufactures. In those developing and transition economies where manufactures constitute a sizeable share of production and exports, the link between the sectoral composition of production and that of exports may well be strengthened by an increasingly globalizing economy in which domestic demand in developing and transition economies will have a greater weight in global demand, output and trade patterns. The ensuing change in the shape of the global distribution of consumption, with a smaller share of consumption by rich consumers and a larger share by lower and middle-income consumers, implies changes in preferences and a wider

variety of new spending patterns. This, in turn, will guide investment decisions and lead to changes in the sectoral focus of investment, with ensuing changes in the composition of domestic production and output.

Some of the issues associated with a change in growth strategies towards a greater role of domestic demand may be illustrated by the experience of Latin American economies following the Great Depression (box 2.1). The remainder of this section examines issues related to the divergence between the sectoral structure of exports and that of domestic demand, focusing on the balance-of-payments constraint. This is followed by an analysis of changes in the product composition of domestic demand as per capita incomes rise.

1. Domestic-demand-oriented growth and balance of payments

Growth dynamics induced on the demand side sit uncomfortably with most of the existing growth theories, whether neoclassical or endogenous. These theories concentrate on the supply side and neutralize demand effects on long-term growth by assuming that the evolution of consumption of each good is proportional to income growth (i.e. changes in per capita income have no effect on the composition of product baskets).[14] By contrast, early development economists (e.g. Rosenstein-Rodan, 1943) emphasized that demand growth for a specific good, and the ensuing growing size of the market for that good, lead to increasing internal returns to scale in producing that good. Larger markets boost productivity either because of effects stemming from learning by doing (Matsuyama, 2002; Desdoigts and Jaramillo, 2009) or through innovations that allow the development of new methods of production to satisfy the rising new demands (Foellmi and Zweimüller, 2006 and 2008).

The resulting scale economies enable the goods to be produced at lower costs, to the benefit of either consumers or other industries that use those goods as inputs in production. As these goods become affordable to an increasingly large number of households and industries, the markets for these goods expand. This, in turn, induces "further improvement in productivity, creating a virtuous circle of productivity

gains and expanding markets" (Mats 1038).[15] But the productivity growth a increasing economies of scale may a paying higher wages, rather than for r The demand growth stemming from enlarges the size of the domestic ma and services, which enables scale ec over a wide range of industrial se Shleifer and Vishny (1989) develo further, showing that such compl demand work via the buying powe class, which eventually determine horizontal complementarities acro of the economy.[16] These considerati more relevant for a development st greater importance to domestic den in the past. Moreover, for such a s cessful, it would also aim at boostin power of income groups below th that there may be scope for econor increasing number of sectors and primarily for the domestic market

However, if a growing mark ger productivity gains, the two-' well cause the domestic econom may happen in an open economy size externalities linked to incre scale benefit mainly foreign p Shleifer and Vishny, 1989; Desd 2009). In this case, the pace of ir tion may be considerably reduce producers will continue to conce technologically simple goods satisfy necessities, while the more complex goods (such as products) will be captured by f

Indeed, to the extent that stemming from domestic dema imports, without a comparable the growth process of the do well face a balance-of-paymer to a halt. According to the dy foreign trade multiplier first (1933), the rate of domestic ou the rate of growth of exports, on the income elasticity of the growth rate of world in country's income elasticity o Prebisch (1950) applied t development context, arguin

Box 2.1 (concluded)

In this context, the economic role of the State was greatly expanded. It fostered industrialization, infrastructure building and the development of domestic firms through several means. In Chile, the Production Development Corporation (Corporación de Fomento de la Producción), created in 1939, developed basic industries; in Brazil, the Government supported industry through trade protection and the creation of State-owned firms (e.g. the steel producer Volta Redonda); Mexico nationalized its oil industry in 1938 and supported its manufacturing sector through the Industrial Promotion Act (1946) and State procurement; in Argentina, the State captured most of the rents from agriculture through its control of foreign trade, and nationalized the transport system, and communication, power and sanitation services (previously owned by foreign investors), while the central bank and State-owned banks extended credit to industrial activities; in Venezuela, the State acquired most of the oil rent and created the Venezuelan Production Corporation (Corporación Venezolana de Fomento) for supporting the steel and agro-industrial sectors; while Bolivia also nationalized its oil sector (1937), and later its tin production (1952), and implemented agrarian reforms (1953) (Thorp, 1997).

This reorientation of development strategy, triggered initially by the crisis of the 1930s, continued to promote economic growth after the Second World War. Latin America grew rapidly in the post-war years, with its GDP growing at an average annual rate of 5.4 per cent between 1950 and 1975, led by the manufacturing sector (6.8 per cent). By 1975, the share of manufactures in its GDP exceeded 25 per cent (ECLAC, 1978), while the proportion of the urban population rose from 42 per cent in 1950 to 62 per cent in 1975. The manufacturing sector also began to diversify, with production evolving from labour-intensive consumer goods to durable consumer goods, industrial inputs and capital goods. By 1965, technology- or scale-intensive industries accounted for around 50 per cent of manufacturing production in the region's largest economies: Argentina, Brazil, Chile, Colombia, Mexico and Peru (ECLAC, 1979). The international environment was also conducive to the region's economic development, as foreign markets regained momentum during the 1960s and foreign direct investment (FDI) in manufacturing contributed to the diversification of industrial production.

However, there were some drawbacks to this development strategy, as evidenced by recurrent imbalances in the balance of payments and persistent inflation. These were the result of structural factors (e.g. rigidities on the supply side, demand elasticities of imports and exports, leading to trade deficits and frequent devaluations; and social tensions related to income distribution) rather than flawed monetary policies (Noyola, 1957; Bajraj, 1977). Retrospective comparison with the East Asian industrial development experiences suggests that the main problem in Latin America was related to the fact that there was comprehensive, rather than selective and well-targeted, protectionism of domestic industries, and government support was not linked to performance requirements (including those related to exports of manufactures). By the beginning of the 1970s, a new phase of the industrialization process seemed to be taking place in the more advanced Latin American countries, which targeted more diversified domestic and external markets. This phase was characterized by high investment and rapid economic growth. However, strong financial shocks and radical policy reorientations, especially after the debt crisis of the early 1980s, brought this development pattern to an abrupt end.

This experience suggests that, while it is possible to anchor industrialization in domestic demand growth, the process of structural changes needs to be carefully managed on both the demand and the supply side. Moreover, the pursuit of such a development strategy needs to be accompanied by macroeconomic and financial policies aimed at keeping inflation low and preventing large external imbalances and financial instability.

---

[a]   This box draws on Calcagno, 2008.

in developing countries requires industrialization; otherwise, growth will be held back. The reason is that an unsustainable current-account deficit emerges when the income elasticity of demand for primary commodity exports in world markets is lower than the income elasticity of demand for imported goods needed by developing countries.

Although the global economic context has evolved, the mechanisms highlighted by Harrod (1933) and Prebisch (1950) continue to apply: if a prolonged economic slump in developed countries leads to a decline in developing countries' export earnings, the latter will find it difficult to sustain a high rate of growth if the need to satisfy accelerating expenditure in the various domestic-demand components triggers a surge of imports. However, if there were to be an expansion of demand in several developing-country trade partners simultaneously, they could constitute a market for each other, and therefore reduce their balance-of-payments constraint. Consequently, regional integration and, more generally, South-South trade may be necessary complements to domestic-demand-led growth strategies.

The import intensity of the three components of domestic demand (i.e. household consumption, government expenditure and investment) varies widely, and generally differs from the importance of the three components in aggregate demand. Household consumption usually accounts for by far the largest share of aggregate demand, whereas "imports tend to be strongly correlated on average with exports and investment and, to a lesser extent, private consumption, while they appear to be uncorrelated with government consumption" (Bussière et al., 2011: 10). Moreover, the correlation between imports and household consumption is particularly high during periods of recession.

These findings, relating to differences in the import intensity of the different components, are based on an analysis of almost only developed economies. However, there is little reason to believe that the patterns will differ to any significant extent in developing countries. The correlation between domestic demand growth and imports of capital goods and durable consumer goods in developing countries probably exceeds that in developed countries. But, the import intensity of exports is probably also higher in developing countries, especially those whose export sectors are closely integrated into global production chains. Indeed, rough calculations reveal little difference between developed and developing countries in the pattern of import intensity across the various elements of aggregate demand (Akyüz, 2011).

If the sectoral composition of domestic production were adjusted to better match the sectoral structure of accelerating domestic demand, it would reduce the import content of that growing demand. It would also allow domestic entrepreneurs to benefit from increasing returns to scale and encourage them to engage in innovative investment. This would also create new employment opportunities. For the domestic economy, it would imply an increase in nominal incomes, which would induce domestic consumers to increasingly engage in discretionary spending. Globally, this could trigger a cumulative process of income and employment growth, as growing demand would spur the output of existing manufacturing industries as well as the creation of new industries. Ideally, this process should take place on a regional scale, with a number of trade partners encouraging domestic demand in a coordinated way. This would boost intraregional trade, which tends to be intensive in manufactured goods, thereby enabling economies of scale and specialization (*TDR 2007*).

The critical importance of the domestic market for domestic industry was stressed long ago by Chenery, Robinson and Syrquin (1986). They noted that growth of domestic demand accounts for about three quarters of the increase in domestic industrial output in large economies, and slightly more than half in small economies. Building on their insights, Haraguchi and Rezonja (2010) showed that the shares in production of different industrial sectors follow a sequence which resembles the changes observed in the sectoral structure of domestic demand. This similarity can be observed particularly with regard to household consumption expenditure in large economies, where the food and beverages sector is a driver of sustained growth at low levels of per capita income, motor vehicles at medium levels, and audio-visual products at high levels. The following section provides further evidence of changes in the product composition of consumer demand as per capita income rises.

2. Changes in the product composition of domestic demand

Demand-side mechanisms which reflect changes in the patterns of demand as per capita income rises have constituted only a relatively small part of the larger search for the stylized facts that characterize economic development. The declining share of aggregate consumer spending on food (i.e. an effect known as "Engel's law") is usually considered the most notable feature of such demand-side effects. Attempts to generalize Engel's law by enlarging the scope of analysis to more categories of expenditure have often focused on changes in the basket of necessities (such as food, housing and clothing), while treating non-necessities (such as durable goods) as a residual of little importance (e.g. Houthakker, 1957; Chenery, Robinson and Syrquin, 1986).

Socioeconomic class is likely to be a very important determinant of individuals' consumption patterns (e.g. Lluch, Powell and Williams, 1977). The reason is that people who are better off dispose of discretionary income and can shift their consumption pattern away from only basic necessities. This shift in consumption patterns may be based on a preference structure related to a hierarchy of needs (Maslow, 1954). It implies that consumers will start spending beyond goods that only satisfy their basic or subsistence needs once their income exceeds a certain threshold. Another important assumption associated with such a preference pattern is that consumer demand for any good reaches a saturation point, so that demand growth for that good will slow down and eventually cease as more and more households reach the levels of income that mark saturation points.[18] The thresholds which trigger an acceleration of demand for specific consumption items cluster at certain levels of per capita income (Mayer, 2013). These levels closely correspond to what is typically used to characterize an individual as becoming "middle class".

There is no generally accepted definition of the term "middle class". However, in economics and applied empirical analysis, it is generally used to describe the social status of individuals who have a certain amount of discretionary income at their disposal which allows them to engage in consumption patterns beyond just the satisfaction of their basic needs, though not – or only occasionally – their desire for luxury items. Given that many individuals aspire to middle-class status, individuals identifying themselves as being "middle class" is also often used as a definition. This may explain why interpersonal effects on consumer demand, such as bandwagon effects, whereby each person's purchasing pattern is influenced by what specific products are bought by a proportion of some relevant group of others, has often been an important element in the discussion of middle-class consumption patterns (e.g. Witt, 2001).

The two boundaries that separate the middle class from the poor, on the one hand, and from the rich on the other, may be defined in relative or absolute terms. Relative approaches use quintiles of income distribution or a band around the median of the distribution. The main drawback of these approaches is that they do not permit international comparisons, whereas the advantage of using an absolute approach is that it does permit such comparisons. An absolute approach is similar in spirit to international poverty measures, and allows the tracing of both the size and the income share of the middle class on a global scale. To ensure comparability across countries, such measures employ purchasing power adjustments to translate income expressed in domestic currency units into an internationally comparable unit (i.e. the international dollar).[19]

Bussolo et al. (2011) have used such an approach, where the two thresholds defining the middle class are set as equal to the per capita incomes of Brazil and Italy.[20] Kharas (2010) has also used this approach to define the global middle class as comprising individuals whose daily expenditures are between $10 and $100 in purchasing power parity (PPP) terms. Both these studies set the lower bound at an annual level of per capita income of about 4,000 international dollars. By contrast, the definition used in Bussolo et al. (2011) implies an upper bound of about 17,000 international dollars, while Kharas (2010) sets the upper bound at about 35,000 international dollars. These differences in the upper bound are reflected in differences in historic measures of the size of the global middle class, as well in its future evolution. Bussolo et al. (2011: 14) estimate that the proportion of the middle class in the total world population will increase from 7.9 per cent in 2000 to 16.6 per cent in 2030, and that over the same period, the number of people in developing countries that are part of the global middle class will grow more than fourfold, to exceed one billion. According to Kharas' (2010: 27) estimates, the size of the global middle class will increase from 1.8 billion people in 2009 to 3.2 billion in 2020 and 4.9 billion in 2030, which implies that the proportion of the middle class in the total world population will increase from 26 per cent in 2009 to 41 per cent in 2020 and 58 per cent in 2030. Asia will account for the bulk of this increase, with the number of people belonging to the middle class in this region estimated to grow sixfold. China and India will account for more than three quarters of the Asian middle class. The size of the middle class in Central and South America will grow by a factor of 2.5, while in sub-Saharan Africa it will triple, yet remain at only 2 per cent of the total; and it will remain more or less unchanged in Europe and North America.[21]

Of course, these numbers are merely illustrative and should not be considered exact predictions. The two studies' projections on the evolution of the middle class in developing countries may be considered optimistic as an extrapolation of past developments (e.g. in terms of investment and technological change). This is because they do not take into account the unsustainability of the policies pursued by the developed countries during the decade preceding the outbreak of the current global economic crisis, which provided the favourable external economic environment that allowed high investment rates and technological change in developing countries. But they may also be considered pessimistic, as they assume that the share of household consumption in GDP remains constant over time and that, in the case of Kharas (2010), growth is distribution neutral, and thus do not take into account the impact of policies to strengthen domestic purchasing power and reduce income inequality, which this *Report* advocates. As discussed in section E of this chapter, a strategy that accords a greater role to domestic demand growth will require a faster increase in wages than in the past. Thus there may be an accelerated increase in the size of the middle class if this strategy is successful.

Evidence on income distribution indicates that the size of the middle class (as defined by Kharas, 2010) varies widely across countries (chart 2.6). In 2005, which is the most recent year for which comprehensive data are available, the middle class constituted 60 per cent of the population in the United States, compared with only 30 per cent in China, and roughly 5 per cent in India, but about 80 per cent in the Russian Federation. More importantly for the future evolution of consumption expenditure is the number of people that are at around the entry level

of the middle class, where the new spending patterns start emerging. Such income brackets are virtually absent in the developed economies, but comprise more than half of the Chinese and about three quarters of the Indian and Indonesian populations respectively.

Many developing economies continue to have substantial pockets of poverty and lagging regions, especially in sub-Saharan Africa and South Asia. Such pockets hamper the expansion of domestic consumption of durable consumer goods. But this also implies that there is considerable potential for increasing the effective demand for, and domestic supply of, basic and non-durable goods, such as food, as well as other fundamental needs, such as clothing, accommodation, heating and lighting, health, education and safety (Chai and Moneta, 2012), including through a change in income distribution.

However, many other developing and transition economies could witness a rapid acceleration of consumption of durable consumer goods in the medium term. Changes in distributional outcomes that could lift individuals from the lower income brackets to middle-class status are closely related to the creation of well-paid jobs. As noted in *TDR 2012*, much of the decline in income inequality in Latin America over the past few years has been due to the creation of such jobs. This has contributed to some developing countries seeing "the emergence of a working middle class, which has now surpassed 40 per cent of the developing world's workforce" (ILO, 2013: 12).

Greater equality of income is widely expected to boost economic growth, which would provide the main impetus to consumer spending. Indeed, there is now broad agreement that growth accompanied by high or rising inequality is unsustainable in the long run, although there may be temporary exceptions in countries with very rapid growth rates, where absolute levels of income may increase sharply despite greater income inequality. Moreover, high levels of income inequality will hold back the pace at which sufficiently large segments of the population attain the thresholds of per capita income that lead to accelerated demand. This could well retard, or even prevent, cumulative processes that drive growth through associated supply responses.

The discussion in this section implies that the process of per capita income growth and/or steps towards a more equal distribution of income are

Chart 2.6

PER CAPITA INCOME AND DIFFERENT INCOME CLASSES, SELECTED COUNTRIES, 2005

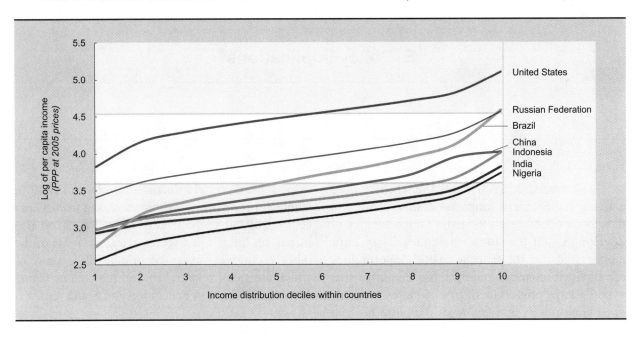

Source: UNCTAD secretariat calculations, based on Milanovic, 2012.
Note: The two horizontal lines are the lower and upper income limits of the middle class. The size of the middle class in each country is indicated by the respective country line that is within the shaded section.

accompanied by the emergence of a range of investment opportunities to produce goods and services to meet the new demand. These investment opportunities will arise at different points in time with respect to both individual products and individual countries. Products will vary because demand for different products will accelerate at different levels of per capita income. Variation across countries will be due to the different size of the slices of the population that are in,

or about to enter, the middle class, whose boundaries mark the levels of per capita income where product-specific demand elasticities are particularly high. The combination of these variations across products and across countries can engender a sustained dynamic growth process driven by interactions between supply and demand over time. The next section focuses on the economic policy implications of these interactions between supply and demand.

E. Policy implications

The preceding sections of this chapter have examined the adverse impacts of slow growth in developed countries on the export opportunities of developing and transition economies. They have emphasized that the reduced export opportunities are likely to concern mainly those countries that export a large proportion of manufactures to developed countries. These countries therefore need to reconsider their growth strategies, giving greater emphasis to domestic sources of demand growth and South-South trade.

This section discusses possible policies that developing and transition economies could adopt in pursuit of such a strategy. It first looks at changes in the relative importance of the domestic demand segments of GDP following the outbreak of the current global economic crisis. It then focuses on policies aimed at: (i) increasing domestic demand by fostering domestic purchasing power, lifting the income of domestic consumers, increasing domestic investment and strengthening the impact of public finances on domestic demand; and (ii) promoting domestic productivity growth and structural change with a view to increasing domestic supply capacities of goods in response to rising domestic demand. Finally, this section looks at the implications of the increased importance of developing countries in the global economy for global development partnerships.

During the period 2008–2009, many developing and transition economies reacted to a decline in their net exports by increasing the share of government consumption expenditure in GDP (chart 2.7). Household consumption expenditure as a share of GDP also increased in some of these countries, such as Brazil, Malaysia and the Russian Federation, while it fell in others, such as China and Indonesia. The latter two countries saw a particularly large increase

in gross fixed capital formation as a share of GDP. In China, for example, this share increased from 39 per cent in 2007 to 45 per cent in 2009. This share also increased, though to a lesser extent, in most of the other economies presented in chart 2.7, many of which are rich in natural resources, such as Chile, Mexico, the Russian Federation and South Africa.

The data for 2011 suggest that there were no similar increases in gross fixed capital formation as a share of GDP, which was possibly a reaction to the euro-zone crisis that gained traction in 2011(chart 2.7). This difference in reaction may be explained by the fact that in 2008–2009 there were expectations of an early recovery, which were supported by episodic signs pointing to a rapid rebound of growth in developed economies. This had led to the assumption of only a temporary decline in otherwise continuously increasing opportunities for exports to these countries. With the euro-zone crisis, by contrast, policymakers in developing and transition economies may have accepted the likelihood of a prolonged period of sluggish growth in developed economies' aggregate demand, which therefore suggested the need to rely less on exports to these economies for their growth. This variation in responses to the adverse effects of the Great Recession and the euro-zone crisis, respectively, may reflect uncertainty and considerations of how best to deal with the challenge of managing a change in emphasis from a growth strategy based on exports towards one based more on domestic demand. This challenge should not be underestimated.

There are many difficulties associated with such a shift in growth strategy. For this shift to be sustainable in developing and transition economies that export mainly manufactures, there will need to be both sustained improvements in technological

Chart 2.7

TYPE OF EXPENDITURE AS A SHARE OF GDP, SELECTED ECONOMIES, 2000–2011

(Per cent)

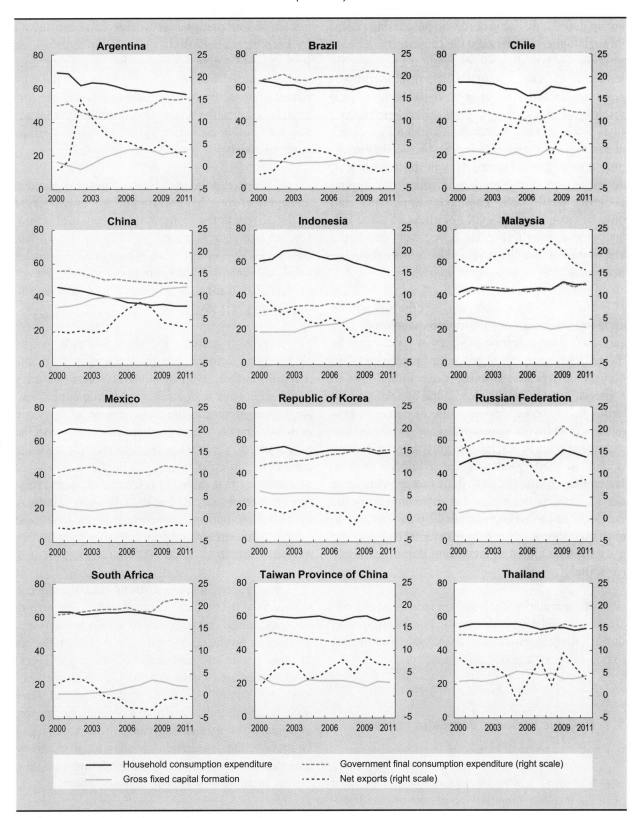

Household consumption expenditure

Gross fixed capital formation

Government final consumption expenditure (right scale)

Net exports (right scale)

Source: *UnctadStat.*
  Note: The shares are based on data measured at current prices in dollars.

dynamism and rising household consumption expenditure based on growth of real disposable income through nominal income growth, rather than cheap imports. And these two goals would have to be achieved simultaneously, because, if domestic productive capacity is not upgraded, any rise in domestic purchasing power through higher earnings and the consequent increase in domestic consumption expenditure would only induce an increase in imports. The resulting import boom would add to the changes in the trade balance resulting from stagnating exports to developed economies. Such multiple pressures on a country's external accounts would risk causing balance-of-payments problems and stall income growth. In that context, an expansion of the markets of other developing countries would be of paramount importance, not only because it would avoid or alleviate trade balance strains, but also because it would provide larger and more dynamic demand, and therefore encourage investment and technological upgrading.

Individuals require real income growth to engage in higher consumption expenditure. This can result from a decline in prices of goods, such as through rising imports of goods that are cheaper than domestically produced ones, made possible by an appreciation of the exchange rate and/or a progressive delinking of the sectoral structure of domestic production from that of domestic demand. However, any attempt to achieve real income growth by increasing imports of cheap goods may cause imports to grow faster than exports and contribute to a growing trade deficit. Thus, policies aimed at enhancing domestic demand need to be accompanied by an appropriate exchange-rate policy to ensure external balance, and by a strategy aimed at increasing domestic supply capacities.

The remainder of this section focuses on policies aimed at fostering both domestic purchasing power through income growth and technological upgrading to boost domestic productive capacity.

1. Policies to boost domestic demand

Since the 1980s, developing countries have placed a growing emphasis on export-oriented production to drive expansion of their formal modern sectors. But while this strategy has been successful in some countries, in most cases domestic demand has not increased at the same pace. This is partly due to weak linkages between the export sector and the rest of the economy, and partly to the strategy of domestic companies and governments to exploit their perceived comparative advantage of cheap labour by keeping wages low in order to strengthen their international competitiveness. But sooner or later such a strategy will reach its limits due to the constraint imposed by low wages on domestic demand growth, especially when global demand weakens and many other countries pursue the same strategy simultaneously.

Therefore, policies to boost domestic demand as an engine of growth are warranted, not only because of the current deflationary trend in the world economy, but also because a strategy of export-led growth based on wage compression, which makes countries overly dependent on foreign demand growth, may not be sustainable for a large number of countries and over a long period of time.

A growth strategy that gives greater emphasis to domestic demand growth must start from the recognition that, even in relatively poor countries and in countries with a relatively large export sector, labour income is the major source of domestic demand. Therefore, policies aimed at increasing the purchasing power of the population overall, and wage earners in particular, need to be the main ingredient of a strategy that favours promoting domestic relative to external sources of growth. In many countries, the two other main components of domestic demand – private investment and public sector expenditure – may also help to advance such a strategy.

In any case, there is a strong interdependence between the three components of domestic demand. First, increased consumption of goods and services that can be produced domestically makes producers of these goods and services more willing to invest in their productive capacity. Second, higher investment will create additional employment and wage income, and thus increase both the purchasing power of domestic consumers and the tax revenue that can be spent by the government. Moreover, productivity gains resulting from additional investment allow a further increase in wages and consumption.

Third, higher public spending can have a positive impact on both private consumption and investment through various channels. It can create additional income for consumers and improve the conditions for private investment. The latter is not only itself a source of domestic demand (even if a large share of the capital goods may have to be imported), but is also indispensable for expanding domestic supply capacity, and consequently for reducing leakages of domestic demand growth through imports. Public investment in infrastructure is often complementary to, if not a prerequisite for, private investment, and helps to increase overall productivity in the economy. To the extent that the pattern of public revenue and public spending contribute to reducing income inequality, consumption will be higher at any given level of total income, because lower income earners spend a larger proportion of their income than higher income earners, and the share of domestically produced goods and services in their consumption tends to be greater because they are less likely to consume imported luxury goods. Finally, if the public sector's contribution to GDP is larger, governments have more possibility to compensate for fluctuations in domestic and external demand through countercyclical fiscal policies, and thus prevent large swings in consumption and investment.

(a) Increasing domestic consumption

Policies that result in a decline of the wage share have often been justified as being necessary to reduce production costs and induce investment. However, as noted above, household consumption constitutes the largest share of effective demand in most countries, developed and developing alike.

Indeed, empirical evidence suggests that changes in the wage share are positively correlated with changes in the share of household consumption in GDP (as reflected in the figures on the left hand side of chart 2.8). Given that most countries show a decline in the wage share, this positive correlation implies a decline in the share of household consumption in GDP.[22] By contrast, there is no clear correlation between changes in the wage share and the share of investment in GDP (figures on the right hand side of chart 2.8). The latter correlation is mildly positive in Africa and nil in developed economies. By contrast, it is negative in East, South and South-East Asia and in Latin America, though smaller in absolute terms than the correlation between changes in wage shares and those in consumption.[23]

Of course, these correlations need to be interpreted with caution, and should not be considered as indicative of causality. In particular, they should not be interpreted as showing that in Asia and Latin America, higher investment rates depend on wage compression. In most South-East Asian countries, investment rates fell significantly after the Asian crisis of 1997–1998, even in countries where wages and consumption also fell as a share of GDP, and were balanced by a commensurate improvement in the current account balance. Regarding Latin America, the comparison between two points in time may be misleading, because 2002–2003 marked a change in the trends of both income distribution and investment rates. In several countries (e.g. Argentina and the Bolivarian Republic of Venezuela), shares of both investment and labour in GDP declined between the early 1990s and 2002, and then recovered in tandem in the subsequent years, showing a positive correlation that is not apparent in the chart. Finally, the case of China illustrates that as long as a declining wage share is accompanied by rapid income growth, it does not imply an absolute fall in living standards.

Soon after the onset of the current financial crisis, GDP growth in developing and transition economies remained relatively high or recovered quickly, as the deceleration or even a decline of their exports was compensated for by faster growth of domestic demand resulting from expansionary monetary and fiscal policies and faster wage growth. The rapid recovery of some large developing and transition economies also provided a market for smaller countries that cannot rely solely on their domestic demand.

In order to sustain these domestic demand dynamics stemming from countercyclical policies, and in some cases also from terms-of-trade gains, growth-supporting monetary and fiscal policies have to become more permanent features, as they were in the developed countries during "the Golden Age" and in those emerging economies that were the most successful in catching up during the 1980s and 1990s. But in order for governments and central banks to pursue fiscal and monetary policies, including supportive public investment and low interest rates that remain favourable to private domestic capital formation over long periods of time, it is also necessary to keep inflation in check. Achieving both objectives – rapid domestic demand growth and relative price stability – could be greatly facilitated if the traditional

Chart 2.8

CHANGES IN WAGE SHARES, PRIVATE CONSUMPTION AND PRIVATE INVESTMENT IN SELECTED GROUPS OF COUNTRIES FROM 1991–1994 TO 2004–2007

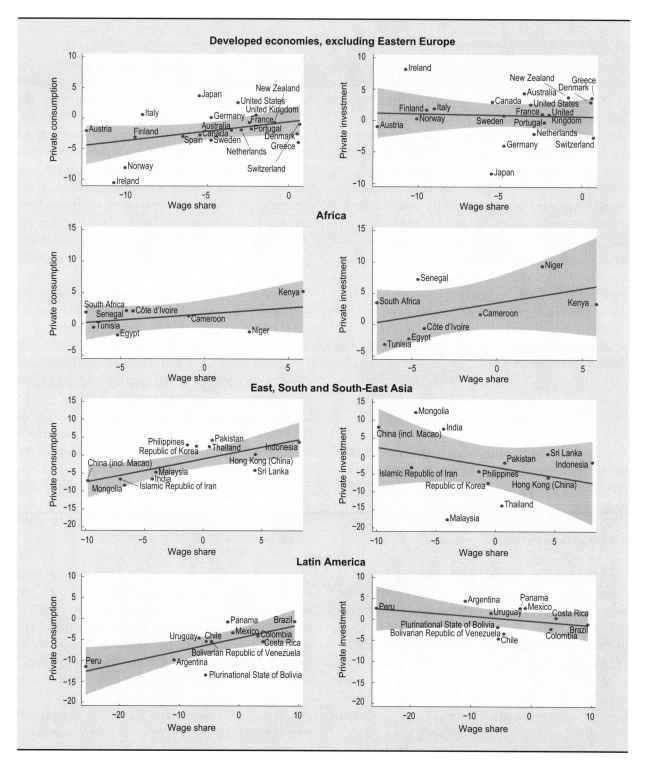

Source: UNCTAD secretariat calculations, based on UN-DESA, *National Accounts Main Aggregates* database; ILO, *Global Wage* database; and *OECD.StatExtracts* database.
Note: Data refer to changes in percentage points of the average GDP for each period. When no observation for wage share was available for the period 1991–1994, the first subsequent observation was used. For Brazil, Mongolia and Niger, data refer to 1995; for Cameroon, Chile, Egypt and Kenya, data refer to 1996; for Panama, data refer to 1997; for Sri Lanka and Uruguay, data refer to 1998; for India, Indonesia, Mongolia and Peru, data refer to 1999; for Pakistan, data refer to 2000. The shaded area represents the 95 per cent confidence interval.

macroeconomic policy toolkit were complemented by an appropriate incomes policy.

A central feature of any incomes policy should be to ensure that average real wages grow at least at a similar rate as average productivity. Previous *TDRs* have repeatedly drawn attention to the merits of establishing such a link with a view to creating employment and avoiding a further deterioration of income distribution (*TDR 2010*, chap.V and *TDR 2012*, chap.VI). These considerations are equally relevant for domestic-demand-led growth strategies, because wage growth in line with productivity growth should be able to create a sufficient amount of domestic demand to fully employ growing productive capacities of the economy without having to rely on continued export growth. At the same time, inflation can be kept within a low range when nominal wages are not adjusted to previous rates of inflation, which would risk causing inflation inertia. Rather, nominal wage adjustments should take into account an inflation target that guides the monetary policy of the respective country (see also *TDR 2012*, chap. VI). This would greatly facilitate the task of the central bank to prevent inflation, and widen its scope to stimulate investment and growth, as proposed in chapter III of this *Report*.

The effectiveness of such an incomes policy that ensures a sustained expansion of domestic demand as well as low inflation could be enhanced by a strengthening of collective bargaining mechanisms (or their introduction where they do not yet exist) and by minimum wage legislation. Collective bargaining of wages, and employment conditions more generally, would also help to achieve greater social consensus about income distribution and enhance social cohesion, provided that both workers' and employers' associations, and possibly government recommendations or guidelines for such negotiations, broadly adhere to the wage adjustment rule. Such mechanisms may be difficult to implement in many developing countries where the institutional framework for structured negotiations for determining wages and employment conditions remains to be created.

The introduction of a legal minimum wage may therefore serve as a useful instrument to protect the weaker social groups, but also, if it is regularly adjusted to average productivity growth in the economy, as a means to expand demand for mostly domestically produced goods and services (*TDR 2012*, chap. VI.D). Minimum wages may push up the prices of some labour-intensive goods and services, but the purchasing power of a large group of employees would also rise, thus helping to create additional income and employment throughout the economy (see also G20, 2012: 12). Moreover, regular adjustment of the legal minimum wage can provide an important reference for wage negotiations in the private sector.

Legal minimum wages already exist in most of the developed countries and in many developing countries, but in countries where there is a large proportion of informal and self-employment, it is often difficult to enforce such legislation. Therefore, in these countries it is important to complement policies aimed at increasing formal employment and increasing the purchasing power of employees in the formal sector with measures to boost incomes and the purchasing power of the informally and self-employed.

In this context, a number of developing countries have introduced public sector employment schemes in order to reduce widespread unemployment and poverty (*TDR 2010,* chap. V; and *TDR 2012*, chap. VI). Such schemes can play an important role within a strategy to raise domestic demand. In countries where a large reserve of surplus labour exists, and where competition between the employed and the unemployed and underemployed tends to drive down earnings, public sector employment not only has a direct demand-generating effect; the terms of such employment, especially the remuneration of workers, can also help to establish a floor to the level of earnings in both the formal and informal sectors. Similar to wages in the private sector and minimum wage levels, remuneration of such employment should also be improved over time at a rate that appropriately reflects the average growth of productivity in the entire economy as well as the increase in tax revenues in a growing economy. The layers of the population that benefit directly or indirectly from the introduction of such schemes are likely to spend most of their incomes, and more than the average, on locally produced goods and services.

In countries with a large rural sector that has many small producers, mechanisms that link agricultural producer prices to overall productivity growth in the economy would be another element of a strategy to increase domestic consumption. At the same time, it would raise productivity, as higher incomes would enable producers to make greater investments in equipment. Such mechanisms have been applied successfully in all developed countries for decades.

Consumers' disposable income can also be influenced by government provision of basic services (financed, for example, though increased taxation of higher income groups), such as health care, care for children and the elderly, education and housing, which will tend to reduce the precautionary savings of the lower and middle-income groups. It can also be influenced by changes in tax rates and transfer payments with a view to reducing income inequality and boosting the purchasing power of low- and middle-income households.

In addition, governments can take discretionary fiscal actions, including promoting the consumption of durable consumer goods, for example through targeted fiscal transfers such as tax rebates on certain consumer goods.[24] In countries with a domestic car industry, passenger cars have often been such a target, including as part of countercyclical measures. A wide range of developed countries, as well as some developing countries (e.g. China) spurred new car sales through so-called "cash-for-clunkers" schemes in 2008–2009. Given that such schemes generally aim at replacing old cars, which are more polluting and less energy efficient, with new ones, these schemes also help to achieve environmental targets. Some other developing countries have successfully adopted similar schemes targeting "first-car purchases".[25] For example, in 2011 Thailand adopted a scheme that allowed first-time car buyers to apply for a tax refund on cars manufactured in Thailand.[26]

Household consumption expenditure can also be spurred by facilitating access to consumer credit for the acquisition of durable consumer goods.[27] An easing of consumer credit may result from changes in credit conditions or from wealth effects based on increased asset prices that make it easier for certain middle-class consumers to provide collateral for loans. However, there are considerable risks involved in encouraging an increase of household consumption based on consumer credit, as amply demonstrated by recent experiences in a number of developed countries, where episodes of fast growth of such credit were at the origin of, or at least contributed to, balance sheet disequilibria that ended in substantial financial turmoil. In the United States household debt

as a share of GDP increased rapidly during the decade prior to the onset of the Great Recession, reaching a peak of 102 per cent in 2007 (chart 2.9). This increase was closely linked to rising house prices, combined with the fact that almost two thirds of household debt stemmed from mortgages. This also resulted in an increase in household debt as a share of household consumption expenditure, which peaked at 145 per cent in 2007.

In most developed countries, households have strongly reduced debt by paying it off, or often they have defaulted, with attendant adverse effects on household consumption expenditure. By contrast, there seems to be an unabated trend towards increased household leveraging in developing countries. This may be the result of a combination of three factors: a quick economic recovery from the downturn in 2008, which contained job losses, sustained low interest rates, and asset price inflation, including in real estate.[28]

Among developing and transition economies, the level of household debt as a share of GDP has become particularly high in Malaysia and the Republic of Korea, where it exceeds 80 per cent (chart 2.10). Both these countries have also seen a significant rise in house prices. At least in the Republic of Korea, the growth of household debt and house prices may be closely linked, as "mortgages and other housing loans make up almost 53 per cent of household debt" (McKinsey Global Institute, 2013: 25). Household debt in Malaysia has increased sharply since 2008, its ratio to disposable personal income rising from 150 per cent to almost 190 per cent. In Brazil, China, Indonesia and Thailand, there has also been a strong increase in this ratio since 2008, though at considerably lower levels (chart 2.10). Such a rapid growth of household debt can rapidly place a heavy burden on household budgets and considerably reduce their consumption expenditure. Brazil for example, witnessed a sharp increase in default rates on consumer loans in 2011, making banks increasingly reluctant to lend, even though a decline of benchmark interest rates to record lows since then has helped stem default rates.[29]

It is difficult to assess what levels and growth rates of household debt are sustainable. However, there are indications that larger and persistent credit growth, as well as growth episodes that start at relatively high debt-to-GDP ratios, pose a greater risk

Chart 2.9

HOUSEHOLD DEBT AND HOUSE PRICES IN THE UNITED STATES, 1995–2012

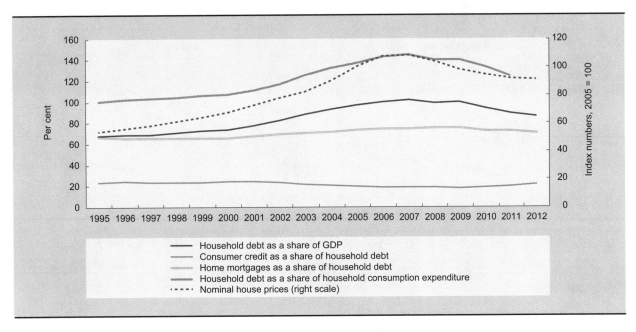

Source: UNCTAD secretariat calculations, based on Bank for International Settlements (BIS), *Credit to Private Non-Financial Sectors* database; the Federal Reserve, *Flow of Funds Accounts of the United States*; and the Federal Reserve Bank of Dallas, *International House Price Database.*

of a credit bust, with ensuing adverse effects on the stability of a country's financial system (Dell'Ariccia et al., 2012). It is also difficult to assess the extent to which rapidly rising and/or elevated debt levels translate into excessive debt servicing burdens and declining consumption expenditure. If any thresholds exist in this area, they will be determined by a wide range of factors, including the income structure of debtors and the maturity and interest-rate structure of loans. Related comprehensive data are not available for developing countries. Macro-level monetary policy easing can smooth the burden of the rising cost of household debt servicing. But for the same reason it can also induce further borrowing, unless such macroeconomic policy easing is combined with micro-level measures such as tighter regulations relating to loan-to-value and debt-to-income ceilings.[30]

There is the possibility of a looming financial crisis in those countries where the growth of household debt steadily exceeds income growth and/or where the size of outstanding household debt considerably exceeds the size of GDP. A crisis could be triggered by a perception that asset prices are overvalued, with an associated collapse of household wealth. But the trigger could also be a sudden sizeable increase in interest rates or a renewed global economic downturn that would cause developing-country exports to decline and domestic incomes to fall. This would make it increasingly difficult for households to service their debt, resulting in turmoil in the financial sector of the country concerned.

To sum up, a policy aimed at spurring household consumption expenditure by easing the constraints on borrowing tends to be risky. Unless such a strategy successfully jump-starts a virtuous process of accelerating domestic demand and supply, it may well cause substantial financial and economic turmoil. The debt servicing burden may rapidly become excessive if interest rates rise, growth of household incomes stalls or property prices fall. Any such development would eventually restrain household consumption expenditure. A more sustainable strategy would thus be the implementation of an incomes policy such as outlined above. But the creation of income opportunities and productivity growth that enables sustained increases in real wages is closely associated with fixed capital formation. The latter has been a driving

Chart 2.10

HOUSEHOLD DEBT AND HOUSE PRICES, SELECTED DEVELOPING COUNTRIES, 2000–2012

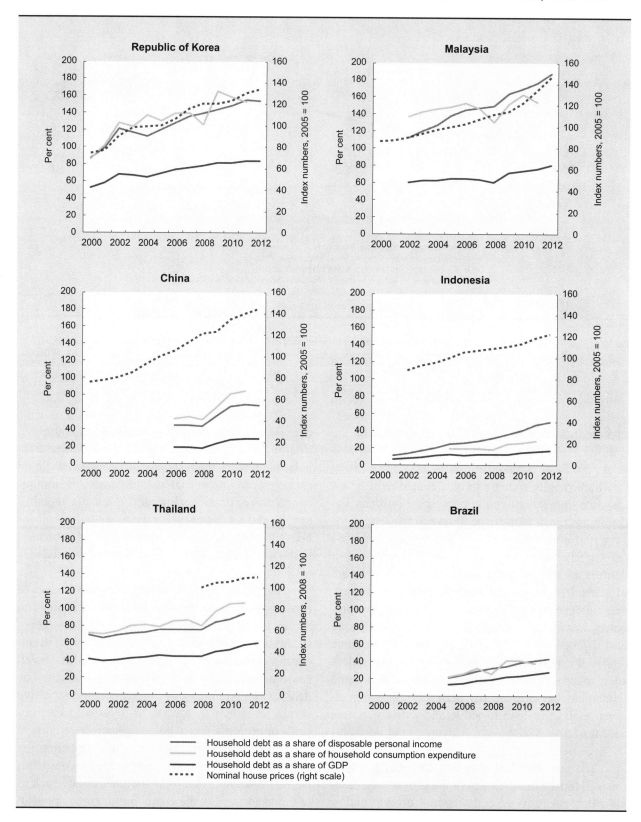

Source: UNCTAD secretariat calculations, based on data from the United Nations Statistics Division; Bank for International Settlements,
         Credit to Private Non-Financial Sectors database; and Federal Reserve Bank of Dallas, *International House Price Database.*
Note: House price data for Brazil were not available.

force for development in those developing countries and emerging market economies that have been the most successful in their efforts to catch up with the developed economies. By contrast, it has remained at relatively low levels in many other developing countries, especially in Africa and Latin America.

(b) Promoting domestic investment

A key determinant of the willingness of entrepreneurs to invest in real productive capacity is the expected profitability of a potential investment, which in turn depends on estimates that help determine whether future demand will be high enough to fully utilize the additional productive capacity.

When wages grow at a slower rate than productivity, the additional supply can only be utilized profitably when there is a continued increase in export demand. In the absence of such demand growth, productive capacity will be underutilized, and this will discourage further productive investment and innovation. Given the current conditions of the world economy, exports are unlikely to grow at the same pace as in the past, thus wage-driven domestic demand growth will become a more important factor in the demand expectations of potential investors. But a favourable environment for domestic investment also requires supportive fiscal policies (discussed in the next subsection) and monetary conditions, including a competitive exchange rate, and financial policies aimed at allowing potential investors access to low-cost credit.

A monetary policy that seeks to strengthen domestic demand and supply capacities would keep the level of interest rates low. In the past, attempts to use only monetary policy to fight inflation often led to high real interest rates, which discouraged private domestic investment for two reasons. First, they meant high financing costs for potential investors, and second, they often attracted foreign capital inflows of a speculative nature, which tended to result in currency overvaluation and a loss of competitiveness. This reduced the export opportunities and demand expectations of domestic producers. An incomes policy based on a regime of productivity-aligned wage growth, as outlined above, would facilitate the pursuit of a monetary policy that fosters domestic investment, because it would also exclude, or at least significantly reduce, the risk of inflation as a result of

rising unit labour costs. Moreover, when exchange rate management and capital account management can ensure a stable real exchange rate, they can prevent unnecessary leakages of domestic demand to foreign markets due to the reduced international competitiveness of domestic producers.

Financial policies should facilitate access to credit for sectors and activities that are of strategic importance for the structural transformation of the economy. Such financial support, which has often been used as an instrument of industrial policy in developed countries and in successful emerging economies in Asia, could also help solve the problem of access to adequate financing faced by many small, often innovative firms, including those in the informal sector and in agriculture, which produce primarily for the domestic market. Examples of such policies include the direct provision of credit by public financial institutions or by intervention in financial markets through such measures as interest subsidies, refinancing of commercial loans and provision of guarantees for certain types of credit.

Such measures are of particular importance where the formal manufacturing sector is still relatively small. In that case, it is not only capital formation in the formal manufacturing sector that can contribute to higher domestic demand and greater domestic supply capacity, but also productivity-enhancing investment in the agricultural sector and in small businesses. Small-scale farmers and the self-employed pursuing non-farm activities in both rural and urban areas are particularly dependent on financial support schemes, because it is often difficult or impossible for them to make even small investments owing to problems or lack of access to low-cost finance from commercial banks (McKinley, 2009).

Productivity in the agricultural sector can also be enhanced through public investment in agricultural research and rural infrastructure and publicly assisted agricultural support organizations. Many such organizations were dismantled during the structural adjustment programmes of the 1990s, partly in the context of sweeping liberalization and privatization, and partly because a number of them had serious governance problems. But if such organizations are equipped with appropriate governance structures, they may be instrumental in fostering income growth in rural areas by providing essential extension services, disseminating information about productivity-enhancing investments and efficient marketing, and facilitating access of small farmers to affordable credit. Ensuring the participation of the agricultural sector in overall productivity growth and the generation of higher purchasing power of those working in this sector may also require protecting farmers against the impact of competition from highly subsidized agricultural products imported from developed countries.

2. The role of the public sector in strengthening domestic demand

(a) Direct and indirect demand effects of public expenditure

Over many years, economic policy was oriented towards a reliance on market forces as key drivers of growth and development, with a reduced size of the public sector in the economy. Government intervention was considered ineffective on the grounds that an increase in public expenditure would cause a reduction in private expenditure. This, it was assumed, would result in greater distortions in resource allocation than those generated by the market mechanism alone, leading to suboptimal outcomes for the economy as a whole. It is certainly true that the public sector has a significant direct and indirect influence on factor allocation, but the "distortions" this creates are not necessarily negative for the economy and society as whole. Moreover, while public finances influence factor allocation at a given level of income, to the extent that they strengthen aggregate demand they raise the level of national income. Taxation and public spending are potentially key instruments for shaping the distribution of purchasing power in the economy and for establishing linkages between companies in the modern sectors, export industries and the rest of the economy, which the market mechanism often fails to accomplish.

Public investment in vital infrastructure to ensure transport, water and electricity supply or services to specific industrial clusters is often a prerequisite for private investment to become viable. Similarly, public expenditure on education and training can influence the quality and skills structure of the labour force and the potential of labour to contribute to productivity growth. This in turn leads to higher

wages and a strengthening of domestic demand. In most developing countries there is also a pressing need to increase public sector provision of essential social services, especially those concerned with nutrition, sanitation, health and education.

Moreover, governments can provide fiscal incentives in the form of targeted tax rebates and temporary subsidies, as well as improved public services to existing firms and potential entrepreneurs. Successful development experiences have shown that if such measures are conceived as elements of a comprehensive industrial policy, they can accelerate the diversification of economic activities and the development of strategic sectors in the economy. At the same time, they can contribute to employment creation, and hence to an expansion of domestic demand.

By influencing income distribution, the structure of taxation has indirect effects on demand, since it has an impact on the pattern of net disposable incomes across different social groups. Aggregate consumption and the incentive for private firms to undertake fixed investments is greater when a given national income is distributed more equally, because lower income groups spend a larger share of their income on consumption, in general, and on domestically produced goods and services, in particular, than higher income groups. Tax-financed social transfers can have similar effects on domestic demand.

Moreover, countercyclical fiscal policy can stabilize domestic demand during periods of slow growth or recession, and thus the demand expectations of domestic investors. The larger the share of the public sector in GDP, the greater will be the potential for stabilization.

(b) Raising public revenues

Higher public spending for purposes of strengthening domestic demand requires an increase in public revenues from taxes or other sources. Alternatively, it may be rational to finance certain types of public expenditure by borrowing. Yet it is often argued that the fiscal space available to governments in developing countries is too limited to extend public sector spending.

Clearly, fiscal space in developing countries, especially in low-income and least developed countries

(LDCs) is smaller than in developed and emerging economies owing to their low level of national income. Moreover, in developing countries, fiscal space is often strongly influenced by international factors that are beyond the control of these countries' governments, such as fluctuations of commodity prices, of interest rates on the public external debt, and of external financing in the form of either private capital inflows or ODA. However, within these constraints, fiscal space is largely determined endogenously; a proactive fiscal policy influences the macroeconomic situation and the overall tax base through its impact on private sector earnings.

Taxes place a burden on the disposable income of the individual taxpayer. Consequently, it is frequently assumed that taxes divert income and purchasing power away from the private sector. But this is a static view that neglects the fact that the perceived tax revenue will flow back to the private sector and increase aggregate income in the economy, thereby enlarging the tax base. It is often forgotten that the net demand effect of a parallel increase in the average tax rate and government expenditure is positive, since some of the additional tax payments are at the expense of the savings of taxpayers, while spending of the tax revenue will cause aggregate demand to rise by the full amount of the tax yield (Haavelmo, 1945). This net effect of additional tax-financed expenditure tends to be greater if more of the additional tax burden falls on the higher income groups (who, of course, will also see their incomes increase, as they participate in the overall income effect of the additional expenditure), and if the larger share of public expenditure is spent on domestically produced goods and services. The scope for using taxation and government spending for strengthening domestic drivers of growth may therefore be greater than is commonly assumed.

Of course, if tax rates are raised above a certain threshold, the behavioural response of those who have to bear the largest share of the tax burden may cause the tax base to shrink along with the economic activity that determines the tax base. However, it is difficult to determine an upper limit for the tax burden, which not only depends on the level of tax rates, but also on how the tax revenue is used. Regarding the income tax rate, it has been found that in developed countries, the top marginal rate at which the total tax yield will be maximized is close to 60 per cent (Piketty, Saez and Stantcheva, 2011),

and there is little reason to believe that it is much lower in developing countries, where incomes often grow faster than in developed countries. Taxing high incomes at higher rates by using progressive scales does not remove the absolute advantage of richer individuals, and neither does it take away the incentive for entrepreneurs to innovate and move up the income ladder. Regarding the corporate tax rate, it is certainly true that fiscal measures to foster private fixed investment are essential, but this does not mean that taxation of profits must be kept to a minimum; reductions of corporate income tax rates have rarely motivated additional investments in fixed capital (*TDR 2012*, chap. V; Devereux, Griffith and Klemm, 2002).

Given the low degree of progressivity in developing and transition economies' tax systems and the large differences between regions and countries in this regard, there may still be scope for more progressive taxation in many of these countries. Levying higher taxes on the modern sector and on highly profitable export activities enables governments to provide financial support for productivity growth and income generation in the traditional and informal sectors. Of course, this requires suitable administrative capacity. In this regard, the conditions in developing countries vary greatly, depending on their level of development, the size of their informal sector and the composition of their GDP. On the other hand, there are a number of other potential sources of revenue that are also available in low-income countries. Taxation of wealth and inheritance is one such source that could be tapped in many developing countries. It requires relatively little administrative capacity and is harder to circumvent than many other taxes. In many resource-rich countries there may be considerable scope for collecting a larger amount of royalties and taxes from companies active in the oil, gas and mining sectors. This is particularly important because the revenue potential from natural resources has grown significantly over the past decade, especially in Africa, and a disproportionally large share of the rents from the extractive industries are captured by transnational corporations (TNCs).

In the manufacturing sector as well, it may be possible to raise additional revenue through a more rational tax treatment of TNCs. Considerable foreign direct investment (FDI) is attracted to developing countries because it allows TNCs to combine the low-cost labour of the host country with more advanced technology and more capital-intensive production techniques than are locally available, resulting in unit profits that are many times higher than they could realize in their home country. Alternatively, TNCs can substantially reduce the sales price of their products and thereby gain market shares. Thus, the benefits of FDI in terms of productivity gains will be captured either by the foreign investor in the form of higher profits, or by foreign consumers in the form of lower purchasing prices. Meanwhile, very little of those, often enormous, productivity gains benefit the host economies.

In some countries that pursue a coherent industrial policy, the market mechanism may lead foreign companies to purchase intermediate inputs for their production from the local market. This should generate some demand and employment in the economy of the host country. However, in many instances, the market mechanism may not generate such linkages, in which case local content requirements in investment agreements might help, provided that the necessary local supply capacities exist. If this is not the case, or in addition to those requirements, adequate taxation of high profits resulting from the low labour costs – which attracted the TNCs in the first place – could be instrumental in ensuring that linkages are created with the rest of the economy. Those linkages could lead to the creation of domestic demand.

TNCs can also contribute to strengthening domestic demand in the host countries by offering wages to their local employees that are more in line with their productivity gains. Moreover, governments in these countries may be well advised to re-evaluate the benefits of foreign investment to domestic income growth: not only low wages, but also fiscal arrangements to attract FDI may be depriving the State of crucially needed public revenue to finance development projects that are a prerequisite for promoting a domestic manufacturing sector. Many countries compete with other countries in offering lower taxes to TNCs to attract their production facilities, similar to wage competition, often resulting in a race to the bottom. Such policies are at the expense of all the countries that enter into such tax and wage competition.

In order to stop a downward spiral of wages and taxation from this process, international arrangements may prove indispensable. These may include an international code of conduct for TNCs, governing the employment conditions they offer to workers in developing countries, and strengthened international cooperation in tax matters. Such cooperation should aim at reducing tax evasion, as with the United Nations Model Double Taxation Convention between Developed and Developing Countries. Equally important, there should be a better balance between ensuring that governments competing for production locations reap a fair share of fiscal benefits from TNCs' operations in their countries, while preserving the advantage that foreign investors can derive from FDI on the basis of labour cost differentials. Taking into account the large differences in unit labour costs between the home and host countries, this balance would likely allow a higher level of tax revenues for the host country, while the level of profits of the foreign investors from their production in the host country may be somewhat lower than before, although still several times higher than if it produced the same goods in its home country.

In several low-income and least developed countries it may still be difficult or impossible to promptly implement any of these measures to increase fiscal space because of their limited administrative and tax collecting capacities. In these cases, the multilateral financial institutions and bilateral donors could help by providing additional resources for social spending, as well as the appropriate technical and financial support for strengthening those capacities.

(c) Debt-financed public spending

Debt financing of public expenditure may be considered an appropriate measure for two strategic reasons. One is the countercyclical effect arising from an increase in public sector demand when private demand is insufficient to maintain economic activity at a level where the labour force and the existing capital stock are fully employed, particularly when this is accompanied by a reduction of net private borrowing, as in the current situation of balance-sheet recession experienced in a number of developed countries. The other is to accelerate domestic capital formation by credit-financed public investment in projects that have a long gestation period, such as infrastructure, which will be used for several years or even decades. These will benefit not only the current generation of taxpayers but also future generations, whose tax payments will then be used to service the debt.

There is a widespread view that, to the extent that public expenditure is financed by government borrowing, private agents will tend to reduce their demand for two reasons. First, increased borrowing by the public sector will push up interest rates, which will cut private investment, and second, consumer demand will fall and savings will rise, because consumers will expect to pay higher taxes some time in the future to enable the government to repay its debt (Barro, 1974). However, both these propositions are flawed. The first is based on the erroneous assumption that the public and private sectors compete for the use of a given pool of financial resources. According to this view, if the public sector absorbs fewer financial resources, more will be available for the private sector for productive use (IMF, 2003: 6 and 110–111). However, there is little, if any, empirical evidence of a crowding out of private investment by public borrowing (*TDR 2010*, box 3.1; Aschauer, 1989). On the contrary, public investment has been found to have an overall crowding-in effect on private investment.

Even a relatively large increase in government borrowing is unlikely to push up interest rates, because this increase would still be marginal compared with the total amount of assets in the capital market. More importantly, the interest rate is itself a policy variable determined by the central bank, which can neutralize any effect that higher government borrowing may have on interest rate levels. But even if there were to be a rise in the domestic interest rate, because monetary policy does not support the increase in the public debt, debt-financed government spending would cause aggregate demand to grow, and this would encourage the private sector to invest in additional productive capacity.

The idea that an increase in the fiscal deficit will restrain current private spending, because it creates an expectation of an increase in the tax rate to enable the State to make net debt repayments in the future, ignores the dynamics of public debt in a growing economy. First, public debt that reaches maturity is usually replaced by new debt for the financing of new expenditure, and the need for a net debt repayment only occurs in exceptional cases. In this respect, sovereign debt differs from that of private agents, since States are supposed to last forever. More importantly, a credit-financed increase in public expenditure will generate new demand and greater output, which in turn will boost both private income and fiscal revenues at a constant average tax rate. In such a situation, it is more likely that higher public expenditure will raise private demand rather than lower it.

These considerations do not imply, of course, that debt financing of public expenditure has no limits. Indeed, an important issue in public sector financing in developing countries and in the assessment of fiscal space relates to the risks involved in the accumulation of public debt. These risks are related to fluctuations in economic growth and to movements in the interest rate on the public debt that are beyond the control of the debtor government, especially when the debt is denominated in foreign currency (see also chapter III of this *Report*). This is one of the reasons why a limit for public indebtedness is difficult to determine. Another reason is that economic growth and the primary budget balance are both partly endogenous variables (i.e. GDP growth and tax revenues are themselves influenced by the size of debt-financed public spending).

Still, unsustainable fiscal policies can lead to sovereign debt crises. It may be preferable for governments to pay all their current and capital expenditure out of current revenues. Balanced budget rules or public deficit ceilings have their merits, but they can also unnecessarily constrain the potential for countercyclical fiscal action when current fiscal revenues fall and reduce the ability of governments to finance public fixed capital formation. The latter is of particular importance for developing and transition economies that have considerable need for substantial investments in infrastructure. Therefore, rules concerning the public sector deficit should not be applied strictly to every single budgeting period; rather, they should adopt a longer term perspective. Also, they should take into account the purposes of public credit financing.

Regarding the first aspect, a rule according to which the public sector deficit should not exceed the long-term trend growth rate of the economy would allow short-term cyclical variations of the deficit. Since the trend growth rate tends to be significantly higher in developing and transition economies than in the developed countries, the former countries may, in principle, have greater scope for deficit financing than the latter. Regarding the second aspect, it is important to bear in mind that some types of spending are bound to have larger multiplier effects on overall income growth than others. In addition, they may have a stronger stimulating effect on private investment. These types of public spending are more suitable for credit financing than others and also are well suited to a strategy of domestic-demand-led growth because they contribute to maintaining, or even enlarging, a country's fiscal space.

A rational approach is certainly to finance current expenditure such as the payment of civil servants' salaries, the consumption spending of public entities, and social expenditure from taxation and other current revenues, except in cases where credit-financing of such expenditure is warranted in the context of countercyclical action. In these situations, the multiplier effects tend to be higher, so that the deficit will generally correct itself as a result of higher tax revenue from the additional income created by the initial deficit spending.

Public expenditure for fixed capital formation is quite different from that of current expenditure, because, owing to the complementarities between private and public investment, it has a strong potential to increase private investment outlays in addition to its immediate demand effect. In a way, the viability of public debt incurred for the financing of public investment can be viewed in a similar way as private debt incurred for the financing of private investment. First, the creation of debt is associated with the creation of new productive assets, and second, similar to the pay-off of private investment through the revenues generated by the use of private productive capacity, public investment can also be viewed as having a pay-off in the form of additional tax receipts due to an enlarged tax base resulting from the overall productivity increases generated by public investment.

This suggests that a rational approach would be to limit debt financing in the medium term to the level of expenditure for public investment. With regard to borrowing in foreign currency, this should be limited to meeting a country's actual foreign exchange needs (i.e. borrowing in foreign currency only to the extent that public investments require the import of capital goods, material and know-how), or if there is a perceived need to accumulate foreign exchange reserves over and above that accruing from current account balances and autonomous capital inflows that are not used by the private sector for the financing of imports.

If the space for public sector borrowing, as determined by these considerations, is not fully used,

an increase in credit-financed public expenditure may be considered as a possible means to raise not only domestic demand but also domestic supply capacities.

3. Policies for fostering domestic productivity growth and structural change

(a) Industrial policies

Within a strategy aimed at giving greater emphasis to domestic demand to drive growth and development, particular attention should be given to strengthening domestic supply capacities. This is necessary in order to avoid a deterioration in the balance of payments and a trade deficit resulting from faster growth of domestic demand coupled with slower growth of external demand, which would increase the dependence on foreign capital inflows to finance such deficits. This is of particular importance for countries that have a large natural resource base but a relatively small manufacturing capacity, because governments of these countries may be tempted to seek short-term welfare gains for their economy by using higher commodity export earnings to pay for imports of consumer goods, with no, or even adverse, effects on development.

Policies promoting structural transformation and technological dynamism[31] will be necessary to overcome the supply and demand challenges arising from what is likely to remain a difficult external environment characterized by a slow recovery and a weak growth path of developed economies.

Developing-country firms are often considered technological laggards that have difficulty supplying products with the characteristics demanded by consumers. This is clearly true for up-market goods produced for export to developed countries. An accelerated and broader transfer of technology from developed to developing countries remains critically important for narrowing this gap. Technology transfer relating to capital goods and equipment also remains crucially important.

However, technological lags play a considerably less important role – or none at all – in meeting the demands of emerging middle-class consumers. Developing-country firms may be well placed to satisfy the demands of these new consumers, not only by adapting existing goods and services to these consumers' specific needs, but also – and perhaps more importantly – by developing new goods and services tailored to their needs or preferences.[32] In addition to technological innovation, the development of new marketing and distribution networks can be crucial for ensuring that new products reach the new consumers in domestic markets. Developing-country firms may have an advantage over developed-country firms in this respect, as they are likely to possess valuable local knowledge for the development of appropriate new distribution networks and marketing strategies for conquering new domestic markets. Less affluent consumers often live outside the largest cities in places where reliable, high-quality and network-driven infrastructure may be scarce, and where distribution systems may differ from those targeting better-off urban consumers. Developed-country firms, on the other hand tend to use "their *existing high-end* products and services through *standard* distribution channels to target the *most affluent* tier of customers in the *largest* cities" (Boston Consulting Group, 2012: 3; emphasis added).[33]

Another issue concerns the increasingly intense competition among firms to gain access to the emerging consumer markets in developing countries, and this is likely to increase even further. Established developed-country firms, especially multinationals, are targeting these new middle classes as potential consumers, especially as sluggish demand growth in their home markets is slowing down their business activities. In addition to building marketing and distribution networks, developing-country firms will need to improve their innovation capabilities and develop appropriate technologies rapidly to successfully compete and capture this new demand in their domestic markets.

The kinds of technologies needed to satisfy the changing demand structures, and the mechanisms required to develop them, are likely to differ from those associated with large technological spurts. The latter are based on advances in scientific understanding which is translated by applied research into the development of commercial products. By contrast, the changes in market conditions, characterized by potentially large new markets in developing countries, requires the identification of "latent demand"

(Schmookler, 1962) and the "steering" of firms to work on problems or requirements specific to those new markets (Rosenberg, 1969).[34] This means that demand may drive both the rate and direction of innovation, so that producers' proximity to markets becomes a valuable asset.

Changes in the production structure of a country required to meet newly rising demand are unlikely to involve a smooth process. The reason is that such structural changes to prevailing specialization patterns require a different distribution of resources across industries. Governments can use industrial policy to encourage this process. Indeed, recent years have seen a revival of the debate on the role of industrial policy in development, prompted by the realization over the past decade that the Washington Consensus, which excluded any role for industrial policy, had not fulfilled its promises. As a result, developing countries, as well as some developed countries, started to look for alternative development strategies. This search for alternatives was accompanied by a revival of interest in classical ideas of economic development, including recognition of the importance of both domestic demand and an economy's sectoral structure for the generation of linkages and productivity growth.[35] These tendencies have been spurred by the economic and financial crisis that has accentuated the debate about market failures and the need for institutions and rules to govern markets. Moreover, accumulated evidence on the contributions of institutions and policies to some of the successes in development (e.g. Fosu, 2013) has become increasingly difficult to ignore and dismiss. As a result, policymakers have been more willing to engage in experimentation and development of home-grown solutions. Many of these experiments include a good dose of industrial policy, such as in Brazil, China and South Africa.[36]

The reorientation required to address post-crisis economic challenges may also be used in industrial policy to boost developing countries' engagement in environmentally sustainable growth strategies.[37] However, it is clear that not all developing countries can develop and use large-scale green production and technologies for their industrial development. Nevertheless, some opportunities exist for early movers that should not be disregarded. A sizeable share of the fiscal stimulus packages adopted in 2008–2009 by a number of countries, especially China and the Republic of Korea, to address the global economic downturn was directed to green measures and investments. These green stimulus packages corresponded to 5 per cent of GDP in the Republic of Korea and to 3 per cent of GDP in China. Measured in absolute dollar terms, the United States spent about twice as much as the Republic of Korea. Yet this amount corresponds to only about half of China's expenditure, and it corresponds to less than 1 per cent of GDP in the United States (Barbier, 2011). The Republic of Korea and China appear to have recognized more generally that investments in clean energy technologies can have a major impact on growth and employment creation. For example, in 2009 the Republic of Korea launched a five-year Green Growth Investment Plan, spending an additional $60 billion on reducing carbon dependence and on environmental improvements, with the aim of creating 1.5–1.8 million jobs and boosting economic growth through 2020 (Zelenovskaya, 2012).

Section B of this chapter has discussed, in addition to the repercussions of shifts in global demand as a result of slower growth in the developed countries, the effects of continuing fast population growth on the demand for food and new climate-change-related challenges to agricultural production. In the light of these effects, there is an urgent need in many developing countries to improve productivity, and thus investment, in the agricultural sector, which has generally been neglected over decades. Increasing agricultural productivity does not necessarily require huge investments in advanced technologies, but primarily catching up with the application of existing technologies. A considerable portion of such investment needs to target basic infrastructure, which can be improved with the help of public works programmes. These would also create additional income and employment in rural areas.

(b)   Issues concerning natural-resource-rich economies

The strong impact of the global financial and economic crisis on natural-resource-dependent countries has again demonstrated the need for these countries to reduce their dependence on the revenues obtained from only a small basket of commodities by diversifying their production and export structures. In this context, the transformation of their natural resource base into physical capital should become a key objective of their development strategies. It will not only generate new employment opportunities and

increase the purchasing power of all the segments of their societies, but also enlarge their fiscal space in the medium to long term.

To the extent that overall demand for primary commodities remains robust and that commodity prices, broadly speaking, plateau at a level that exceeds that in the 1980s and 1990s, natural-resource-rich economies will continue to benefit from improving terms of trade. Nevertheless, they should remain alert to the cyclicality of prices. Moreover, a situation of relatively high commodity prices also implies that these countries should not allow the exploitation of their natural-resource wealth to jeopardize their growth in the long term. They can prevent this by ensuring that the revenues accruing from resource exploitation are used for investing in new activities that spur production and export diversification.

This challenge relates to how to deal with two potentially offsetting forces: "Over the short run, positive terms-of-trade shocks will always (*ceteris paribus*) raise GDP, and the empirical issue is … [by] how much. Over the long run, however, a positive terms-of-trade shock in primary product-producing countries will reinforce comparative advantage, suck resources into the export sector from other activities, and cause deindustrialization" (Hadass and Williamson, 2003: 640–641). Improvements in the terms of trade and the resulting increase in government revenues should be used to reduce income inequality and avoid deindustrialization through public investment and the provision of social services which target those segments of the population that do not directly benefit from resource revenues. Also needed are policies that spur industrial production, such as maintaining a competitive exchange rate and pursuing a monetary policy that stimulates private investment. These issues have been discussed in some detail by UNCTAD (2012).

(c)   Implications for development partnerships

Since the launch of the Millennium Development Goals (MDGs) in 2000 and the adoption of the Monterrey Consensus in 2002, the global partnership for development has concentrated largely on the provision of concessional development assistance with a view to alleviating poverty in developing countries. It has also focused on increased access for developing countries to developed-country markets with a view to spurring economic development in developing countries through export-oriented growth strategies.

The increased provision of both aid and market access was closely related to the greater integration of developing countries, especially China, into global markets. The focus of the global partnership for development on aid and market access has often been criticized for its neglect of the crucial importance of investment and the creation and expansion of productive supply capacities (see, for example, *TDR 2006*). Moreover, the onset of the Great Recession casts serious doubts on the pertinence of this focus on aid and market access. It is highly unlikely that donor countries will meet the targets for development assistance set at various international summits any time soon in view of their fiscal problems associated with the effects of the Great Recession. It is also clear that the rules and regulations of trade and investment agreements, as well as the conditionalities attached to loan agreements with the International Monetary Fund (IMF) and the World Bank, have reduced the policy space of developing countries. Yet, such policy space is needed to develop the domestic productive capacities required to benefit from improved market access conditions and enhance development.

This shortcoming needs to be redressed by ensuring that the global partnership for development takes into account the structural shifts that have been taking place in the world economy since the early 2000s. One of these shifts, on which this chapter has focused, concerns the likely emergence of about 2 billion additional middle-class consumers over the next decade. This shift could be accelerated by the implementation of a development strategy that gives greater importance than in the past to the expansion of domestic demand. Such a strategy, if successful, may also lead to increased purchasing power among the lower income groups in developing countries. This will open up new opportunities for the enhancement of productive capacity and economic growth. The quest for market shares in the large, but only slowly growing markets of developed countries, as well as in the yet small, but rapidly growing markets in developing countries, will be associated with greater international competition. In order to manage such increased competition, developing countries may need to make full use of whatever policy space they still have at their disposal after the conclusion of various regional and bilateral trade and investment agreements and the Uruguay Round trade agreements.

However, these shifts also have much broader implications. Even though the vastly increased importance of developing countries in global economic growth, trade, FDI and capital flows remains concentrated in only about a dozen of them, this systemic change opens up new possibilities. For one, it gives greater weight to their voice and increases their bargaining power as a group for reshaping the rules and institutions that constrain the policy space available to countries that are latecomers to development. There is also greater scope for regional and South-South cooperation in many spheres and through different forms of institutional arrangements that pool markets and resources for development. But perhaps most importantly, the international community should now realize that, with the structural shifts in the world economy, "it is time to move away from unidirectional or asymmetrical relationships" so that development partnerships between developed and developing countries, as well as among developing countries, move towards a greater consideration of "the logic and the spirit of international collective action" (Nayyar, 2012: 23).

4. Conclusions

Developing and transition economies are likely to face sluggish import demand for their goods as a result of a protracted period of slow growth in developed countries. Thus, for policymakers in the former set of countries, reverting to the pre-crisis policy stance with its emphasis on export-oriented growth is not an option. The external economic environment that benefited such a growth strategy, especially during the five years prior to the Great Recession, was built on unsustainable global demand and financing patterns. Countercyclical macroeconomic policies can boost growth for some time, but will eventually result in fiscal or balance-of-payments constraints unless they are followed by policies that adopt a more comprehensive and longer term perspective.

A longer term policy to support rapid and sustained economic growth in developing and transition economies in the vastly changing global environment will need to consider adopting a more balanced growth strategy that gives a greater role to domestic demand to complement external demand. The possibility of rapidly undertaking such a shift in strategy and the policy mix needed to support this shift will largely depend on the extent to which the sectoral structure of domestic production is delinked from that of domestic demand. This, in turn, will be influenced by the size of the domestic market. While natural-resource-rich countries may be able to continue to benefit from historically high commodity prices, they should ensure that the resulting revenues are used for investing in new activities that spur production and export diversification.

Particularly in countries where manufactures already account for a sizeable share of production, a shift in growth strategy should seek to achieve an appropriate balance between increases in household consumption, private investment and public sector expenditure. The specifics of this balance will largely depend on the circumstances of individual countries, but in general it will require a new perspective on the role of wages and the public sector in the development process. Export-oriented growth strategies emphasize the cost aspect of wages; by contrast, a more domestic-demand-oriented strategy would emphasize the income aspects of wages, as it would be based on household spending as the largest component of domestic demand. Employment creation combined with wage growth that is in line with productivity growth should create sufficient domestic demand to fully utilize growing productive capacities without having to rely on continued export growth. Household spending could also be encouraged by facilitating access to consumer credit. However, such an approach is risky, as amply demonstrated by recent experiences in a number of developed countries. The public sector can further boost domestic demand by increasing public employment or undertaking investment, which is often a precondition for private investment. In addition, changes in the tax structure and the composition of public expenditure and transfers could shape the distribution of purchasing power in the economy towards those income groups that spend a larger share of their income on consumption.

Increased aggregate demand from household consumption and the public sector would provide an incentive to entrepreneurs to invest in increasing real productive capacity. Industrial policy could support the associated investment decisions so that the sectoral allocation of investment better corresponds to the newly emerging patterns of domestic demand. Given their better knowledge of local markets and local preferences, developing-country enterprises may well have an advantage over foreign ones in catering to these new demand patterns. They could thus prevent the rise in domestic demand from causing a surge in imports from developed countries.

Perhaps most importantly, distinct from export-led growth, a growth strategy with a greater role for domestic demand can be pursued by many countries simultaneously, including even the largest, without causing adverse spillover effects on other countries and without inducing wage and tax competition. Indeed, if many developing and transition economies were to move towards a more balanced growth strategy simultaneously, their economies could become markets for each other, spurring regional and South-South trade, and thus further growth in all of them.

Notes

1 Evidence in chart 2.1 suggests that China suffered only mildly from the trade collapse in 2008–2009. However, the data for China probably underreport the actual effects by a sizeable margin. It is well known that much of China's exports are recorded as transshipments and re-exports from Hong Kong, Special Administrative Region of China (Hong Kong, SAR) (e.g. Ferrantino and Wang, 2008), for which the adverse effect shown in chart 2.1 is very strong.

2 For a more detailed account of the contribution of different product categories to changes in the terms of trade in selected developing countries, see UNCTAD, 2012: 17–19.

3 Standard Chartered (2010:1) defines a supercycle in general as a "period of historically high global growth, lasting a generation or more, driven by increasing trade, high rates of investment, urbanization and technological innovation characterized by the emergence of large, new economies, first seen in high catch-up growth rates across the emerging world".

4 Based on the United Nations Population Division's medium-variant estimates (see *World Population Prospects*, available at: http://esa.un.org/wpp/).

5 More recently, China has even surprised the markets by importing rice (*Wall Street Journal*, China rice imports unsettle market, 7 January 2013). OECD-FAO (2013) also reports considerable growth in China's imports of some other commodities in recent years, including pig meat, dairy products, maize and sugar.

6 See, for instance, *Wall Street Journal*, "China to speed up reform of hukou system", 18 December 2012.

7 UNCTAD secretariat calculations, based on data from USDA, Background profile on corn, at: http://www.ers.usda.gov/topics/crops/corn/background.aspx (accessed June 2013).

8 See, for instance, *Wall Street Journal*, "African oil exports plunge amid swelling U.S. output", 28 February 2013.

9 For a more detailed analysis of the potential implications of shale oil, see Helbling, 2013; Maugeri, 2012; Morse et al., 2012; and PWC, 2013.

10 See Farooki and Kaplinsky (2012) for a more detailed discussion on commodity supply response and production constraints.

11 As discussed in more detail later in this *Report*, this could also exert downward pressure on the prices of certain internationally traded manufactures, possibly causing producers of such goods to use any productivity increase to reduce unit labour costs. This, in turn, would have a negative impact on the purchasing power of workers in these industries, and thus on domestic demand growth, especially in developing countries that continue to pursue a development strategy that relies on export-oriented growth of their manufacturing industries.

12 Durable consumer goods include commodities which have an expected life span of more than three years and are of relatively high value, such as refrigerators and washing machines, together with other commodities with a useful life of three years or more, such as audio-visual products. Semi-durable consumer goods include commodities which have an expected life span of more than one year but less than three years and are of relatively lower value, such as textiles, apparel, footwear and toys. Non-durable consumer goods include commodities with an expected life span of less than one year, such as parts of apparel and pharmaceuticals. These three categories combined accounted for 55 per cent of China's total exports to the United States in 2007.

13 United States imports of automobiles (chart 2.4) have also rebounded to their pre-crisis dynamism. However, developing countries account for only a small share of those imports.

14 This assumption relates to what economists refer to as "homothetic preferences".

15 The structure of this theoretical approach is similar to the theory of consumption proposed by Pasinetti (1981) in that it is based on a generalization of Engel's law (i.e. an income-driven non-proportional expansion of demand and learning processes by consumers which cause them to alter their preferences). However, rather than emphasizing demand, Pasinetti based these learning processes on the appearance of new products that result from technical progress on the supply side.

16 Indeed, Murphy, Shleifer and Vishny (1989: 538) view the middle class as a necessary "source of buying power for domestic manufacturers".

17 See the annex to this chapter for a more detailed discussion of these mechanisms.

18 For empirical evidence supporting these assumptions with regard to passenger cars, see Dargay, Gately and Sommer, 2007.

19 The international dollar is a hypothetical currency unit that is generally expressed in terms of constant prices in a certain base year and has the same purchasing power as the dollar in the United States in that year. For the various issues concerning the use of purchasing power parity and international average prices of commodities to calculate the unit, see United Nations, 1992.

20 "Italy's per capita income was used as the upper threshold because it was the country with the lowest income among the G7; Brazil's per capita income corresponded to the official poverty line used in rich countries like the US and Germany (about $ PPP 10 per capita per day)" (Bussolo et al., 2011: 14).

21 The estimates in Kharas (2010) are based on projections of GDP for the period 2008–2050, where GDP is a function of the accumulation of labour (based on prospects for the evolution of the working-age population provided by the United Nations) and capital (based on the average investment rate for the period 1995–2005), as well as total factor productivity growth (based on historic long-term technology growth and an assumed process of convergence with the United States). All these are combined with projections of long-term exchange-rate movements and purchasing-power conversion rates, as well as with data on income distribution and estimates of mean consumption per capita. The estimates in Bussolo et al. (2011) result from a broadly similar methodology, though this focuses on the impact of economic growth in China and India on global growth and distribution, and employs growth rates that are disaggregated by economic sector in order to better model the evolution of income distribution. While the methodological approaches used in these two studies may be subject to criticism, they are, nevertheless, useful for illustrating the key issue raised here, namely that the developing countries are progressively accounting for a larger share of global consumption.

22 The correlation between the growth of labour income and the growth of household consumption is significant at the 10-per cent level of confidence.

23 These findings are supported by a comprehensive study by Onaran and Galanis (2012) which shows that, taking the world economy as a whole, a simultaneous and continuing decline in the wage share leads to a slowdown of global growth. Furthermore, taking countries individually in a more detailed investigation of 16 members of the G20, the authors observe that 9 of them show a positive correlation between wage growth and GDP growth. Moreover, 4 of the remaining 7 economies which show negative correlations between wage growth and GDP growth when taken individually, effectively register lower growth when the wage shares of all the economies fall simultaneously.

24 The recent debate on higher aggregate demand that results from an increase in government spending (i.e. "the multiplier effect") indicates that this effect is generally higher – and exceeds unity – in recessions than in more normal times.

25 It should be noted that any scheme that attempts to increase the sales and use of private cars may conflict with urbanization strategies that give priority to expanding public transport systems.

26 JP Morgan, "Thailand: autos slowing but domestic demand not stalling", *Global Data Watch*, 22 March 2013.

27 Revenue from capital investments (e.g. dividends) may also boost disposable personal income. However, such sources are unlikely to be of much significance to most of the segments of the population that are targeted as agents of increased household consumption spending (i.e. lower and middle-income classes).

28 In some countries, such as Brazil, the rapid growth of household credit has also been affected by capital inflows (which have provided ample liquidity to banks) and by the development of domestic credit markets. Chapter III of this *Report* addresses these issues in detail.

29 R. Colitt, "Brazil consumer default rate drops to lowest level in 16 months", Bloomberg, 26 March 2013; available at: http://www.bloomberg.com/news/2013-04-26/brazil-consumer-default-rate-drops-to-lowest-level-in-16-months.html.

30 This trade-off is part of the debate (further discussed in chapter III) about whether central banks should be concerned exclusively with price stability (e.g. by pursuing inflation targeting), or whether they should also be responsible for maintaining financial sector stability, which may imply preventing the formation of asset price bubbles. A central bank that pursues inflation targeting would maintain low interest rates when the inflation rate is low. The low interest rates, in turn, would allow households to contain an increase in their debt burden, even if their outstanding debt increases. However, a sudden change in risk perception, caused, for example, by the bursting of an asset price bubble, will lead to a sudden and sizeable rise in the interest rate on outstanding debt, with ensuing adverse effects on spending.

31 It is clear that the need for technological dynamism does not concern only manufacturing, which is the focus of this section. However, the primary and services sectors often provide few or only poorly

paid jobs, and productivity growth in these sectors usually lags behind that in manufacturing.

32 A related issue concerns the impact of a shift of major segments of the end markets for manufactures from developed to developing countries on the functioning of global supply chains. Industrialization through participation and upgrading in global value chains has played a crucial role in many countries' export-oriented development strategies over the past two decades. However, empirical evidence suggests that supporting exporters' domestic embeddedness, rather than favouring participation in supply chains, is crucial for product upgrading and for achieving profitability and value added (see, for example, Jarreau and Poncet, 2012; and Manova and Yu, 2012). The existence of such backward linkages may become even more important for the resilience of developing countries, as some segments of the end markets for consumer goods shift to their domestic economies (i.e. closer to the production sites of such goods), thereby also increasing the forward linkages of such production sites. This may eventually provide an opportunity for developing-country firms to lead supply chains, rather than merely integrate into existing chains, and develop by trying to increase the value-added content of their activities.

33 It is interesting to note in this context that some market analysts have started to warn even Western producers of luxury goods that the time may soon be over when luxury goods embodying familiar French and Italian cultural values sell well, and that they will increasingly need to offer less standardized items, which take account of values embedded in the cultures of their destination markets (V. Accary, "Le marché du luxe dans les pays émergents est en train de changer, il faut s'y adapter!", *Le Monde Economie*, 25 March 2013; available at:. http://www.lemonde.fr/economie/article/2013/03/25/le-marche-du-luxe-dans-les-pays-emergents-est-en-train-de-changer-il-faut-s-y-adapter_1853658_3234.html).

34 Miles (2010: 3) provides a detailed review of the "schism between Schumpeter's emphasis on technology breakthroughs and Schmookler's stress on innovation responding to the pull of market demand."

35 Both these issues were discussed in detail in *TDRs 2003* and *2006*.

36 These experiments are not only related to the development of domestic supply capabilities required for satisfying growing domestic consumer demand, which is the focus here; they also concern issues related to global supply chains, where industrial policy involves regulating links to the global economy, such as through trade, FDI and exchange rates (see, for example, Milberg, Jiang and Gereffi, 2013).

37 Industrial policy can also be a vehicle for greater regional integration, especially for small countries (for Uruguay, see Torres, 2013).

References

Aglietta M (2012). Chine: Horizon 2030, in *L'économie mondiale 2013*. Paris, Centre d'Etudes Prospectives et d'Informations Internationales (CEPII).

Akyüz Y (2011). Export dependence and sustainability of growth in China. *China & World Economy*, 19(1): 1–23.

Aschauer D (1989). Is public expenditure productive? *Journal of Monetary Economics*, 23(2):177–200.

Bajraj R (1977). La inflación argentina en los años setenta. *El Trimestre Económico*, 44 (176), October-December: 947–996.

Barbier E (2011). A global green recovery and the lessons of history. *The European Financial Review*, 17 February; available at: http://www.europeanfinancialreview.com/?p=2497.

Barro R (1974). Are government bonds net wealth? *Journal of Political Economy*, 82 (6): 1095–1117.

Berkelmans L and Wang H (2012). Chinese urban residential construction. *Reserve Bank of Australia Bulletin*, September.

Bems R, Johnson RC and Yi KM (2010). Demand spillovers and the collapse of trade in the global recession. *IMF Economic Review*, 58(2): 295–326.

Bems R, Johnson RC and Yi KM (2013). The great trade collapse. *Annual Review of Economics*, forthcoming.

Bloxham P, Keen A and Hartigan L (2012). Commodities and the global economy — Are current high prices the new normal? Multi Asset, August, HSBC Global Research.

Boston Consulting Group (2012). Unlocking growth in the middle: How business model innovation can capture the critical middle class in emerging markets. *bcg. Perspectives*; available at: bcgperspectives. com/content/articles/growth_globalization_unlocking_growth_in_the_middle/.

BP (2011). *BP Energy Outlook 2030*. British Petroleum.

BP (2013). *Statistical Review of World Energy*. British Petroleum.

Brown L (2012). Full planet, empty plates: The new geopolitics of food scarcity. Earth Policy Institute.

Bussière M, Callegari G, Ghironi F, Sestieri G, Yamano N (2011). Estimating trade elasticities: Demand composition and the trade collapse of 2008–09. Working Paper 17712, National Bureau of Economic Research, Cambridge, MA.

Bussolo M, de Hoyos RE, Medvedev D and van der Mensbrugghe D (2011). Global growth and distribution: China, India, and the emergence of a global middle class. *Journal of Globalization and Development*, 2(2), Article 3.

Calcagno AF (2008). Reformas estructurales y modalidades de desarrollo en América Latina. In: Déniz J, de León O and Palazuelos A, eds. *Realidades y desafíos del desarrollo económico de América Latina*. Madrid, Los Libros de la Catarata.

CBA (2012). The resource boom — entering a new phase. CBA Research, Commonwealth Bank.

Chai A and Moneta A (2012). Back to Engel? Some evidence for the hierarchy of needs. *Journal of Evolutionary Economics*, 22(4): 649–676.

Chenery H, Robinson S and Syrquin M (eds) (1986). *Industrialization and Growth: A Comparative Study*. Oxford University Press, Oxford and New York.

Citi (2013). From Commodities Supercycle to Unicycles – 2Q 2013. *Commodities Market Update*. Citi Research.

Coates B and Luu N (2012). China's emergence in global commodity markets. *Economic Roundup Issue* 1. Australian Government, The Treasury.

Credit Suisse (2013). *2013 Global Outlook*.

Dargay J, Gately D and Sommer M (2007). Vehicle ownership and income growth, worldwide: 1960–2030. *The Energy Journal*, 28(4): 143–170.

Dell'Ariccia G, Igan D, Laeven L and Tong H (2012). Policies for Macrofinancial Stability: How to Deal with Credit Booms. Staff Discussion Note SDN/12/06, International Monetary Fund, Washington DC, 7 June.

Desdoigts A and Jaramillo F (2009). Trade, demand spillovers, and industrialization: The emerging global middle class in perspective. *Journal of International Economics*, 79(2): 248–258.

Devereux MP, Griffith R and Klemm A (2002). Corporate income tax reforms and international tax competition. *Economic Policy*, 17(35): 451–495.

ECLAC (1978). *Series históricas de crecimiento*. Cuadernos de la CEPAL No. 3, Santiago, Economic Commission for Latin America and the Caribbean.

ECLAC (1979). *América Latina en el umbral de los años 80*. Santiago, Economic Commission for Latin America and the Caribbean.

ECLAC (2012). *Latin America and the Caribbean in the World Economy: Continuing Crisis in the Centre and New Opportunities for Developing Economies*. Santiago, Economic Commission for Latin America and the Caribbean.

Erten B and Ocampo JA (2012). Super-cycles of commodity prices since the mid-nineteenth century. Working Paper No. 110, United Nations Department of Economic and Social Affairs (UN-DESA), New York, February.

FAO (2011). *The State of the World's Land and Water Resources for Food and Agriculture: Managing Systems at Risk*. Rome.

FAO (2012a). *The State of Food Insecurity in the World*. Rome.

FAO (2012b). *The State of Food and Agriculture: Investing in Agriculture for a Better Future*. Rome.

Farooki M and Kaplinsky R (2012). *The Impact of China on Global Commodity Prices: The Global Reshaping of the Resource Sector*. London and New York, Routledge.

Ferrantino MJ and Wang Z (2008). Accounting for discrepancies in bilateral trade: The case of China, Hong Kong, and the United States. *China Economic Review*, 19(3): 502–520.

Foellmi and Zweimüller (2006). Income distribution and demand-induced innovations. *Review of Economic Studies*, 73(4): 941–960.

Foellmi and Zweimüller (2008). Structural change, Engel's consumption cycles and Kaldor's facts of economic growth. *Journal of Monetary Economics*, 55(7): 1317–1328.

Fosu A (ed.) (2013). *Achieving Development Success: Strategies and Lessons from the Developing World*. Oxford, Oxford University Press.

Furtado C (1976). *La economía latinoamericana, formación histórica y problemas contemporáneos*, editorial Siglo XXI (eighth edition in Spanish, reprinted in 1998), Mexico, DF.

G20 (2012). Boosting jobs and living standards in G20 countries. A joint report by the ILO, OECD, IMF and World Bank. June. Available at: http://www.ilo. org/wcmsp5/groups/public/---dgreports/---dcomm/ documents/publication/wcms_183705.pdf.

Goldman Sachs (2012). *The Old Economy Renaissance: 2013-2014 Issues and Outlook*. Goldman Sachs Commodities Research, December.

Gopinath G, Itskhoki O and Neiman B (2012). Trade prices and the global trade collapse of 2008–09. *IMF Economic Review*, 60(3): 303–328.

Haavelmo T (1945). Multiplier effects of a balanced budget. *Econometrica*, 13: 311–318.

Hadass YS and Williamson JG (2003). Terms-of-trade shocks and economic performance, 1870–1940:

Prebisch and Singer revisited. *Economic Development and Cultural Change*, 51(3): 629–656.

Haraguchi N and Rezonja G (2010). In search of general patterns of manufacturing development. Working Paper 02/2010, United Nations Industrial Development Organization, Vienna.

Harrod R (1933). *International Economics*. Cambridge, Cambridge University Press.

Heap A (2005). China – The engine of a commodities super cycle. Citigroup Smith Barney.

Helbling T (2013). On the rise. *Finance & Development*, March issue. Washington, DC, International Monetary Fund.

Houthakker HS (1957). An international comparison of household expenditure patterns, commemorating the century of Engel's law. *Econometrica*, 25(4): 532–551.

IEA (2012a). *World Energy Outlook*. Paris, International Energy Agency.

IEA (2012b). *Medium Term Oil Market Report*. Paris, International Energy Agency.

ILO (2013). *Global Employment Trends 2013 – Recovering from a Second Jobs Dip*. Geneva, International Labour Office.

IMF (2003). Evaluation report: Fiscal adjustment in IMF-supported programmes. Washington, DC, Independent Evaluation Office.

Jarreau J and Poncet S (2012). Export sophistication and economic growth: Evidence from China. *Journal of Development Economics*, 97(2): 281–292.

Kharas H (2010). The emerging middle class in developing countries. Working Paper No. 285, OECD Development Centre, Paris. January.

Lawson S and Dragusanu R (2008). Building the world: Mapping infrastructure demand. Goldman Sachs Global Economics Paper, 166.

Levchenko AA, Lewis LT and Tesar LL (2010). The collapse of international trade during the 2008–09 crisis: In search of the smoking gun. *IMF Economic Review*, 58(2): 214–253.

Lluch C, Powell AA and Williams RA (1977). *Patterns in Household Demand and Saving*. New York and Oxford, Oxford University Press.

Manova K and Yu Z (2012). Firms and credit constraints along the value-added chain: Processing trade in China. Working Paper 18561, National Bureau of Economic Research, Cambridge, MA.

Maslow AP (1954). *Motivation and Personality*. New York, Harper and Row.

Matsuyama K (2002). The rise of mass consumption societies. *Journal of Political Economy*, 110(5): 1035–1070.

Maugeri L (2012). Oil: The next revolution. Cambridge, MA, Harvard Kennedy School, Belfer Center for Science and International Affairs.

Mayer J (2013). Towards a greater role of domestic demand in developing countries' growth strategies.

UNCTAD Discussion Paper (forthcoming). Geneva, UNCTAD.

McKinley T (ed.) (2009). *Economic Alternatives for Growth, Employment and Poverty Reduction*. London and Basingstoke, Palgrave Macmillan.

McKinsey Global Institute (2013). Beyond Korean style: Shaping a new growth formula.

MEG (2013). *Worldwide Exploration Trends 2013*. Metals Economics Group.

Milanovic B (2012). Global income inequality data, 1988–2005; available at: http://econ.worldbank.org/WBSITE/EXTERNAL/EXTDEC/EXTRESEARCH/0,,contentMDK:22261771~pagePK:64214825~piPK:64214943~theSitePK:469382,00.html.

Milberg W, Jiang X and Gereffi G (2013). Industrial policy in the era of vertically specialized industrialization. In: Kozul-Wright R and Salazar-Xirinachs JM, eds., *Growth, Productive Transformation and Employment: New Perspectives on the Industrial Policy Debate* (forthcoming).

Miles PI (2010). Demand-led innovation. *Global Review of Innovation Intelligence and Policy Studies*. Manchester, University of Manchester; available at: http://grips-public.mediactive.fr/ministudies/view/11/demand-led-innovation/.

Morse E, Lee EG, Ahn DP, Doshi A, Kleinman S and Yuen A (2012). Energy 2020: North America, the new Middle East? *Global Perspectives and Solutions (Citi GPS),* March.

Murphy KM, Shleifer A, Vishny R (1989). Income distribution, market size, and industrialization. *Quarterly Journal of Economics*, 104(3): 537–564.

Nayyar D (2012). The MDGs after 2015: Some reflections on the possibilities. Paper prepared for the UN System Task Team on the Post-2015 UN Development Agenda; available at: http://www.un.org/en/development/desa/policy/untaskteam_undf/d_nayyar.pdf.

Nomura Equity Research (2012). How much metal can China use? Nomura China Non-Ferrous Metals Special Report.

Noyola JF (1957). Inflación y desarrollo económico en Chile y México. *Panorama económico*, 11(170). Santiago, Chile, Editorial Universitaria, July.

Ocampo JA and Parra MA (2010). The terms of trade for commodities since the mid-19th century. *Journal of Iberian and Latin American Economic History*, 28(1): 11–43.

OECD-FAO (2013). *Agricultural Outlook 2013–2022*. Paris and Rome.

Onaran O and Galanis G (2012). Is aggregate demand wage-led or profit-led? National and global effects. *Conditions of Work and Employment Series* No. 40. Geneva, International Labour Office.

Oxfam (2012). Extreme weather, extreme prices.

Pasinetti LL (1981). *Structural Change and Economic Growth: A Theoretical Essay on the Dynamics of the Wealth of Nations*. Cambridge, Cambridge University Press.

Piketty T, Saez E and Stantcheva S (2011). Optimal taxation of top labor incomes: A tale of three elasticities. NBER Working Paper 17616, National Bureau of Economic Research, Cambridge, MA.

Prebisch R (1950). The economic development of Latin America and its principal problems. Reprinted in *Economic Bulletin for Latin America* (1962), 7(1): 1–22.

PWC (2013). Shale oil: The next energy revolution.

Rosenberg N (1969). Direction of technological change – inducement mechanisms and focusing devices. *Economic Development and Cultural Change*, 18(1): 1–24.

Rosenstein-Rodan PN (1943). Problems of industrialisation of Eastern and South-Eastern Europe. *Economic Journal*, 53(210/211): 202–211.

Sainz P and Faletto E (1985). *Transformación y crisis: América Latina y el Caribe 1950-1984*. ECLAC, Santiago, Chile.

Schmookler J (1962). Economic sources of inventive activity. *Journal of Economic History*, 22(1): 1–20.

Smale D (2013). Review and outlook for copper, nickel, lead and zinc. Presentation to the UNCTAD Multi-year Expert Meeting on Commodities and Development. International Lead and Zinc Study Group, International Copper Study Group, International Nickel Study Group, Geneva, 20–21 March.

Standard Chartered (2010). *The Super-Cycle Report*.

Thorp R (1997). Las economías latinoamericanas 1939-c.1950. In: Bethell L, ed., *Historia económica de América Latina*, Vol. 11. Barcelona, Editorial Crítica.

Torres S (2013). Industrial policy in Uruguay. In: Kozul-Wright R and Salazar-Xirinachs JM, eds., *Growth, Productive Transformation and Employment: New Perspectives on the Industrial Policy Debate* (forthcoming).

UNCTAD (2012). Excessive commodity price volatility: Macroeconomic effects on growth and policy options. Contribution of the UNCTAD secretariat to the G20 Commodity Markets Working Group; available at: http://unctad.org/meetings/en/Miscellaneous%20 Documents/gds_mdpb_G20_001_en.pdf.

UNCTAD (*TDR 2003*). *Trade and Development Report, 2003. Capital accumulation, growth and structural change*. United Nations publication, Sales No. E.03. II.D.7, New York and Geneva.

UNCTAD (*TDR 2005*). *Trade and Development Report, 2005. New Features of Global Interdependence*. United Nations publication, Sales No. E.05.II.D.13, New York and Geneva.

UNCTAD (*TDR 2006*). *Trade and Development Report, 2006. Global Partnership and National Policies for Development*. United Nations publication, Sales No. E.06.II.D.6, New York and Geneva.

UNCTAD (*TDR 2007*). *Trade and Development Report, 2007. Regional Cooperation for Development*. United Nations publication, Sales No. E.07.II.D.11, New York and Geneva.

UNCTAD (*TDR 2009*). *Trade and Development Report, 2009. Responding to the Global Crisis: Climate Change Mitigation and Development*. United Nations publication, Sales No. E. 09.II.D.16, New York and Geneva.

UNCTAD (*TDR 2010*). *Trade and Development Report, 2010. Employment, Globalization and Development*. United Nations publication, Sales No. E.10.II.D.3, New York and Geneva.

UNCTAD (*TDR 2011*). *Trade and Development Report, 2011. Post-crisis Policy Challenges in the World Economy*. United Nations publication, Sales No. E.11.II.D.3, New York and Geneva.

UNCTAD (*TDR 2012*). *Trade and Development Report, 2012. Policies for Inclusive and Balance Growth*. United Nations publication, Sales No. E.12.II.D.6, New York and Geneva.

United Nations (1992). *Handbook of the International Comparison Programme*. Studies in Methods, Series F, No. 62, document ST/ESA/STAT/SER.F/62. New York, Department of Economic and Social Development, Statistical Division, United Nations.

UN-DESA (2009). Global Vulnerability to Trade Shocks. *World Economic Vulnerability Monitor* No. 1. United Nations, New York, 12 August.

UN-DESA (2012). *World Population Prospects: The 2011 Revision*. Population Division. United Nations, New York.

USDA (2013). *USDA Agricultural Projections to 2022*. Outlook No. (OCE-131), February. Washington, DC, United States Department of Agriculture.

Witt U (2001). Learning to consume: A theory of wants and the growth of demand. *Journal of Evolutionary Economics*, 11(1): 23–36.

Zelenovskaya E (2012). Green growth policy in Korea: A case study. International Center for Climate Governance; available at: http://www.iccgov.org/ FilePagineStatiche/Files/Publications/Reflections/08_ reflection_june_2012.pdf.

Zhou Z, Tian W, Wang J, Liu H and Cao L (2012). Food consumption trends in China. Report submitted to the Australian Government Department of Agriculture, Fisheries and Forestry, April 2012.

Annex to chapter II

SHIFTING GROWTH STRATEGIES: MAIN IMPLICATIONS AND CHALLENGES

Many developing countries have pursued export-oriented growth strategies over the past three decades. The success of such strategies depends on rapidly growing global demand and the identification of new export markets or the expansion of existing ones, combined with the ability of an exporting country to enter market segments with high growth and potential for productivity growth.

With the onset of the global crisis, such strategies are no longer viable. Demand growth in developed-country markets, especially the United States and Europe, has declined sharply. Despite an early swift rebound, it is widely expected that slow growth in the developed countries will reduce export opportunities to these countries for a long time. This raises the question as to whether developing and transition economies, and especially the large ones among them, can shift from an export-oriented to a more domestic-demand-oriented growth strategy. This annex addresses what such a shift would entail.

1. The national income accounting identity and economic growth

The orientation of a country's growth strategy, whether more towards exports or more towards domestic demand, implies differences in the growth contribution of the various elements of the national income accounting identity expressed as:

$$Y=C+I+G+(X-M) \qquad (1)$$

where a country's output (Y) is the sum of household consumption expenditure (C), investment (I), government expenditure (G) and the current-account balance, i.e. the difference between exports (X) and imports (M).[1] Each element on the right-hand side of the equation has two components, one of which is autonomous and the other a function of national income, which in turn equals output (Y). An export-oriented growth strategy will pay particular attention to the relationship between exports and imports, while the other three components will be of greater interest in a more domestic-demand-oriented growth strategy.

Most models of economic growth pay little attention to the various components of the national income accounting identity. Such models are supply-driven, with output growth being a function of factor inputs and factor productivity. Aggregate demand for output is assumed to be sufficient for full utilization of capacity. Trade is the one component of the accounting identity that enters supply-based growth analyses, sometimes through the terms of trade (defined as the ratio of export prices to import prices), but more usually on the assumption that "trade openness" contributes to capital accumulation or productivity growth. Different studies measure openness differently: some through tariff rates or non-tariff barriers, but most commonly as some ratio of trade flows to output (Harrison and Rodriguez-Clare, 2010).

From such a supply-based perspective, "export-oriented growth" refers to a high ratio of exports and imports relative to output $((X+M)/Y)$, i.e. being very open to trade. A high degree of openness to trade may contribute to growth if imported inputs are more productive than domestic inputs, or if there are technological spillovers or other externalities from exporting or importing. The literature on global value chains suggests that a high degree of trade openness will have a positive effect on growth, particularly in countries that export a large proportion of manufactures and succeed in "moving up the value chain", i.e. they increase the value-added content of their exports. A high degree of trade openness is also of microeconomic relevance, since it determines the degree to which the sectoral structure of domestic production is delinked from that of domestic demand. This gap will be particularly wide for countries that export a high proportion of primary commodities; but it will also be substantial for countries that produce goods, such as consumer electronics, which few domestic consumers can afford.

The national income accounting identity is of immediate relevance for the macroeconomic causation of growth if it is considered from the demand side. From a demand-based perspective, "export-oriented growth" refers to a large difference between exports and imports relative to output $((X-M)/Y)$, i.e. running a large trade surplus. The reason why this perspective considers the degree of openness as being less relevant for growth is that, focusing on the share of household consumption in

output, the national income accounting identity can be rearranged as:

$$\frac{C}{Y} = 1 - \frac{(I+G)}{Y} - \frac{(X-M)}{Y} \qquad (2)$$

where any given share of household consumption in output (i.e. C/Y) is compatible with an unlimited range of values of trade openness (i.e. $(X+M)/Y$). A country can have a high share of consumption in output and still export most of its output. By contrast, the larger the trade surplus (i.e. $(X-M)/Y$), the larger will be the growth contribution of exports, and the smaller will be the contributions of the domestic demand elements (i.e. C, I and G) required to attain a given rate of growth.

A related demand-based meaning of export-oriented growth emphasizes the role of the balance-of-payments constraint in limiting output growth. From this perspective, export orientation is relevant for a country's growth strategy for at least two reasons (Thirlwall, 2002: 53).[2] First, exports are the only truly autonomous component of demand, i.e. they are unrelated to the current level of national income. The major shares of household consumption, government expenditure and investment demand are dependent on income. Second, exports are the only component of demand whose revenues accrue in foreign currency, and can therefore pay for the import requirements of growth. Growth driven by consumption, invest-ment or government expenditure may be viable for a short time, but the import content of each of these components of demand will need to be balanced by exports. Of course, such balancing is not necessary if a country accumulates external debt, absorbs a rising amount of net capital inflows or lets the real exchange rate depreciate. However, the length of time any of these three strategies can be pursued depends very much on the external economic environment (e.g. the size of the rate of interest on international capital markets), and they can quickly spiral into a balance-of-payments crisis.

At what point in time the balance-of-payments constraint is felt depends on the import content of the various components of aggregate demand (Y_D) which are a part of leakage, i.e. the fraction of a change in national income that is not spent on current domestic production, but instead saved (s), paid in taxes (t)

or spent on imports (*m*). Thus, the determination of aggregate demand can be schematically expressed as:

$$Y_D = \frac{I + G + X}{s + t + m} \qquad (3)$$

A special case of this equation is the dynamic version of Harrod's foreign trade multiplier. In this case, household consumption, investment, and government expenditure have no autonomous element and trade is assumed to be balanced in the long run (i.e. *X=M*), because all output is either consumed or exported and all income is consumed either on domestic goods or imports. This means that savings and taxes must equal investment and government expenditure (i.e. *s+t=I+G*). Thus, the growth rate of country *i* (*g_i*) is determined by what is known as "Thirlwall's law", and expressed as:

$$g_i = \frac{\varepsilon_i z}{\pi_i} \qquad (4)$$

where ε_i is the world's income elasticity of demand for exports from country *i*, π_i is the income elasticity of demand for imports by country *i*, and *z* is the rate of world income growth (Thirlwall, 1979). According to equation (4), a country's growth rate is determined by the ratio of export growth to the income elasticity of demand for imports. The growth of a country's exports (x_i) – with $x_i=\varepsilon_i z$ – is determined by what is going on in the rest of the world. It influences the growth of Y_D, and hence the growth of output (in the short run via the rate of capacity use and in the long run by motivating the expansion of capacity).[3] Given the current situation of slow growth in developing countries' main export markets, equation (4) implies that developing countries' economic growth will be constrained by a slowdown in the expansion of their exports.

In addition to the impact on the expansion of exports taken as a bundle, the extent to which an exporting country's growth rate is affected by economic growth in the rest of the world also depends on its pattern of specialization.[4] If a country exports goods and services with a relatively large potential for innovation and technological upgrading, output growth could be boosted through improved factor productivity or through an increase in the income elasticity of demand stemming from innovation-based improvements in the quality of goods. If a country

exports from sectors with more rapid international demand growth, it could benefit from a larger income elasticity of demand for its exports, thus boosting output growth by attaining a higher ε/π ratio. Sectors in which there is significant potential for innovation may be called "supply dynamic", while sectors that benefit from a rapid growth of international demand may be called "demand dynamic" sectors. And there is a significant degree of overlap between the two groups (Mayer et al., 2003). Compared with primary commodities, manufactures are usually considered as having both greater potential for innovation and technological upgrading as well as better international demand prospects. Export-oriented industrialization is a strategy that exploits this overlap during periods of favourable export opportunities with a view to increasing a country's ε/π ratio (especially through an increase in ε) and therefore its growth rate. On the other hand, this also means that, in the current context, the adverse impact of slow growth in developed countries is likely to be greater on developing countries that pursue an export-oriented growth strategy that relies mainly on exports of manufactures than on developing countries whose similar strategy relies mainly on exports of primary commodities.

The argument made in this chapter adopts a demand-side perspective mainly because it facilitates an examination of the processes involved in shifting the orientation of a country's growth strategy from one component of demand (i.e. exports) to another (i.e. domestic demand). But taking a demand-side perspective on growth also allows establishing a link between the orientation of growth strategies and the current debate on rebalancing, much of which relates to the share of household consumption in aggregate demand. The G20 Leaders' Statement (2009) at the Pittsburgh Summit called for a rotation of global demand from countries with a current account deficit (especially the United States) towards countries with a current account surplus (such as China and Germany), where domestic expenditure in deficit countries would no longer exceed their income but rapid global growth would be maintained. This is because surplus countries would, at least for a period of time, record accelerated domestic demand growth in excess of their income. Finally, some of those countries whose export opportunities may be adversely affected by a prolonged period of slow growth in developed economies may risk falling into the so-called "middle-income trap", as the decline in their manufactured exports may significantly slow down economic growth. It is generally argued that those countries will increasingly need to rely on

innovation (i.e. investment in the national accounting identity), and household consumption expenditure in order to continue to catch up with the income levels and standards of living of the developed countries.

2. A demand-side perspective on the transition from an export-oriented to a more domestic-demand-orientated growth strategy

Considered from a demand-side perspective, there are three main challenges in switching from a growth strategy based on exports to one based more on domestic demand. One relates to the size of the domestic market. According to equation (2), the increase in the sum of C, I and G must be sufficiently large to compensate for the decline in the trade surplus caused by a fall in exports without having a negative impact on growth. With Δ denoting changes, this can be expressed as:

$$\frac{\Delta(C + I + G)}{Y} = -\frac{\Delta(X - M)}{Y} \quad (5)$$

Concentrating on household consumption, the claim that a sizeable segment of the population in some of the most populous developing and transition economies (e.g. Brazil, China and the Russian Federation) has attained middle-class status, and that this status is not far from being attained in some other economies as well (such as India and Indonesia) (e.g. Bussolo et al., 2011; Kharas, 2010) suggests that these economies have a sufficiently large domestic market for rising household expenditure to compensate for at least a major part of any decline in export demand due to low growth in developed countries.

The second challenge concerns the risk that a switch in growth strategy will rapidly become unsustainable by triggering a surge in imports and ensuing balance-of-payments problems.[5] Differences in the import intensity of the different components of

aggregate demand imply that the relative importance of C, G and I determines the evolution of imports. Rewriting equation (1), with m_C, m_I, m_G, and m_X denoting the import intensity of C, I, G, and X, leads to

$$Y=(C-m_C C)+(I-m_I I)+(G-m_G G)+(X-m_X X) \quad (6)$$

which shows that these differences imply that changes in the composition of a country's aggregate demand will cause significant changes in imports, which occur even if the level of national aggregate demand does not change. Statistical evidence indicates that in most countries the import intensities of exports and investment exceed that of consumption, and that the import intensity of household consumption exceeds that of government consumption, since the latter includes a large proportion of non-tradables such as services (e.g. Bussière et al., 2011). A variation in the import contents of the different elements of aggregate demand implies that changes in the trade balance have different indirect impacts on growth.[6] As noted by McCombie (1985: 63), "an increase in exports allows other autonomous expenditures to be increased until income has risen by enough to induce an increase in imports equivalent to the initial increase in exports."

Maintaining some export growth will most likely be necessary in order to finance the imports of primary commodities and capital goods required for ongoing urbanization and for an expansion of domestic productive capacity. In the current context, maintaining some export growth may be more feasible for developing-country exporters of primary commodities, especially energy. For developing countries exporting manufactured goods to developed countries, it will depend on the evolution of import demand in developed countries, but would probably also require seeking other destination markets, mainly in developing countries where consumption expenditure is increasing. Maintaining export growth could also be achieved by the inclusion of more sophisticated goods in the export basket, such as through upgrading in global value chains which could both raise exports and reduce imports, but much of the scope for doing so will also depend on the evolution of import demand in developed countries. However, it must be borne in mind that from the perspective of the global economy, any country's trade surplus must be absorbed by a commensurate growth in other countries' imports.

The third challenge relates to the fact that, unlike exports, the bulk of the other components of aggregate demand (i.e. household consumption expenditure, government expenditure and investment) is not autonomous, but induced by income (e.g. $C=cY$, where c is the marginal propensity to consume). This means that for a shift in growth strategy to be sustainable, an initial increase in expenditure in the, usually small, autonomous segments of C, G and I must trigger an increase in expenditure in those segments of C, G and I that are induced by income, and income itself must be generated in the process. The remainder of this annex discusses how the autonomous segments of the various components of domestic demand can be increased, and how such increases can create income that, in turn, would enable growth in those segments that are a function of income.

Some part of government expenditure is autonomous, and can be financed by issuing government bonds or imposing higher tax rates. However, much of government expenditure and revenue is endogenous (such as payments for unemployment benefits and tax receipts), and is therefore a function of income. The income effects of an increase in government expenditure, in turn, depend on its multiplier effects and on the degree of internationally coordinated fiscal expansion. There is an ongoing debate about the size of the multiplier effect, but it is generally agreed to be higher in a slump than in more normal

times (Blanchard and Leigh, 2013). In 2008–2009, simultaneous fiscal expansion played a crucial role in compensating for the adverse growth effects of declining export opportunities for developing countries. However, these countries may not have the necessary fiscal space to enable the adoption of such measures a second time (or even on a continuous basis over a given period). Moreover, there are questions as to how much of a country's fiscal expansion undertaken individually spills over to other countries through rising imports. Coordinated fiscal expansion would greatly bolster the growth prospects of all participating countries, but this requires considerable solidarity among States and peoples, which is unlikely in the foreseeable future.

Investment also has an autonomous component, particularly public investment in infrastructure and housing. However, the bulk of investment is endogenous and is determined by the opportunity cost of capital. This is mainly a function of the short-term interest rate set by the central bank and expectations of future growth of sales. If entrepreneurs expect a strong and sustained increase in demand for what they produce, they will engage in large investment expenditures financed, for example, through the creation of liquidity by commercial banks. This means that a country's overall share of investment in GDP must be compatible with its overall share of consumption in GDP to achieve a balanced expansion of domestic demand. If investment continuously outpaces consumption, the productive capacity created will be underutilized, which will depress revenues and, to the extent that investment is debt financed, it will create problems in the domestic financial system.

Turning to the third component of domestic demand (i.e. household consumption expenditure), the financial ability of a sizeable group of consumers to delink, at least temporarily, consumption from current income will facilitate a broad-based increase in consumption expenditure. Such a delinking might occur, for example, in anticipation of a higher future income or for reasons of social interdependencies in consumption. Both these factors may well be considered key characteristics of middle-class households. Usually, low-income households will not have the discretionary income or the savings required to engage in spending unrelated to current income, even if tax policies and government transfers to low-income households affect consumption spending by this category. High-income households are likely to prefer spending on conspicuous, luxury goods, and their number will generally be smaller than that of middle-class households. Moreover, generally it is middle-class households that seek access to consumer credit which finances purchases of durable consumer goods. An initial provision of the purchasing power required for accelerated consumption expenditure through sources delinked from wage income would also limit any adverse consequences for international competitiveness that can be due to a shift from an export-oriented growth strategy, which has often relied on low wages, to a growth strategy that relies more on private consumption. However, to be sustainable, this will eventually require a higher wage income.

The autonomous part of middle-class consumption could also be financed by borrowing from abroad, which would appear as an external deficit in the national income accounting identity (equation 1), or through various possibilities that would reduce leakage by increasing the size of s (=1 minus the marginal propensity to consume out of income) in equation (2): a reduction of spending or savings by another class of households, for example by a redistribution of income (through taxes or transfers) from high-income to middle-class households, borrowing from domestic lenders, and/or improved social security systems.

However, if a greater role of household consumption in a country's growth strategy is to be sustainable in the current context, where the growth of its exports is constrained by slow growth in its destination markets, the bulk of the rise in consumer demand must be met by domestic production rather than by imports. Some of this domestic production may consist of those goods that were formerly exported to developed countries, but the rest will need to come from increased domestic production made possible by induced investment. This in turn

will create employment and income for domestic consumers and lead to an increase in consumption linked to current income. Thus the creation of domestic purchasing power through jobs and income is an essential condition for a shift from an export-oriented to a more domestic-consumption-oriented growth strategy to be sustainable, as it will boost the non-autonomous component of household consumption.

This latter point illustrates that even a growth strategy based on an increase in domestic demand needs to give strong emphasis to the supply structure of the economy. Induced investment may be particularly sensitive to two factors. First, the tastes and preferences of middle-class consumers in developing countries may well differ from the existing high-end products much sought after by consumers in developed countries and by the most affluent groups of consumers in the largest cities of developing countries, who are the standard targets of developed-country firms. It may be easier for domestic producers than foreign producers to develop goods whose characteristics match the preferences of local middle-class consumers. Second, emphasizing that trade is not costless, and that geographical distance to markets still matters, the literature on international trade and economic geography has shown how market size and relative geographic position affect specialization patterns. In particular, greater domestic demand for manufactured consumer goods "will lead to higher wages which, in the presence of non-homothetic preferences combined with positive trade costs, will shift local production towards the manufacturing sector" (Breinlich and Cuñat, 2013: 134). In taking advantage of the associated innovation opportunities, developing-country firms would need to combine investment in supply- and demand-dynamic sectors, thereby reducing the import content of rising domestic consumption expenditure, i.e. increasing their country's ε/π ratio, as expressed in equation (4), especially through a decline in π associated with private consumption.

Notes

1   Treating the current account as exactly equal to net exports is an approximation, which assumes transfers to equal zero. Transfers in the form of workers' remittances play a significant role in the national income of poor countries.

2   For a discussion of other demand-oriented growth models, see Setterfield, 2010.

3   This relationship is subject to a number of assumptions, including constant relative prices (or the real exchange rate), and the Marshall-Lerner condition being just satisfied (i.e. the sum of the price elasticities of demand for imports and exports equals unity), so that the growth of exports is solely determined by the growth of world income. Thirlwall (2013: 87–90) concludes from a review of a "mass of studies applying the model in its various forms to individual countries and groups of countries" that the "vast majority of studies support the balance of payments constrained growth hypothesis for two basic reasons. The first is that it is shown overwhelmingly that relative price changes or real exchange rate changes are not an efficient balance of payments adjustment mechanism either because the degree of long-run change is small, or the price elasticity of exports and imports is low. ... The second reason why the model fits so well is that even if balance of payments equilibrium is allowed ... there is a limit to the current account deficit to GDP ratio that countries can sustain". For further discussion of the debate about this relationship, see McCombie (2011). For a full discussion about how Thirlwall's law relates to Kaldorian growth theory

and about the robustness of its basic hypothesis to extensions such as taking account of relative price dynamics, international financial flows, multi-sector growth, cumulative causation, and the interaction between the actual and potential rates of growth, see Setterfield (2011).

4   For an extension of Thirlwall's law to a multi-sectoral economy, see Araujo and Lima (2007) and Razmi (2011).

5   While induced imports may be the main factor in the leakage identified in equation (3), savings and taxation also play a role. Savings cause households' expenditure to be lower than their total income. Households' net acquisition of financial assets and other forms of wealth reduces the amount of disposable income that constitutes consumption expenditure. However, depending on the age structure of the population and the availability of social security systems, especially for senior citizens, this reduction is likely to be small for most individuals, especially those belonging to middle-class households. Data on the distribution of household wealth indicate a high concentration, with the share of the top 10 per cent of adults holding over two thirds of global wealth (Davies et al., 2010). Moreover, accumulated wealth is usually used to finance housing, rather than durable goods consumption.

6   The composition of private consumption between tradable goods and non-tradable services also plays a role. Workers in the latter sector demand more imports but do not contribute to exports, with ensuing adverse effects on the balance of payments.

References

Araujo RA and Lima GT (2007). A structural economic dynamics approach to balance-of-payments-constrained growth. *Cambridge Journal of Economics*, 31(5): 755–774.

Blanchard O and Leigh D (2013). Growth forecast errors and fiscal multipliers. Working Paper No 13/1, International Monetary Fund, Washington, DC.

Breinlich H and Cuñat A (2013). Geography, non-homotheticity, and industrialization: A quantitative analysis. *Journal of Development Economics*, 103 (July): 133–153.

Bussière M, Callegari G, Ghironi F, Sestieri G, Yamano N (2011). Estimating trade elasticities: Demand composition and the trade collapse of 2008–09. NBER Working Paper 17712, Cambridge, MA, December.

Bussolo M, de Hoyos RE, Medvedev D and van der Mensbrugghe D (2011). Global growth and distribution: China, India, and the emergence of a global middle class. *Journal of Globalization and Development*, 2(2): Article 3.

Davies JB, Sadström S, Shorrocks A and Wolff EN (2010). The level of distribution of global household wealth. *The Economic Journal*, 121(1): 223–254.

G20 (2009). Leaders Statement: The Pittsburgh Summit. At http://www.g20.utoronto.ca/2009/2009communique0925.html.

Harrison A and Rodriguez-Clare A (2010). Trade, foreign investment, and industrial policy for developing countries. In: Rodrik D and Rosenzweig M, eds. *Handbook of Development Economics,* Vol. 5. North-Holland, Amsterdam: 4039–4214.

Kharas H (2010). The emerging middle class in developing countries. Working Paper No. 285, OECD Development Centre, Paris. January.

Mayer J, Butkevicius A, Kadri A and Pizarro J (2003). Dynamic products in world exports. *Review of World Economics*, 139(4): 762–795.

McCombie JSL (1985). Economic growth, the Harrod foreign trade multiplier and the Hicks' super-multiplier. *Applied Economics*, 17(1): 55–72.

McCombie JSL (2011). Criticisms and defences of the balance-of-payments constrained growth model, some old, some new. *PSL (Paolo Sylos Labini) Quarterly Review*, 64(259): 353–392.

Razmi A (2011). Exploring the robustness of the balance of payments-constrained growth idea in a multiple good framework. *Cambridge Journal of Economics*, 35(3): 545–567.

Setterfield M (ed.) (2010). *Handbook of Alternative Theories of Economic Growth*. Cheltenham and Northampton, MA, Edward Elgar.

Setterfield M (2011). The remarkable durability of Thirlwall's law. *PSL (Paolo Sylos Labini) Quarterly Review*, 64(259): 393–427.

Thirlwall AP (1979). The balance of payments constraint as an explanation of international growth rate differences. *Banca Nazionale del Lavoro Quarterly Review*, 32(128): 45–53.

Thirlwall AP (2002). *Trade, the Balance of Payments and Exchange Rate Policy in Developing Countries*. Cheltenham and Northampton, MA, Edward Elgar.

Thirlwall AP (2013). *Economic Growth in an Open Developing Economy: The Role of Structure and Demand*. Cheltenham and Northampton, MA, Edward Elgar.

Chapter III

FINANCING THE REAL ECONOMY

A. Introduction

A redesign of development strategies involves structural change as well as an expansion of productive capacities and their adaptation to new demand patterns, all of which require financing. The availability and conditions of such financing have evolved significantly over the past few decades. In addition, the recent economic and financial crisis presents new challenges for the financial sector and its capacity to provide long-term credit for investment. This chapter analyses the challenges and options currently available to developing and emerging market economies[1] to finance their development.

Investment financing in developing countries, especially low-income countries, has been frequently linked to foreign capital. The view that foreign financing is necessary and efficient is based on the neoclassical assumption that, since capital is scarce in developing countries and abundant in developed ones, the marginal return on capital is higher in developing countries, thus providing strong incentives to investment in the latter. Moreover, since the level of income is low in developing countries, and the majority of the population consumes most of it, resulting in a shortage of savings, it is argued that with open capital accounts, foreign capital could fill the savings-investment gap. The owners of that capital would obtain a higher return in developing countries than in their home country, while the rate of investment would rise in the recipient economy

without reducing the already low levels of domestic consumption there. In addition to the long-term benefits of higher investments in capital-poor economies, access to foreign capital would enable short-term smoothing of the economic cycle. For instance, a negative external shock that reduces export earnings could be cushioned through a foreign loan, which would be reimbursed when export earnings rise again. Access to foreign finance would therefore support domestic expenditure during bad times and moderate it during bonanzas, producing an overall countercyclical effect.

However, empirical evidence has repeatedly invalidated these theoretical assumptions. For sure, foreign capital in amounts that can be productively absorbed by the domestic economy may be very helpful in accelerating productivity growth, diversification and industrialization when it is properly oriented to investment in real productive capacity. But, as discussed in this chapter, unrestricted capital inflows generally have not been accompanied by a sustained increase of investment in real productive capacity; nor have they led to higher and more stable GDP growth rates. First, not all capital inflows are used for the financing of productive investment. Foreign loans may be channelled through domestic financial intermediaries towards financial speculation or imports of consumer goods. They may also be used for servicing foreign debt or re-channelled abroad through an increase in external private financial assets ("capital flight"). And second, foreign capital inflows have often been procyclical, accentuating (or even generating) the business cycle in the recipient countries. Indeed, they have played a key role in all the "twin crises" (i.e. balance-of-payments and domestic financial crises) of the last three decades in the developing world.

Empirical studies conducted by economists from fairly diverse theoretical schools of thought have failed to find a positive correlation between openness to international capital flows and development (Bhagwati, 1998). Indeed, capital flows have not only been a source of instability; they have also proved to be either ineffective, or even negative, for long-term growth (Prasad et al., 2003; Prasad, Rajan and Subramanian, 2007; Jeanne, Subramanian and Williamson, 2012). This also explains why, since the late 1990s, an increasing number of developing-country governments have become more cautious about receiving massive amounts of capital inflows which are often triggered by events on international markets and by monetary policies in developed countries. Policies in developed countries that might generate such capital movements, such as the recent huge injections of liquidity as part of "non-conventional" expansionary monetary policies, are criticized for not taking into account their possible macroeconomic effects on developing countries and for their potential to fuel a "currency war".

The recent global financial crisis is more than just the latest episode in a long list of boom-bust cycles over the past three decades; it is an event that should lead policymakers to call into question, even more seriously than before, the governance of the international financial system and to seek ways to improve it. This crisis, and the global imbalances that have contributed to it, have revealed fundamental flaws in the functioning of financial systems, not only in the major financial centres but also at the global level. The crisis has also revealed the shortcomings of monetary policies that narrowly focus on monetary stability, understood as low consumer price inflation. There is a pressing need for monetary authorities to pay greater attention to financial stability and to the strengthening of the real economy, in addition to monetary stability. After all, it is the real economy that determines financial soundness and the capacity of borrowers to pay back their debts. From this point of view, the critical question is not how much money is generated by the monetary authorities or the commercial banks (as monetarist theory suggests), but whether that money is used for productive or unproductive purposes.

In a world of accelerated financial expansion and large international capital movements, developing countries face a dual challenge. On the one hand, they need to have effective mechanisms to protect themselves against destabilizing financial shocks caused by huge capital inflows and outflows. On the other hand, they need to ensure that the financial system – or at least the largest part of it – fulfils its main function, which is to serve the real economy by financing productive investment and supporting the development of firms and the economy as a whole. In order for domestic financial systems to fulfil these functions, they have to be organized and managed in such a way that they provide sufficient and stable long-term financing and channel credit flows to productive uses. This will probably require reduced dependence on foreign short-term capital and a greater reliance on domestic sources of finance, which are often much larger than is commonly assumed. Hence, a major policy issue in the financial sphere is: how can developing countries advance their development goals despite the crisis that continues to weaken financial and economic conditions in the developed world and the international financial system?

Section B of this chapter takes a longer term perspective on this issue by tracing the evolution of global finance since the 1970s, and considering how this has affected developing and transition economies. Section C then discusses the impacts on developing countries of both the global financial crisis and the policies followed in systemically important financial centres. Finally, section D discusses the lessons that can be derived from these experiences and the policy options that are available to developing and transition economies to reduce their macroeconomic and financial vulnerability and ensure that the structural changes needed in the new global environment can be financed in a sustainable way.

B. Global trends in finance and their impacts on developing and transition economies

1. Trends in cross-border capital movements and financial flows to developing countries

Since the mid-1970s, foreign capital flows to developing countries have increased dramatically, but they have been very volatile. The acceleration of financial globalization, spurred by far-reaching liberalization and deregulation of financial systems worldwide, led to a rapid increase in cross-border capital flows, which jumped from $0.5 trillion in 1980 (equivalent to 4 per cent of global GDP and 25 per cent of the value of international trade) to $12 trillion in 2007 (equivalent to 21 per cent of global GDP and 84 per cent of international trade) (chart 3.1A). Much of these capital movements took place among developed countries, which accounted for 80 per cent of the stock of foreign-owned financial assets by 2007 (Lund et al., 2013).

However, the relative importance of developing countries as recipients of international capital flows has changed significantly over the past few decades. These countries saw an increase in such inflows between 1976 and 1982 and again between 1991 and 1996, followed in both cases by abrupt decreases. Their share in total capital inflows reached its highest level soon after the onset of the global financial crisis (26.4 per cent of total inflows during the period 2008–2011). This reflected not only an increase of flows to developing countries, but also a sharp fall of flows to developed countries (table 3.1 and chart 3.1B).

Large and volatile capital movements remain a challenge for developing countries, and this has not diminished with the crisis. Indeed, in 2010–2011

capital flows actually exceeded their levels of 2007 in Africa, Latin America and China. Moreover, the structural factors contributing to their pre-crisis surge are still in place. There is still considerable potential for international investors in developed countries to diversify their portfolios, particularly to emerging market economies, in search of high returns. This is due to a gradual diminishing of the "home bias" in investment portfolios, a bias that makes investors hold domestic financial assets in excess of the share of such assets in global market capitalization (Haldane, 2011). Given the magnitude of global financial assets (estimated at $225 trillion, or more than three times the world's gross product),[2] even minor portfolio adjustments oriented towards developing countries would represent an increase in such flows at a rate that could destabilize the economies of these countries.[3]

Another major change that has surfaced in the last few decades is related to the composition and use of capital flows. In the decades immediately following the Second World War, foreign financing was relatively scarce and consisted mainly of foreign direct investment (FDI) or loans from official sources, either bilateral or multilateral. Bilateral financing was mainly in the form of trade credits provided directly by public agencies of developed countries or insured by them. Such credits were directly linked to imports, particularly of capital goods. Multilateral loans from the World Bank and regional development banks were also oriented towards specific real investment projects. Loans from the International Monetary Fund (IMF) were of a different nature, since they sought to cover balance-of-payments deficits arising from macroeconomic disequilibria. On the borrowers' side, a large share of financing went to the public sector (including State-owned firms) or to private entities in the form of publicly-guaranteed loans.

Chart 3.1

NET CAPITAL INFLOWS BY ECONOMIC GROUP, 1976–2011

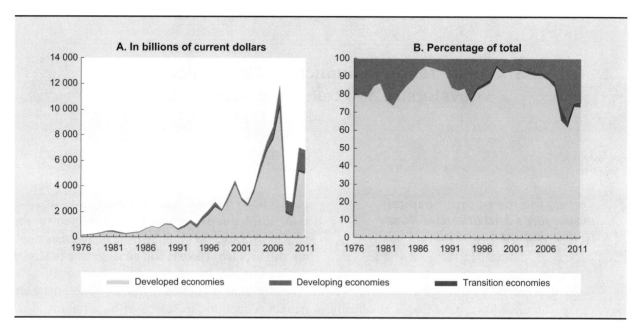

Source: UNCTAD secretariat calculations, based on IMF, *Balance of Payments Statistics* database.
Note: Net capital inflows by economic group correspond to net FDI, portfolio and "other investment" inflows.

From the mid-1970s, private lenders increasingly replaced official lenders as the main sources of external financing for developing countries. International banks recycled petrodollars by providing syndicated loans at variable interest rates to developing countries, particularly in Latin America. By 1979–1981, such commercial bank loans accounted for some 57 per cent of net capital flows to emerging economies, while official lending (bilateral loans or credit from international financial institutions) declined to barely more than 20 per cent (table 3.2).

However, with the Latin American debt crisis in 1982 and a "sudden stop" of bank credit in the region, official financing again had to fill part of the gap. It was used for servicing debt to private creditors (in a scheme termed "revolving door") in order to prevent an outright debt default. But this increase in official lending did not last long. As international banks managed to recapitalize and build up provisions, and were therefore in a sufficiently strong position to be able to offload their loans that had been deeply discounted in secondary markets, they engaged in a debt restructuring process supported by the so-called "Brady Plan". Under this plan, implemented

in several highly indebted countries in the region in the late 1980s and early 1990s, bank loans were transformed into long-term securities, which were then partly sold by the original bank creditors to a variety of financial investors. This was part of the larger trend of "securitization", which was accompanied by a change in the structure of creditors in which other (non-bank) private sources became an important source of finance for emerging economies (table 3.2).

Another major change in the composition of external financial flows to developing countries since the 1990s has been the rapid rise in FDI, which grew from around 15 per cent of net inflows during the period 1976–1982 to more than 50 per cent in the 2000s. This was a fairly general trend among developing countries as a whole, including both middle-income and least developed countries (LDCs).

During the 1980s, external financing from official sources to middle-income countries declined further, and recovered only for short periods in response to the various financial crises (in 1982–1986, 1998 and 2009). By contrast, external financing

Table 3.1

NET CAPITAL INFLOWS BY ECONOMIC GROUP AND REGION, 1976–2011

	1976– 1982	1983– 1990	1991– 1996	1997– 2000	2001– 2007	2008– 2011	Cumulative total
	In $ billion (annual average)						*($ billion)*
Developed economies	289	652	1084	2930	5543	3459	78 094
Transition economies	...	...	12	22	99	146	1 436
Developing economies	71	54	218	239	586	1291	12 462
of which:							
Africa	12	9	17	27	30	100	978
Asia	22	33	123	109	449	912	8 386
Latin America and the Caribbean	37	12	78	102	107	277	3 087
Memo item:							
LDCs	4	6	6	6	8	27	297
World	360	706	1314	3190	6227	4896	91 992
	As a percentage of total						
Developed economies	80.2	92.3	82.5	91.8	89.0	70.7	84.9
Transition economies	...	...	0.9	0.7	1.6	3.0	1.6
Developing economies	19.8	7.7	16.6	7.5	9.4	26.4	13.5
of which:							
Africa	3.4	1.3	1.3	0.8	0.5	2.0	1.1
Asia	6.1	4.7	9.4	3.4	7.2	18.6	9.1
Latin America and the Caribbean	10.3	1.7	5.9	3.2	1.7	5.7	3.4
Memo item:							
LDCs	1.2	0.8	0.4	0.2	0.1	0.6	0.3
Total	100	100	100	100	100	100	100
	As a percentage of GDP						
Developed economies	4.1	5.0	5.0	12.1	16.8	8.4	8.3
Transition economies	...	...	6.3	4.9	8.4	6.6	6.8
Developing economies	4.0	2.0	4.7	3.9	5.7	6.8	4.3
of which:							
Africa	4.3	2.2	3.8	5.4	3.3	6.3	3.9
Asia	2.8	2.2	4.7	3.0	6.7	7.3	4.3
Latin America and the Caribbean	5.3	1.5	4.8	4.9	3.9	5.8	4.1
Memo item:							
LDCs	5.3	4.5	4.2	3.7	3.1	5.2	4.3
World	4.1	4.5	4.9	10.4	14.2	7.8	7.4

Source: UNCTAD secretariat calculations, based on IMF, *Balance of Payments Statistics* database.

in the form of bilateral and multilateral loans remained important for LDCs until the mid-1990s, when, with the start of the Heavily Indebted Poor Countries (HIPC) Initiative in 1996, grants increasingly replaced concessional loans. Consequently, their capital account balance (which includes grants) increased significantly, from an average of 0.4 per cent of the GDP of LDCs countries for the period 1987–1996 to 1.9 per cent on average for 1997–2011.[4] The low share of private capital in the composition of capital inflows in LDCs reflects the historical reluctance of private capital to undertake what they considered to be risky investments in LDCs. It effectively shielded LDCs from the waves of capital flows that affected and often destabilized other developing and transition economies over the last two decades.

Table 3.2

COMPOSITION OF EXTERNAL FINANCING TO EMERGING MARKET ECONOMIES, 1979–2012

(Annual average, per cent)

	1979– 1981	1982– 1990	1991– 2000	2001– 2007	2008– 2012
Official flows	21.0	42.9	15.8	-1.0	9.1
FDI	9.9	25.1	40.0	57.5	41.1
Portfolio equity investment	3.2	4.1	9.3	3.7	-0.9
Commercial banks	56.8	9.5	10.2	19.0	13.5
Other private creditors	9.2	18.5	24.7	20.9	37.2
Total	100	100	100	100	100

Source: UNCTAD secretariat calculations, based on Institute of International Finance, *Capital Flows* database.
Note: Numbers do not add to 100 due to rounding.

LDCs' lack of access to private capital was also due to the stringent limits on private borrowing set by the Bretton Woods Institutions in order for them to continue to access concessional borrowing in the context of debt reduction programmes. Countries with more severe debt problems remain dependent on high levels of concessional financing to maintain debt sustainability (IMF, 2010).[5]

In the middle-income countries, the general shift to private sources of finance occurred in parallel with a change in recipients within each country and in their use of financing. Since the mid-1970s, foreign financing has been directed increasingly to private banks and firms, much of it associated with purely financial movements, such as "carry trade" operations and financial speculation in the recipient country, eventually leading to large capital outflows. Concomitantly, there has been less external financing directed at imports of capital goods and productive inputs. This implies that it was often the decision of lenders (international investors) to invest in developing countries rather than the decision of borrowers to seek loans, but the receiving countries initially welcomed such inflows as a sign of their creditworthiness and as recognition of their economic performance and potential. However, the increasing "privatization" of capital flows, and the fact that they frequently represented purely financial operations rather than transactions related to real investment, contributed to their greater instability, as they became prone to sudden stops and reversals. Given the very

large amounts of funds involved relative to the size of the recipient developing economies, financial globalization became a major destabilizing factor for many of them.

2. Capital flows, booms and busts in emerging market economies

External financial flows to developing and transition economies have repeatedly proved to be a double-edged sword. On the one hand, they have often been a way of alleviating balance-of-payments constraints on growth and investment. On the other hand, the large size of financial inflows and their instability have often led to an overvaluation of currencies, lending booms and busts, asset price bubbles, inflationary pressures and the build-up of foreign obligations without necessarily contributing either to growth or to improving a country's capacity to service those obligations. And the drying up or reversal of such inflows has frequently resulted in pressures on the balance of payments and on the financing of both the private and public sectors. The magnitudes involved in these swings can be large vis-à-vis the size of the asset markets of the developing countries concerned and also relative to the size of their economies. Reliance on private capital inflows has therefore tended to increase macroeconomic and financial instability that has hampered, rather than supported, long-term growth.

The experience of past episodes of strong net capital inflows[6] followed by sharp slowdowns or reversals offers important lessons for the present situation. There were three major waves of capital inflows to emerging market economies prior to the most recent financial crisis: in 1977–1981, 1990–1996 and 2002–2007 (chart 3.2). All these episodes presented some common features. First, they all started when there was abundant liquidity in the developed countries resulting from their pursuit of expansionary monetary policies, and/or their large balance-of-payments deficits which were financed by the issuance of debt in international currencies (mainly in dollars). At the same time, developed countries experienced significant slowdowns related to different shocks: the oil shock in the second half of the 1970s, the Savings and Loan crisis in the United States, the crisis of the European Exchange Rate

Chart 3.2

NET PRIVATE CAPITAL INFLOWS TO EMERGING MARKET ECONOMIES, 1978–2012

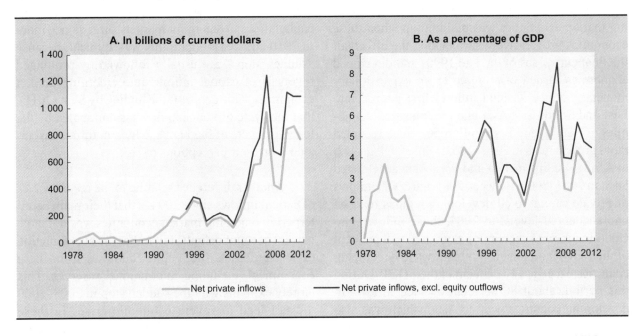

Source: UNCTAD secretariat calculations, based on Institute of International Finance, *Capital Flows* database; and *UNCTADstat*.
Note: Data for 2012 are estimates.

Mechanism (ERM) and the financial crisis in Japan in the early 1990s, and the bursting of the dot-com bubble in the early 2000s. On all these occasions, the monetary authorities in the developed countries lowered their policy interest rates to support their economies and financial systems. Given these developments, developing countries appeared to present attractive alternatives for international investors, as their economies were growing faster than those in the North and were providing opportunities for higher returns (Akyüz, 2012).

Second, the reduction or reversal of capital inflows in emerging market economies in the late 1970s, mid-1990s and mid-2000s followed increases in policy interest rates in developed countries. Although expansionary monetary policies in developed countries were a major factor contributing to those capital movements, these policies alone were not enough to generate strong outflows to developing countries; for instance, the reduction of interest rates in developed countries between 1984 and 1986 did not generate large outflows to emerging market economies because banks needed to recapitalize and create adequate provisions due to their risky Latin

American assets resulting from the debt crisis in that region.

Third, how the capital inflows were used by recipient countries has been an important additional factor determining their impact on these countries. When a large proportion of the inflows was used to finance a higher oil-import bill or investment projects which required imports of capital goods, they helped to stabilize the domestic economy and support growth. In other cases, however, where capital inflows were directed mainly to private banks for financing consumption or speculative financial investments, or to firms for financing current expenditure, they had (often strong) destabilizing effects. If capital inflows are not used primarily for imports, they can lead to a strong real appreciation of the local currency and severely harm domestic industries. In some countries, where currency appreciation was the cornerstone of anti-inflationary policies, capital inflows were mainly channelled to the private sector through deregulated financial systems. This generated an uncontrolled expansion of domestic credit, which led to financial fragility associated with real estate and financial bubbles, currency appreciation and significant current account deficits, eventually resulting in a crash.

The last major wave of capital inflows to emerging market economies was building up when these economies progressively surmounted the effects of the financial crises of the late 1990s and developed economies turned once again to an expansionary monetary stance. Capital inflows first poured into East and South-East Asia and the transition economies of Central and Eastern Europe, which resumed rapid growth rates in 2000–2002, while GDP growth in Africa, Latin America and West Asia accelerated later, in 2003–2004. Between 2005 and 2007, inflows of private capital to all developing regions reached unprecedented levels: in 2007, those inflows into emerging market economies amounted to 8 per cent of their GDP and total capital inflows to developing countries exceeded 10 per cent of their GDP. During this period, about 80 per cent of such inflows to developing countries went to Asia, which was also the region where private capital inflows accounted for the largest proportion of GDP (more than 10 per cent on average during that period compared with 4.9 per cent in Latin America and 4.2 per cent in Africa). The transition economies also received very large amounts of foreign capital during that period (12.4 per cent of GDP).[7]

This last major wave of capital inflows came to a halt in 2008 and 2009. This was atypical, because the reversal did not occur in response to an increase in interest rates in the major developed countries; on the contrary, those countries had lowered interest rates in efforts to mitigate the crisis. Rather, what is likely to have caused the reversal this time was that the crisis

in the most advanced financial markets was still fresh in the minds of investors, making them extremely risk averse and eager to minimize the overall risk of their portfolios. However, this proved short-lived, as capital flows to emerging markets surged once more in 2010 and 2011. Again this was atypical, because "sudden stops" are usually followed by prolonged reversals of capital inflows into emerging market economies. This confirms the finding by Shin (2011), that the cycle of financial flows is dominated by the leverage cycle of big banks, which in turn is associated with their perceptions of risk.

Another difference relating to the recent waves of capital inflows since 2004 is that their main counterpart in emerging market economies was not large current account deficits, but rather the accumulation of foreign assets (i.e. capital outflows from these economies), including international reserves. This largely explains why the sudden stop in 2008–2009 did not lead to severe economic crises in these countries. The main exceptions to this rule were the emerging market economies in Europe, which saw huge current account deficits and experienced a severe economic setback due to a reversal of foreign capital inflows.

The most recent experience shows that large capital inflows followed by a "sudden stop" do not necessarily trigger an immediate financial collapse as in previous "waves" of capital flows. This raises the question as to whether the financial vulnerability of emerging economies has changed, and if so, why. What are the challenges they now face and how can they be overcome? These questions are addressed in the next two sections.

C. The global crisis and the challenges ahead

1. The financial situation and monetary policies in developed countries

(a) Impacts of the crisis and policy responses

In order to understand the challenges for developing countries, especially emerging market economies that are potential destinations of a new wave of capital flows, it is worth recalling some important features of the latest crisis and the policy response of developed countries.

The recent financial crisis resulted from a surge of private indebtedness in developed countries. A widespread view five years after the outbreak of the crisis is that excessive public debt was the cause, and that it is also the main obstacle to recovery. However, it was the private sector debt that increased rapidly from the mid-1990s onwards, while public sector debt, for the most part, remained flat or even declined (chart 3.3). It is only since 2008, following the onset of the global economic crisis, that public sector debt began to rise as a result of large-scale government bailout packages, the effect of automatic stabilizers and additional fiscal policy measures to stabilize aggregate demand. Notwithstanding this rise, private debt is still a multiple of public debt. It is surprising that neither the economic authorities, nor the credit rating agencies or the managers of financial institutions, seemed to be aware of the mounting risks caused by such a rapid increase in private debt. All of them appear to have had extreme, but unjustified, confidence in the efficiency of financial markets and in the ability of private sector debtors (unlike the public sector) to honour their debt obligations.[8]

Once the financial crisis broke out, followed by the broader economic crisis, there was a marked change in the financial behaviour of all actors – households, financial and non-financial firms and governments – in the major developed countries. Following years of mounting prosperity, during which financial markets had fuelled the build-up of asset price bubbles, households and firms suddenly saw a dramatic deterioration of their balance sheets. They found it more and more difficult, if not impossible, to revolve their debts, let alone increase their borrowing, as the prices of their collateral plunged. On the other side of the ledger, banks found themselves burdened with poor-quality or non-performing loans and securities of dubious value. The sudden disruption of credit flows forced a process of deleveraging in the private sector that led to a sharp downturn of economic activity. The contractionary effect of the crisis on economic activity in the developed economies could be contained only by increasing debt-financed public spending by governments, which acted as borrowers, investors and consumers of last resort. These abrupt changes are reflected in the net lending or borrowing positions of the private and public sectors (chart 3.4).

When the crisis erupted, governments in developed countries reacted with strong monetary and fiscal measures. Public spending rose quite significantly, while central banks provided emergency liquidity to the financial system in order to compensate for the sharp fall in interbank lending and reduced interest rates. When the worst of the crisis seemed to be over, and many governments and international institutions (wrongly) believed that the major hindrance to a sustained recovery was not the lack of global demand but the rise in public debt, this multipronged supportive approach came to an end. The view that their "fiscal space" was exhausted led to a shift towards fiscal austerity, and monetary policy appeared to be the sole available instrument of support.

Chart 3.3

PRIVATE SECTOR AND GROSS PUBLIC DEBT, SELECTED DEVELOPED COUNTRIES, 1995–2012

(Per cent of GDP)

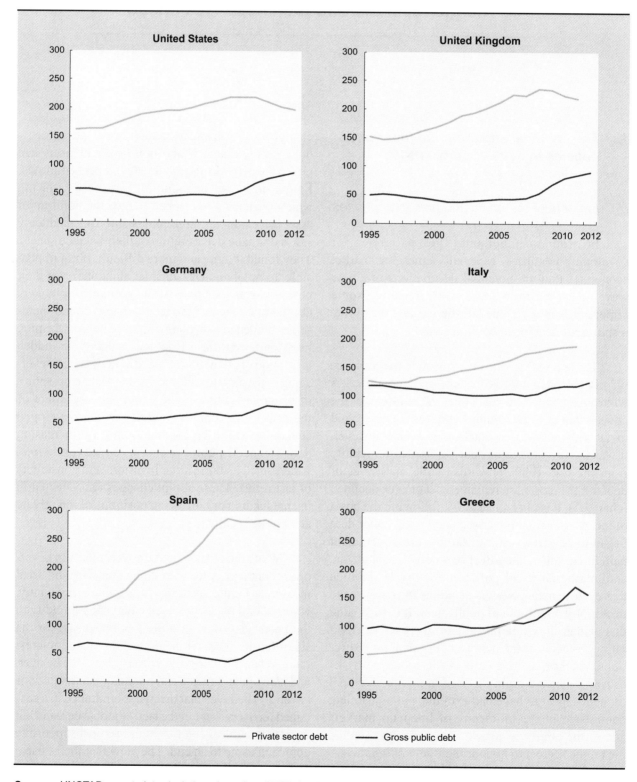

Source: UNCTAD secretariat calculations, based on *OECD.StatExtracts* database.

Note: Data for the United States on "gross public debt" refer to "debt of central government". Data on "gross public debt" for 2012 are projections.

Chart 3.4

NET LENDING/BORROWING BY SECTOR, UNITED STATES AND EURO AREA, 2000–2012

(Per cent of GDP)

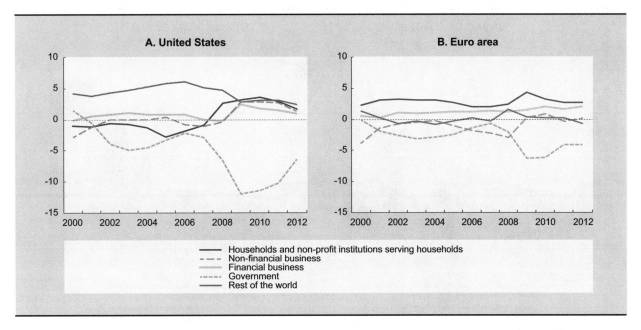

Source: UNCTAD secretariat calculations, based on United States, Bureau of Economic Analysis; and European Central Bank, *Statistical Data Warehouse*.
Note: Net lending positions are indicated by positive values, net borrowing by negative values.

As interest rates were already at or approaching the lowest possible limits, central banks in all the major developed economies turned increasingly to "unconventional" policies, which led to a rapid expansion of their monetary base. Moreover, in addition to rescuing private financial institutions in trouble, they sought to revive credit and demand, and also to reduce the perceived risk of financial assets. Most importantly, the central banks agreed to buy (or to finance the acquisition of) their own governments' sovereign bonds. This expanded their role of lender of last resort and also blurred the boundaries between fiscal and monetary policies. Their efforts resulted in a ballooning of their balance sheets. For instance, between the onset of the subprime mortgage crisis in August 2007 and the end of 2012, the balance sheet of the Bank of England grew by 380 per cent, and those of the European Central Bank (ECB) and the United States Federal Reserve System grew by 241 per cent and 221 per cent respectively.

The central banks used different instruments, depending on the structure and needs of their economies. This is reflected in the different compositions and profiles of their balance sheets. The ECB, given the more bank-centric nature of the euro-area economy, supplied liquidity directly to the banking sector, mainly through a long-term refinancing operation (LTRO) (chart 3.5A).[9] In addition, it implemented bond purchase programmes, including a new Outright Monetary Transactions programme. The United States Federal Reserve, by contrast, supplied liquidity through security purchases, not only Treasury securities, as it had traditionally done, but also private mortgage-backed securities (chart 3.5B). These large-scale asset purchases aimed to stop the decline of asset prices, revive consumer spending and support economic growth. A similar approach was followed by the Bank of England and, more recently, by the Bank of Japan.

Their strategies have been partially successful. In particular, the commitment by the ECB to buy (in the secondary market) unlimited quantities of sovereign bonds of euro-zone periphery countries (Greece, Ireland, Italy, Portugal and Spain) led to a reduction of their sovereign risk premiums. However, neither in Europe nor in the United States has the large

Chart 3.5

ASSET COMPOSITION OF THE EUROPEAN CENTRAL BANK AND THE UNITED STATES FEDERAL RESERVE, 2003–2013

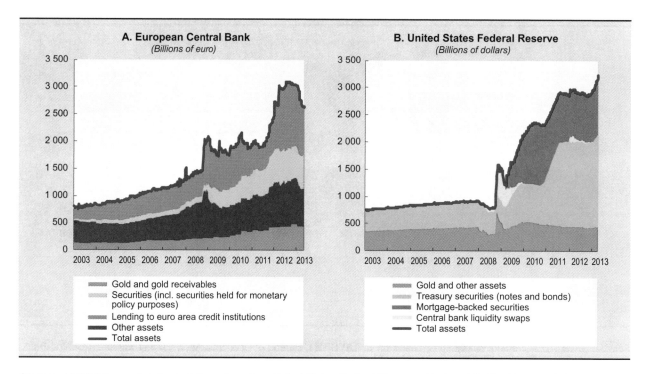

Source: UNCTAD secretariat calculations, based on United States Federal Reserve, *Factors Affecting Reserve Balances (H.4.1)* database; and European Central Bank, *Statistical Data Warehouse.*

injection of "high-powered money" translated into increased bank lending to the private sector; on the contrary, outstanding credit to the private sector has actually declined as a percentage of GDP (chart 3.6). The question is whether the failure of banks to increase lending is due to their reluctance to lend or the unwillingness of companies and households to borrow. What is clear is that the credit crunch is not due to banks lacking liquidity or access to central bank refinancing.

Euro-zone banks appear to have been using the additional liquidity created by the ECB as a means of refinancing themselves or for accumulating deposits at the ECB itself: commercial bank deposits with the ECB increased to the historically high level of €800 billion during 2012. At the same time, ECB surveys of small and medium-sized enterprises (SMEs) in the euro zone show that lending activity is still very low, not only because of weak demand for credit but also because firms are finding it difficult to obtain loans. This is seen as evidence that credit markets in the euro-area remain highly dysfunctional.

Economic history provides evidence that credit is slow to recover after a major financial crisis, and this time is no different. Private actors in the euro zone, Japan and the United States are increasing their savings, hoarding cash or paying down debt, and therefore their demand for credit is largely limited to refinancing loans that are reaching maturity. Many of them that are willing to borrow more are experiencing difficulty in accessing credit due to uncertainty about their future income stream and the value of their collateral. In addition, many banks need to be recapitalized owing to a deterioration of their loan portfolios, which is further limiting their credit supply.

The failure of monetary expansion to boost private expenditure is a reminder of the "liquidity trap" analysed by Keynes (1936/1973), which occurs when economic agents prefer to keep cash holdings rather than investing funds in areas that present a high risk of capital loss. Anecdotal evidence suggests that this may be happening to some extent: liquid reserves held by industry and the banking system

Chart 3.6

MONETARY BASE AND BANK CLAIMS ON THE PRIVATE SECTOR, 2001–2012

(Per cent of GDP)

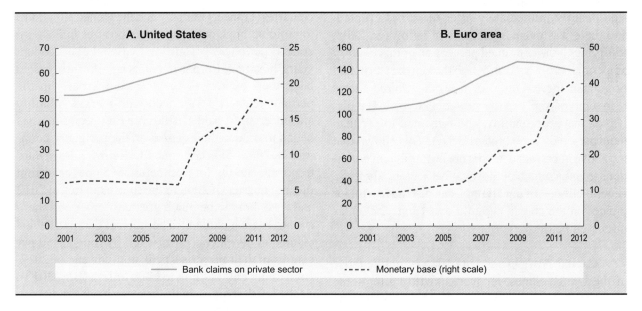

Source: UNCTAD secretariat calculations, based on IMF, *International Financial Statistics* and *World Economic Outlook* databases.
Note: Monetary base for euro area corresponds to currency issued and central bank's liabilities to depository corporations.

in the United States at the end of 2012 amounted to more than $3 trillion, four times as high as the stimulus package of $831 billion provided under the 2009 American Recovery and Reinvestment Act. One recent study argues that almost half of this amount was in "excess" of reasonable precautionary requirements, estimating that if it had been redirected into productive investments it would have helped create millions of jobs and lower the unemployment rate to below 5 per cent (Pollin et al., 2011).

Other major economies have similar stockpiles, suggesting that the "precautionary motive" for holding liquid assets is undermining policymakers' attempts to use cheap capital as a means of injecting life into a nervous and demand-deficient economy. In Japan, for example, recent estimates put companies' liquid assets at around $2.8 trillion, up 75 per cent since 2007. Similarly, in the euro zone, households currently hold some €7,000 billion in currency and deposits, and non-financial companies hold around €2,031 billion.[10]

This coexistence of idle liquidity held by a group of economic agents and liquidity shortages faced by

others is new evidence of the "broken transmission mechanism" on the monetary and financial markets. It suggests that policy responses should include better targeting of the recipients of money creation. In other words, monetary authorities should find a means of making credit available to agents that really need it for using in a productive way.

(b) Impact on capital flows

The previous subsection has described typical conditions that are conducive to strong capital outflows from developed countries. Indeed, they are likely to be even more conducive to a surge in outflows than those at the beginning of previous "waves". This is because there is a large interest rate differential in favour of developing countries, a huge amount of liquidity in the banking system and low demand for credit in developed countries. Although immediately following the onset of the financial crisis there was a sharp increase in public sector borrowing, the subsequent policy switch to fiscal austerity and public debt reduction is causing demand for public credit to fall as well. But these conditions have not induced strong and sustained capital outflows from developed countries; rather such outflows have been very volatile.

Capital outflows from the United States fell significantly immediately after the crisis erupted, and there was even an increase in inflows in 2008, testifying to the continued perception of this country as a "safe port in a storm" even though the storm had originated there. Outflows from the United States recovered partially in the subsequent years, but displayed marked volatility, and remained lower than their pre-crisis levels (chart 3.7A). This shows that the above-mentioned factors are not sufficient conditions to induce such outflows; other factors, such as a general climate of uncertainty, can also have a major impact on the size of capital flows (Shin, 2011), as discussed below.

Capital flows in and out of Japan, unlike those of the United States, recovered swiftly after some contraction in the years immediately following the onset of the crisis, and even surpassed pre-crisis flows, accounting for between 10 and 15 per cent of GDP in 2010–2011. Portfolio outflows in 2011 remained relatively high, as investors and speculators took advantage of close-to-zero interest rates to borrow in yen and invest abroad. This recovery of capital outflows from Japan was partly bolstered by its supportive regional environment of East and South-East Asia, which contrasts sharply with that of Europe.

In Europe there was a simultaneous contraction of both inflows and outflows of capital (chart 3.7B). By 2011, capital flows were equivalent to less than 20 per cent of GDP, compared with over 30 per cent during the period 2005–2007. And some components of those flows declined sharply. For example, euro-zone portfolio outflows fell from $1,386 billion in 2005 to just $288 billion in 2010, and even turned negative in 2011. The contraction of capital flows to and from European countries reflects the sudden stop in intraregional credit movements due to the crisis. Prior to the crisis, easy availability of all kinds of cross-border financing had fuelled mounting imbalances within the EU, which have been a major cause of its present problems. Also of relevance has been the "balance sheet recession" that has deterred banks from lending both domestically and abroad, and which has been deeper and longer in Europe than in other developed economies where banks' recapitalization has progressed more rapidly (Koo, 2011).

Capital movements within Europe reproduce much of the "centre-periphery" pattern that many developing countries have endured in the past. In the lead-up to the crisis, integrated financial markets allowed commercial banks in the core European countries (France, Germany and the United Kingdom) to build up large cross-border exposures in the euro zone's "periphery" countries. During the subsequent years, however, European banks significantly scaled back their exposures to their counterparts in the periphery (chart 3.8). Faced with market volatility and uncertainty, banks in the core European countries began to reduce their claims on the periphery countries in 2008. This continued to follow a downward trend, accounting for a reduction of 51 per cent from the first quarter of 2008 to the fourth quarter of 2012 and it is likely to be much greater if other periphery countries are included.[11] The stock of German banks' claims on peripheral Europe fell by roughly 50 per cent from their pre-crisis peak until the end of 2012, from under €600 billion to €300 billion (BIS, 2013). At the level of individual European banks, outstanding loans to periphery banks declined by 30–40 per cent. For example, HSBC reduced its holdings in euro-zone periphery banks by 39.5 per cent in just four months, and Lloyds reduced them by 28 per cent over the same period (Goff and Jenkins, 2011).

The pattern of capital outflows differed among developed countries, which may be due to the different recipients of these outflows. The strong decline in capital flows into and out of euro-zone countries was mainly due to intraregional developments. Japanese capital outflows, on the other hand, were not strongly affected by the financial crisis, probably because they targeted mainly emerging market economies and developing countries in Asia that were not as severely impacted by the crisis. As for the United States, as a major financial centre, it has strong links with both other developed economies and emerging market economies. However, the major generators of capital movements are large banks whose main offices in various countries handle capital movements based on their interests, and they generate gross outflows towards third countries that may have originated from several different countries. Consequently, there is not necessarily a direct link between the macroeconomic and monetary conditions prevailing in a specific country and the value of its capital inflows and outflows. Those conditions may promote or hinder the incentives for international banks to increase their international capital flows, which may therefore originate from their branches in different countries.

Chart 3.7

NET CAPITAL INFLOWS AND OUTFLOWS, 2005–2012

(Billions of current dollars)

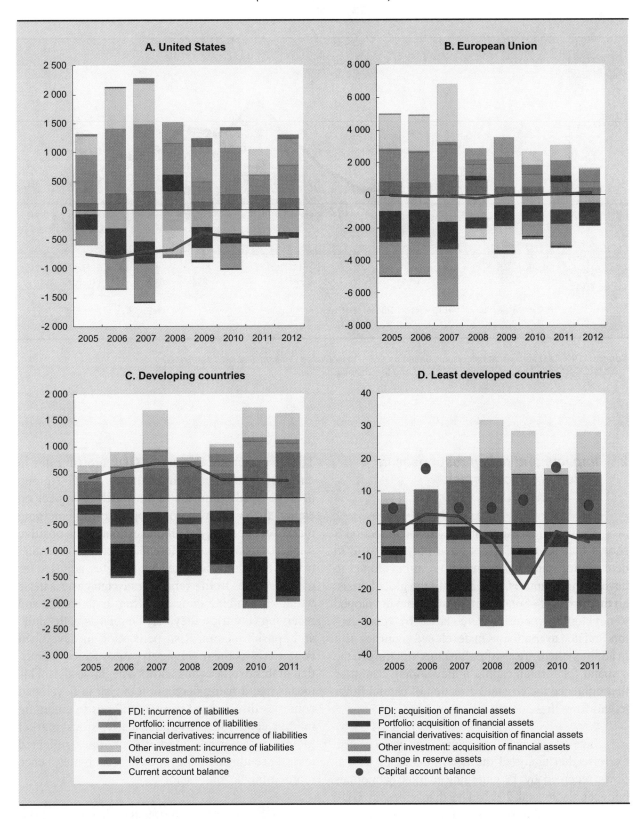

A. United States

B. European Union

C. Developing countries

D. Least developed countries

Legend:
- FDI: incurrence of liabilities
- Portfolio: incurrence of liabilities
- Financial derivatives: incurrence of liabilities
- Other investment: incurrence of liabilities
- Net errors and omissions
- Current account balance
- FDI: acquisition of financial assets
- Portfolio: acquisition of financial assets
- Financial derivatives: acquisition of financial assets
- Other investment: acquisition of financial assets
- Change in reserve assets
- Capital account balance

Source: UNCTAD secretariat calculations, based on IMF, *Balance of Payments Statistics* database.
Note: Data were available for only 67 developing countries (excluding LDCs) and for 28 LDCs.

Chart 3.8

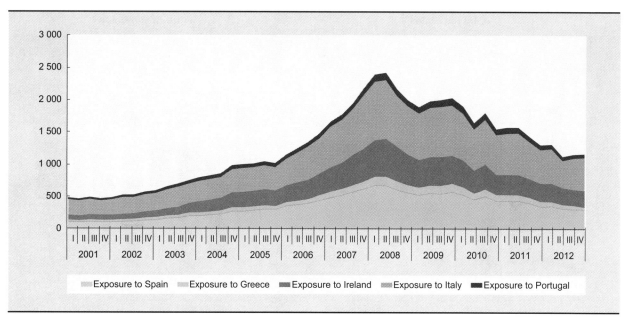

EUROPEAN UNION: CORE COUNTRIES' COMMERCIAL BANK EXPOSURE TO PERIPHERY COUNTRIES, 2001–2012

(Billions of dollars)

Source: UNCTAD secretariat calculation, based on BIS, *Consolidated Banking Statistics* database.
  Note: Core countries are France, Germany and the United Kingdom.

2. Impacts and policy responses in developing economies

The historical experience discussed in section B shows that several factors have played a role in determining capital movements from developed to developing countries. At least until the global crisis, all the waves of strong capital flows from developed to developing countries were started by "push factors" related to conditions in developed countries. But in addition there are also "pull factors" relating to the demand for foreign capital in developing countries that influence the size and direction of capital flows to and from these countries.

Box 3.1 presents the results of an econometric exercise that analysed the determinants of capital flows received by 19 emerging market economies between 1996 and 2012. The disparities in GDP growth rates and in returns on financial investments appear to be significant explanatory variables.

The first indicates that faster GDP growth rates in emerging market economies than in the G-7 group of developed countries had a positive impact on capital flows from the developed to the emerging market economies; the second estimates the positive impact of interest rate differentials between emerging market economies and the United States, adjusted for gains or losses from exchange rate changes. As these variables combine indicators from both source and receiving countries, they may be seen as both "pull" and "push" factors. Risk perception in developed countries was the main purely "push factor" identified in this exercise, and shows a negative sign. This means that a rising perception of risk in developed countries discouraged capital outflows to emerging market economies. Symmetrically, stock market indices in emerging market economies reflected investor sentiment in the receiving economies, hence representing a "pull factor".

All these factors appear to have had a significant impact on capital flows. However, different factors may also have had opposite effects simultaneously, as seems to have been the case during most of 2011 and 2012, and also in the first half of 2013. Some push factors (particularly monetary conditions) in developed countries appear to have had a positive impact on capital outflows to emerging market economies, while other push factors, such as an increase in perception of financial risk discouraged such movements. This may explain the considerable volatility of these capital flows, and uncertainty about a possible new big wave of capital inflows to emerging market economies similar to that of 2003–2007.

While the occurrence of new waves of capital outflows depends to a large extent on circumstances in the developed countries, the impact it can have on developing countries largely depends on the economic situation and government policies in the latter. In that respect, there were some unique features in the most recent crisis that can provide valuable lessons for the future. Unlike previous financial crises, a sudden stop of capital inflows did not generally translate into balance-of-payments problems or domestic financial crises, the main exceptions being a number of Central and East European countries (as mentioned above). Consequently, fiscal policy could be used for supporting the real economy rather than bailing out the banking system, leading to a rapid recovery of GDP growth, although not to pre-crisis rates.

The impact of the financial shocks on developing countries depended critically on their pre-crisis situation. External balances played a major role: historically, capital reversals had a greater adverse impact on countries already running large current account deficits, as they were forced to suddenly undertake recessionary adjustments when they could no longer finance external imbalances. Hence, one reason for the relative resilience of emerging market economies is that, in general, they were not running current account deficits, at least not on the same scale as occurred during previous surges of foreign capital inflows. Several countries, including China, even had "twin surpluses" – an unusual situation of surpluses in both the current and the financial account – the counterpart of which was a strong accumulation of official foreign currency reserves and, in some cases, a net repayment of external debt. Some of the reasons for the healthy current accounts of most emerging market economies before the crisis were favourable terms of trade for commodity exporters and/or an increase in export volumes owing to strong demand

from developed countries. These favourable factors had not existed in previous "waves" of capital flows. Another factor explaining the relative resilience of the emerging market economies was that in many of them the authorities had been able to prevent excessive currency appreciation through intervention in the foreign exchange market or through some form of capital account management. These measures helped them avoid, or at least contain, an appreciation of their real exchange rate. Other countries, such as Brazil, Chile, China and the Russian Federation, though less successful in this regard, had rather undervalued currencies (from a historical perspective) at the time their currencies began to appreciate (around 2004–2005) (chart 3.9).

The lower vulnerability of emerging market economies to financial shocks also resulted from the fact that many of them had already experienced financial crises between the mid-1990s and the early 2000s, which had led to a significant contraction of outstanding bank loans to the private sector (chart 3.10). Consequently, in the years following those crises many banks were unwilling or unable to increase their credit operations as they sought to consolidate their balance sheets. At the same time, firms and households restrained their demand for credit. This explains why capital inflows did not have a strong impact on domestic credit expansion in several of those countries that had been hit at the end of the "second wave" of capital inflows in the late 1990s, such as Argentina, Indonesia, Malaysia, Mexico, the Philippines and Thailand. In other countries, such as Brazil, the Russian Federation, Turkey and Ukraine, which had also experienced financial crises earlier, but had again received massive capital inflows in the years preceding the 2008–2009 global crisis, domestic credit expanded rapidly.

In LDCs as a group, financial plus capital inflows accounted for about 6 per cent of GDP in 2010–2011, a level similar to that of other developing countries. Most of the inflows were in the form of FDI and official development assistance (ODA) in the capital account, which represented rather stable capital. In addition, the LDCs have been able to accumulate reserves for several years in a row and reduce their current account deficit to about 1 per cent of GDP (chart 3.7). However, the situation varies considerably among these countries, with oil-exporting LDCs posting current account surpluses

Box 3.1

CAPITAL INFLOWS INTO EMERGING MARKET ECONOMIES:
SOME ECONOMETRIC RELATIONSHIPS

This box presents the results of an econometric exercise that analysed the determinants of capital inflows received by 19 emerging market economies between 1996 and 2012.

The dependent variable is capital inflows, as measured by net capital inflows as a percentage of GDP.

The retained explanatory variables are:

• The differential between the real GDP growth of the emerging market economies and the G7 GDP growth rate (G-DIFF). A positive differential indicates that the emerging market economies grew faster than the developed economies, whereas a negative differential indicates the opposite.

• The national stock exchange indices (NSEI) measures the equity market performance of the companies covered by the index. A change in the index represents changes in investors' expectations of the yields and risks.

• The Chicago Board Options Exchange Spx Volatility Index (VIX) measures the expected stock market volatility over the next 30-day period from the prices of the S&P 500 index options. The VIX is quoted in percentage points, and higher values indicate that investors expected the value of the S&P 500 to fluctuate wildly over the next 30 days.

• The emerging markets investment returns (EMIR) represent the differential between the interest rates of emerging markets and the United States at the beginning of the quarter, adjusted by the ex-post appreciation rate of the corresponding emerging market currency. It corresponds to what a foreign investor can obtain by borrowing in a currency at a low interest rate and investing in domestic assets that give a higher interest rate, corrected by the exchange rate appreciation.

The data

The capital inflows data for these estimations covered 19 emerging market economies: Argentina, Brazil, Chile, China, Colombia, Ecuador, India, Indonesia, Malaysia, Mexico, Morocco, Peru, the Philippines, Poland, the Republic of Korea, Romania, Singapore, South Africa, Thailand and Uruguay. Quarterly data from the first quarter of 1996 to the fourth quarter of 2012 were extracted from the IMF Balance of Payments database and complemented by national sources.

Quarterly real GDP data were taken from the IMF International Financial Statistics and national sources. They were seasonally adjusted using the census X12 method. Data for the remaining variables were taken from the Bloomberg database, the IMF's International Financial Statistics and national sources.

Results

The table below shows the regression results based on panel data. The panel data model with fixed effects was estimated using feasible generalized least squares (GLS) along with robust standard errors.

Column (1) shows that for the full period the four explanatory variables were statistically significant for explaining capital inflows in emerging markets. More specifically, the results indicate that a wider differential growth in GDP, an increase in the stock exchange market index of emerging market economies and an increase in the investment return differential had a positive impact on capital inflows into emerging

Box 3.1 *(concluded)*

market economies. Conversely, a higher degree of investor risk aversion (as measured by the VIX index) was associated with lower capital inflows in emerging market economies.

Recursive coefficient estimates were used to evaluate stability of the coefficients. Results show changes in the coefficients across time, indicating that there was a break around 2005. Therefore the full period was separated into two sub-periods: 1996–2005 (first quarter) and 2005–2012. The regression results are presented in columns (2) and (3). They show that, except for the volatility of the S&P 500 index, the impact of the explanatory variables was much larger in the period after 2005 than in the earlier period. Even the GDP growth differential is not meaningful for the 1996–2005 period. These results are consistent with the observation that carry trade strategies of investors contributed to capital inflows into emerging market economies during the period of low interest rates in the United States. The coefficients of the other two variables were found to remain stable.

Short-term capital inflows (i.e. the difference between net capital inflows and net inward FDI) were also regressed based on the four explanatory variables. For the full period (column 4), as expected, the impact of investment returns on short-term capital inflows was larger than that on total capital inflows, whereas the other three variables showed lower coefficients. Columns (5) and (6) show results for the two sub-periods. They present similar patterns to those observed for total capital inflows: the impacts of the GDP growth differential, emerging market stock market indexes and investment returns were much greater in the period 2005–2012 than in the period 1996–2005.

REGRESSION RESULTS FOR EMERGING MARKET ECONOMIES, 1996–2012

(Dependent variable: capital inflows as a percentage of GDP)

Period	Capital Inflows			Capital Inflows (excl. FDI)		
	(1) 1996–2012	*(2)* 1996–2005	*(3)* 2005–2012	*(4)* 1996–2012	*(5)* 1996–2005	*(6)* 2005–2012
Pull factors						
Ln(NSEI) (+)	1.704***	1.068***	3.421***	1.272***	0.800***	3.117***
Push factors						
VIX (-)	-0.115***	-0.097***	-0.111***	-0.094***	-0.080***	-0.090***
Combination of both factors						
G-DIFF (+)	0.135***	0.050	0.321***	0.110***	0.069**	0.263***
EMIR (+)	0.183**	0.099**	0.250***	0.204***	0.129**	0.277***
Number of observations	68	37	32	68	37	32
Number of countries	19	18	19	19	18	19
Total pool (unbalanced observations)	1 066	525	559	1 066	525	559
R-squared	0.445	0.447	0.509	0.336	0.326	0.416
F-test	33.096***	19.389***	25.302***	23.94***	11.572***	17.347***
Durbin-Watson	1.442	1.533	1.740	1.465	1.616	1.710
F-test on fixed effects	31.010***	19.038***	25.201***	15.938***	9.264***	15.947***
R-squared (without fixed effects)	0.148	0.092	0.094	0.153	0.115	0.103

Note: Estimation used Generalized Least Squares with cross-section weights and was based on panel data and quarterly data.

  *** Significant at 1 per cent.
   ** Significant at 5 per cent.
    * Significant at 10 per cent.

Chart 3.9

REAL EFFECTIVE EXCHANGE RATES (REER), SELECTED COUNTRIES, 1990–2012

(Index numbers, average for 1990–1995 = 100)

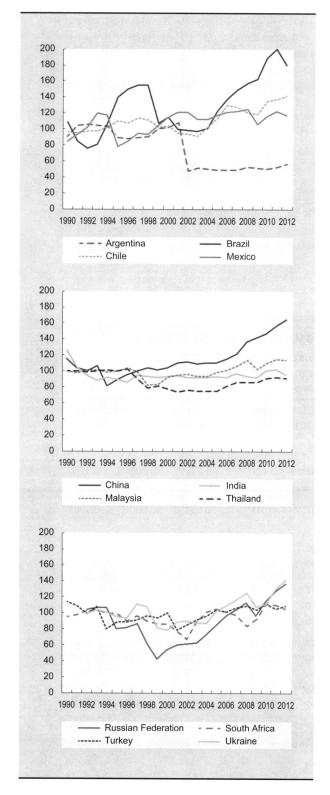

and non-oil exporters relying on foreign capital for financing important current account and fiscal deficits (UNCTAD, 2012).

Foreign reserve accumulation and improved debt management have been two effective strategies adopted by developing countries to shield themselves from the volatility of capital flows and international financial shocks. During the 2000s several developing countries accumulated large external reserves through market intervention in order to avoid currency appreciation arising from capital inflows, and as a self-insurance strategy against the risk of sudden stops and liquidity crises. Foreign exchange accumulation in pre-crisis times enabled developing countries to withstand adverse consequences of capital outflows in the months following the collapse of Lehman Brothers. Contrasting with many of those countries' responses to financial crises in the late 1990s, this time they did not defend fixed exchange parities at any cost by adopting tight monetary and fiscal policies; rather, they allowed their currencies to depreciate, with central banks selling part of their international reserves in order to avoid an uncontrolled depreciation. This reflected pragmatic and flexible approaches to exchange rate policies, which preferred intermediary regimes rather than "corner solutions" (i.e. free floating or irrevocably pegged exchange rates). It gave them more room for manoeuvre in handling the financial crisis and for implementing countercyclical policies in response to the global recession. It also showed that, in the absence of an international lender of last resort, foreign reserves offer a natural protection against financial market shocks.

The greater resilience of several developing and emerging market economies to adverse financial events was also due to their lower levels of external debt and its more favourable currency composition compared with earlier episodes. Prior to the global financial crisis, most of these countries had managed to sharply reduce their average debt ratios and to develop or expand domestic markets for the issuance of debt instruments denominated in local currencies. A greater reliance on domestic capital markets for the financing of public expenditure helps developing countries to reduce their vulnerability to lending booms and exchange-rate effects generated by surges of capital inflows followed by sudden stops and reversals of such flows. Although it does not solve the eventual problem of a foreign exchange

Chart 3.10

BANK CLAIMS ON THE PRIVATE SECTOR, SELECTED COUNTRIES, 1990–2012

(Per cent of GDP)

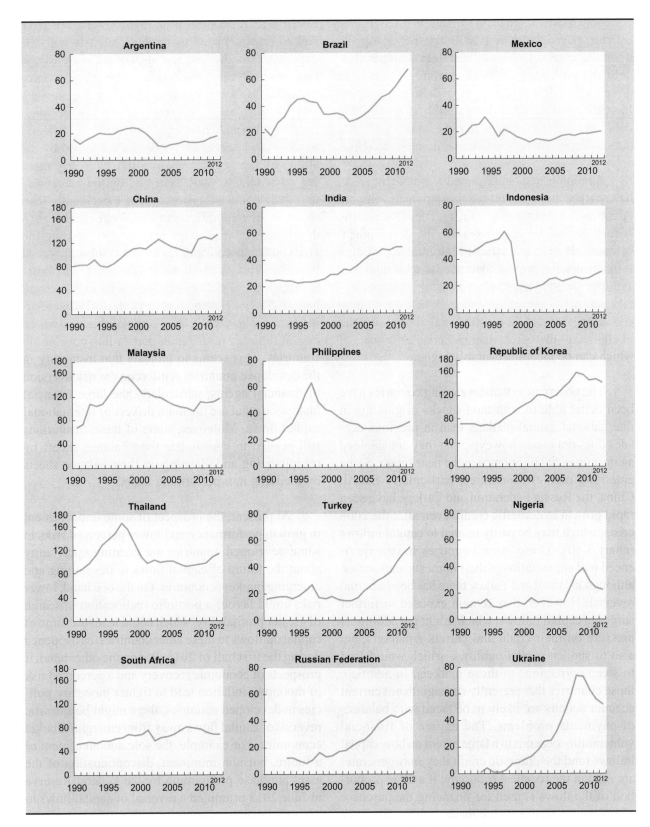

Source: UNCTAD secretariat calculations, based on IMF, *International Financial Statistics* database.

shortage, it should be the first option for financing expenditure in domestic currency. Debt denominated in local currency also increases policy space because it allows external shocks, such as sudden capital outflows, a rise in global interest rates or the widening of sovereign yield spreads, to be countered by currency devaluations without increasing the domestic currency value of that debt. Furthermore, debt denominated in local currency allows the government a last-resort option of debt monetization in a time of crisis. The sole possibility of monetizing debt dramatically reduces the insolvency risk, and consequently lowers the risk premium on the debt.

Summing up, policies aimed at minimizing risks have played an important role in helping developing countries ride out the global crisis. These include the accumulation of foreign reserves, the development of domestic debt markets and the issuance of debt instruments that provide insurance against domestic and external shocks. Although such insurance policies may entail some costs,[12] they reduce developing countries' vulnerability to financial shocks and the likelihood of disruptive financial crises, the costs of which can be incommensurably higher.

The observation that developing countries have been better able to withstand shocks originating in international capital markets than in previous decades does not mean, however, that they are shielded against financial turbulence in the near future. Some emerging market economies, particularly Brazil, China, the Russia Federation and Turkey, have seen rapid growth in domestic credit, even after the 2008 crisis, which may be partly related to capital inflows (chart 3.10). These same countries have experienced real appreciation of their domestic currencies, although in Brazil and Turkey there has been a partial reversal. However, they remain exposed to further surges in capital inflows, which might put additional pressure on their credit and currency markets, but also to sudden capital outflows, which would lead to steep corrections in those markets. In addition, those countries that presently run significant current account deficits are likely to be faced with balance-of-payments problems. The degree of financial vulnerability depends to a large extent on how capital inflows (and the domestic credit they may generate) are used in the recipient economy: if a large proportion of the flows is used for financing the purchase of real estate, leading to a housing bubble, there is a risk of greater financial fragility than if it is used for productive investment.

The instability of capital movements to developing countries since the crisis, with a temporary return to their previous peak in the first half of 2011 and a subsequent fall thereafter, contrasts with the experience of the last few decades. Previously, it took several years after a crisis before a new wave of capital flows to developing countries commenced, and it would last for several years before receding. Investors driven to developing countries in 2010 and most of 2011 seem to have been encouraged by the ability of these countries to resume their very rapid pre-crisis GDP growth rates and by the perception that their financial systems were more stable than those of developed countries. However, by then developed countries were also recovering from the crisis, and consequently investments there appeared less risky. But, as paradoxical as it may seem, worsening prospects in developed countries in the second half of 2011, including higher perceived risks relating to the sovereign debt of some of them, curtailed capital flows towards better performing developing countries. This seems to indicate that instability in the developed countries reinforced the risk aversion of financial agents, particularly the large financial institutions that are the main drivers of international capital flows. Moreover, some of these institutions still needed to consolidate their balance sheets by recapitalizing and cleaning up their balance sheets by shedding non-performing loans.

At present, the prospect of some improvement in growth performance and lower perceived risks in some developed countries are creating uncertainty about the future of capital flows to developing and emerging market economies. On the one hand, lower risks could favour a portfolio reallocation in search of greater profitability, which could lead to a surge of capital outflows to these latter countries, as happened during the first half of 2013. But on the other hand, if prospects of economic recovery and a perceived risk of mounting inflation lead to tighter monetary policies in developed countries, there might be a drastic reversal of capital flows away from emerging market economies. For example, the sole announcement of a future, but non-imminent, discontinuation of the asset purchase programme by the Federal Reserve in June 2013 prompted a reversal of capital flows to emerging market economies.

In conclusion, it is necessary to exercise caution with regard to cross-border capital flows, especially in a climate of high uncertainty, when sentiments more than facts tend to drive capital movements, potentially leading to self-fulfilling prophecies. Developing countries should adopt precautionary measures, as discussed in the next section, bearing in mind that "the seeds of emerging market crises are sown in the build-up phase, as inflows dwarf the absorptive capacity of recipient countries' capital markets" (Haldane, 2011: 2).

D. Lessons and policy recommendations

1. The role and impact of financial markets: a reassessment

(a) Financial instability

In his *History of Economic Analysis*, Schumpeter observed: "People may be perfectly familiar with a phenomenon for ages and even discuss it frequently without realizing its true significance and without admitting it into their general scheme of thought" (Schumpeter, 1954: 1081). He made this remark in the chapter on money, credit and cycles. Indeed, this is the area where the gap between conventional theory – based on the hypothesis of efficiency, rationality, neutrality and self-regulating market mechanisms – and actual experience is the most evident. The present crisis is a new reminder of the inadequacy of that theoretical framework. This time the message seems to be stronger, because at the epicentre of the crisis are the most sophisticated and "deep" financial systems of developed countries. Thus, financial dysfunction can no longer be attributed to underdeveloped financial institutions or governance shortcomings, which were commonly considered to be the cause of the repeated financial crises in developing and transition economies in the 1980s and 1990s. There is now increasing recognition of the need to reintroduce the notion of financial instability in the theoretical framework (Borio, 2013; Blanchard, 2013).

One essential lesson of the crisis relates to the assumed self-correcting mechanisms of financial markets and their supposed stabilizing role for the entire economy. Historically, repeated financial crises have followed fairly similar patterns, regardless of where and when they have occurred, which suggests that their cause lies in the very nature of finance. External shocks and occasional mismanagement may accentuate financial vulnerability or trigger a financial crash, but they do not by themselves destabilize what are considered intrinsically stable markets (Kindleberger, 1978; Galbraith, 1994; Reinhart and Rogoff, 2009). Rather, recurrent financial instability results from the fact that financial markets do not function like goods markets, where suppliers and purchasers are clearly distinct and where some material factors (e.g. productivity, costs and stocks) set limits to price movements. In financial markets, such limits are much scarcer or simply do not exist (Aglietta and Brand, 2013; Wicksell, 1935). Unlike in other markets, most agents can be buyers as well as sellers in financial markets. This may lead to "manias", when most investors anticipate price increases and buyers outnumber sellers, followed by "panics", when prices are expected to fall and buyers disappear from the market. In times of "euphoria", strong expectations of price appreciation will drive up demand for some financial assets, which in turn will increase the prices of those assets, thereby generating (at least for some time) a self-fulfilling prophecy.

Consequently, on financial markets, unlike other markets, rising prices encourage – rather than discourage – demand for financial assets, and the opposite is true when demand is falling, thus leading to over-shooting. Investors can maximize their gains by incurring debt: when the expected gains are higher than the cost of the debt, higher leveraging increases the ratio of profits to capital. If borrowers are able to provide collateral in the form of financial assets that are rising in price, lenders will be willing to meet their demand for credit. And as that credit is partly used for buying more financial assets, their prices will continue to increase, thereby feeding back the whole process and inflating a speculative bubble. In other words, there is a close correlation between credit supply and demand: they both grow in parallel during expansionary phases and validate the increase in asset prices, with no endogenous adjustment forces in the financial markets to stop the process (Aglietta and Brand, 2013). What eventually leads from manias to panics is anecdotal: at some point a number of financial investors and banks change their perception of risk, and the ensuing herd behaviour makes the financial markets abruptly turn from bullish to bearish. The downward phase is normally more abrupt and spectacular than the upward phase, although equally irrational. Financial crises are thus rooted in the euphoria phase.

The perception that financial markets are inherently unstable and potentially irrational challenges the orthodox view that they are essentially not only stable and efficient themselves, but also help to stabilize the economy as a whole. In that view, access to credit is supposed to smooth expenditure, as non-financial agents can borrow during bad times and repay their debts during good times. Financial markets are therefore seen as playing a countercyclical role. In addition, it is argued that financial markets help "discipline" policymakers, as they will react against "market unfriendly" policies that might undermine economic stability. Therefore, so the argument goes, policymakers should not regulate intrinsically stable financial markets beyond some basic microeconomic precautionary rules (such as capital ratios); instead, the markets should regulate policymakers. However, actual experiences, some of which have been reviewed in this chapter, show that, on the contrary, financial markets have a strong procyclical bias, and in many countries they have encouraged, rather than restrained, unsustainable macroeconomic policies.

(b) International capital flows

The divergence between these two views is particularly sharp with respect to cross-border capital

flows (Brunnermeier et al., 2012). For many years, the prevalent view considered almost any kind of foreign capital flows to developing countries as beneficial. They were seen as constituting "foreign savings" that would complement national savings of the recipient countries and lead to higher rates of investment there.

This view has been challenged on both a theoretical and empirical level. Theoretically, a pre-existing stock of savings is not a precondition for investment, according to the alternative (Keynesian/ Schumpeterian) view. Investment can be financed through bank credit, and savings are an endogenous variable resulting from the income generated in the economic process (see *TDR 2008* chap. III and IV; Dullien, 2009). In other words, as the causality runs from investment to (ex-post) savings, larger flows of foreign capital do not automatically increase investment. This conceptual view is supported by the evidence of huge capital inflows coexisting with stagnating investment rates (e.g. Africa and Latin America in the 1990s) and substantial increases in fixed investment, despite strong outflows or negative "foreign savings" (e.g. Argentina and China in the 2000s). Moreover, it cannot be assumed that all foreign capital finances investment in productive sectors. It is not because they are called "foreign savings", and that "savings equals investment", that capital inflows will automatically increase domestic investment. Even FDI does not necessarily consist of real investment, since some of those flows include mergers and acquisitions – including privatizations – and credits from headquarters to affiliates of transnational corporations (TNCs).

As noted earlier, experience with international capital flows shows that they repeatedly affected economic stability: they led to excessive expansion of domestic credit and generated bubbles in equity, real estate and other financial markets; they also caused an appreciation of the domestic currency, reduced the competitiveness of domestic producers in international markets, boosted demand for imported goods and services, and generated or increased the current account deficit.[13] Of course, there are also examples of capital inflows financing higher investment rates, either directly, as with greenfield investments, or indirectly through loans effectively used for fixed capital formation and/or for financing imports of capital goods. Therefore, what matters for developing countries is not simply access to external financing, but also a degree of control over how that financing is used. Countries need to be selective in terms of the quantity, composition and their use of foreign capital.

(c) Money, credit and banks

The fact that savings are not a prerequisite for higher fixed capital formation leads to the conclusion that the provision of credit (more specifically bank credit), rather than money, should be the focus of the analysis (Stiglitz, 2013). Credit expansion creates deposits, and consequently money, and not the other way around (Schumpeter, 1954: 1079–1080). This contrasts with the monetarist tradition that assumes that "high-powered money" issued by central banks determines the amount of credit and other monetary aggregates – an assumption that has been invalidated by recent experience, which shows how massive money creation by a central bank can have little, if any, impact in terms of increasing credit to the private sector. More importantly, by focusing excessively on the quantity of money, economists and monetary authorities have given less importance to how it should be utilized. Money is not neutral, in particular because it is not distributed evenly among all economic actors when it is created. Oversimplified monetarist views of monetary creation miss this essential point, and yet it is central to the writings of Cantillon, Wicksell and Schumpeter, for instance.

The channel through which supplementary purchasing power is introduced in an economy, the kinds of agents that receive it and how it is utilized have an impact on the amount and composition of aggregate demand (i.e. credit has different effects depending on whether it is used for consumption, investment, imports or exports) and on the sectoral structure of an economy (i.e. the relative importance of agriculture, manufactures and services). They also have an impact on economic power; for example, credit may concentrate property by financing the rich or reduce its concentration by supporting micro-, small- and medium-sized firms. Banks are key mechanisms through which this purchasing power is introduced in an economy. In order to perform efficiently, they must discriminate between good and bad projects, and reliable and unreliable borrowers, instead of behaving like passive intermediaries following mechanical protocols, or losing interest in their borrowers after having securitized their loans and transferred the risk to another entity.

Shifting attention from money to credit also implies making policymakers responsible not only for monetary stability but also for financial stability. The latest crisis has revealed that monetary stability, in the sense of price stability, can coexist with severe financial instability. Even worse, in some cases monetary stability has increased financial instability. In the euro zone, for example, the elimination of exchange rate risk and the prevalence of low inflation favoured large capital flows from banks in the core countries of the common currency area to countries in the periphery, and there was a virtual disappearance of interest rate differentials between these two sets of countries. However, those capital flows were not used for spurring competitiveness and production capacities: instead, they fed asset bubbles and increased current account deficits. This amplified intraregional disparities, rather than reducing them, and led to the difficult situation in which Europe finds itself today. This shows that, importantly, it was not the amount of money creation or the overall availability of financial resources, but who received those resources and how they were used, that mattered. Monetary stability based on a fixed nominal exchange rate led to similar outcomes in many developing and transition economies in previous decades, particularly in Latin America and South-East Asia.[14]

2. Countering financial instability

Given that financial systems are prone to significant instability with system-wide implications, and that self-regulation and self-correcting mechanisms cannot be relied upon, monetary authorities and supervisory institutions need to assume greater responsibility for financial stability in developed, transition and developing countries alike. This involves macroprudential policies relating to international financial integration, which aim at addressing the potentially destabilizing effects of cross-border capital flows. At the national level, it also requires policy measures and institutional reforms that should avoid excessive leveraging without discouraging credit for productive investment. Indeed, proactive policies by central banks may be needed to spur investment and growth, and create conditions conducive to financial stability. Financial stability will not be sustained in the long run in an economy that does not grow and create jobs, because sooner or later banks will accumulate non-performing loans in their balance sheets. There is also a need to reconsider how the financial sector is organized, such as separating commercial banking and investment banking, and extending transparency requirements, regulations and taxation to cover "shadow banking" and offshore centres as well. Finally, reform of the macroeconomic framework is essential, as the existing framework has contributed significantly to the generation of unsustainable financial processes.

(a) Exchange rates and capital account management

The potentially positive role of foreign capital in economic development is undermined by the risk of it becoming a major source of instability. This highlights the problems arising from an international financial system in which a small number of national currencies of developed countries (particularly the United States dollar) are used as international money. In each international credit cycle, monetary policy in these countries has been determined by domestic considerations and goals, such as supporting domestic economic activity and easing financial distress in some cases, or controlling domestic inflation in others. Little or no consideration is given to the effects of these policies on the global economy through their impact on exchange rates and current account balances.

Moreover, often, "sudden-stop" episodes of capital inflows have had a negative impact on emerging market economies by triggering balance-of-payments crises, usually combined with banking and fiscal crises. And when such inflows have been too large to be productively absorbed in those countries, they have generated price distortions and macroeconomic imbalances, eventually leading to capital reversals and financial collapse. Thus, often, it is not only volatile capital movements to and from emerging markets, but also, and primarily, the magnitude of those movements vis-à-vis the recipient countries that have adversely affected their macro economy. This can lead to the "big fish small pond problem", as stressed in Haldane (2011): as big fish (i.e. large capital flows originating in developed countries) enter the small pond (the relatively modest financial markets of capital-importing emerging market economies) they can cause ripples right across the international monetary system, and never more so than in today's financially interconnected world.

The existing international monetary and financial system is not equipped with mechanisms that promote exchange rate stability, prevent large and persistent current account imbalances and ensure smooth and orderly adjustments to, and corrections of, disturbances. It has been unable to restrain destabilizing capital movements and organize an exchange rate system that would reasonably reflect economic fundamentals. These shortcomings have become ever more evident and damaging with the deepening of financial globalization and the increasing volume of cross-border capital flows.

In the present (non-)system, the burden of adjustments to global imbalances falls entirely on deficit countries that depend on external financial resources, and not on any of the major actors: big surplus economies do not need financing, and the country with the largest deficit issues the major international reserve currency. This introduces a recessionary bias into the system, because the less powerful deficit countries are forced to cut demand, while there is no obligation for surplus countries to increase demand.

The existing international financial arrangements have also failed to prevent the disorderly increase in short-term capital movements, which is a major factor contributing to economic instability. Countries wishing to avoid the procyclical and destabilizing impact of capital flows have to resort to unilateral measures, such as foreign-exchange market intervention or capital controls. Such measures have been relatively successful in curbing undesired capital movements or their impact on the domestic economy. However, an effective control of potentially destabilizing financial flows requires multilateral arrangements, which are also in the interest of countries from which such flows originate. The global financial crisis has shown that unregulated capital flows generate risk not only in recipient countries, but also in source countries, since solvency of the latters' banks may be threatened if they are involved in foreign countries' asset bubbles. Thus, financial supervision needs to be applied at both ends of capital movements.

Greater stability of external financing for developing countries is difficult – if not impossible – to achieve without broader reform of the international financial and monetary system. The experience of the financial and economic crisis has made it clear that weak international arrangements and institutions, and the absence of international rules and regulations in this area, carry high risks not only for developing countries but also for the most advanced developed countries. Yet the will for international cooperation to undertake the necessary reforms is still lacking. Under existing monetary and financial conditions, and in the absence of international reforms, developing and emerging market economies need to design national, and, where possible, regional strategies aimed at reducing their vulnerability to international financial shocks.

As long as there are no multilaterally agreed rules governing the exchange-rate system, the task of reducing the risks of currency misalignment and exchange rate volatility remains with the governments and monetary authorities of each country. These risks are likely to increase in the current global context of persistent growth disparities between the major reserve currency countries and emerging market economies, and could well be accentuated as the latter and other developing countries shift to a strategy that places greater emphasis than in the past on increased domestic demand as a driver of growth and development.

Following their experience of the high costs of adopting "corner solutions" for exchange rates (i.e. fully flexible or irrevocably pegged), most emerging market economies have turned towards a more pragmatic managed floating regime. This allows flexible intervention by central banks to avoid both excessive volatility and unsustainable real exchange rates resulting from speculative financial operations rather than from fundamentals.[15]

In addition, regional financial cooperation can support efforts to stabilize macroeconomic conditions. Since the 1960s, some regions have used certain mechanisms that make it possible to reduce dependence on foreign currency for regional trade, such as clearing payment systems and the use of domestic currencies for bilateral trade. Other institutions provide balance-of-payments financing without undesirable conditionalities attached. Some regional arrangements also facilitate the managing of exchange rates, for instance through credit (or swap) agreements among central banks or the pooling of reserves (e.g. the Latin American Reserves Fund (FLAR), the Arab Monetary Fund (AMF) and the Chiang Mai Initiative). As these regional institutions offer support without harsh conditionalities, they provide an effective tool for countercyclical policies.

Destabilizing effects and a procyclical bias caused by capital flows can also be prevented, or at least mitigated, by resorting to capital controls, which are permitted under the IMF Articles of Agreement. There is extensive experience with such controls in both developed and developing countries. They were the rule in the United States in the 1960s and in Europe until the 1980s. In the 1990s and 2000s, some emerging market economies (e.g. Chile and Colombia) sought to discourage short-term capital inflows through taxation or the imposition of non-remunerated deposits, while others imposed barriers on short-term capital outflows (e.g. Argentina and Malaysia). More recently, Brazil also introduced taxes on capital inflows. The use of capital controls is being increasingly accepted in international forums, although still with some reservations. For instance, the IMF has accepted that capital controls are legitimate instruments, but it suggests resorting to them only in situations when a balance-of-payments crisis is already evident and after all other measures (e.g. monetary and fiscal adjustment) have failed.[16] The problem with such an approach is that it does not recognize the macroprudential role that controls can play in preventing such a crisis in the first place.

(b) A broader mandate for central banks

To achieve the goal of financial stability, central banks and other economic authorities need to adopt a coordinated policy approach. Not only should the mandates of the former be broadened, but also the number and kinds of instruments they can use should be increased, including for macroprudential regulation and for keeping track of what is being financed in the economy. All this requires a reassessment of the idea that central banks must maintain their independence (Blanchard, 2013). The rationale for their independence was to keep them free from political pressures as they implemented their (supposedly) technical responsibility of controlling inflation. Even in cases where their mandate was limited to one single goal (monetary stability) with one single instrument (policy interest rates), their "technical" nature was debatable. With the progressive broadening of their mandate and their use of more instruments (already under way), they have assumed wider responsibilities in a comprehensive approach to macroeconomic and financial policy.

The need for reconsidering the role of central banks, and with it the concept of their "independence" for undertaking the sole task of ensuring stability of prices of goods and services, has never been more evident than during the latest financial crisis. The crisis obliged central banks to take more and more "unconventional" measures, which highlighted the gap between the theoretical basis for the concept of central bank independence and the need, derived from experience, to involve the monetary authorities in efforts to stabilize financial markets in the interests of the economy as a whole. The conventional view holds that the private financial sector is efficient, even to the extent of being able to ease the impact of shocks on the real economy. It excludes the possibility of mismanagement by financial institutions and markets on the assumption that they always have correct information about current and future economic developments, and that it is government mismanagement that leads to financial crises. The present crisis has turned that hypothesis upside down, as it was caused by the private sector. Central bank independence from government did not prevent the financial crisis, and the combined action of central banks and governments was indispensable for responding to the crisis, including bailing out institutions that were considered "too big to fail".

A further step forward would be to accept that central banks must play an active role in the implementation of a growth and development strategy. Monetary stability, in the sense of price stability, is insufficient to secure stable financial conditions for the real economy. Moreover, financial stability depends on the performance of the real sector of the economy, because, in severe crisis situations, banks have tended to accumulate non-performing loans and eventually fail. Thus, supporting economic growth should not be considered merely a supplementary responsibility of central banks; it constitutes the very basis of financial and monetary stability.

(c)   Reconsidering regulation of the financial system

Financial systems in developing countries require appropriate regulations aimed at ensuring that they serve the real economy and the development process.

Moreover, in seeking to achieve financial stability, the regulations should not hamper growth by unduly restricting credit. In particular, they should encourage long-term credit to finance productive investment. Indeed, there is a two-way relationship between financial stability and growth, in the sense that without financial stability it would be difficult to achieve growth; on the other hand, in a situation of economic stagnation, loans could very easily become non-performing, thus posing a risk to financial stability.

Several developed countries, having been severely affected by financial crises, are introducing or considering far-reaching changes in bank regulations. Some of these changes have been formulated by the Basel Committee on Banking Supervision (BCBS) through the Basel III rules, and others by the Financial Stability Board (FSB) as well as other bodies. Moreover, these new rules are being introduced or considered not only in developed countries, but also, to a large extent, they are shaping regulatory systems in developing and emerging market economies. For instance, Basel III capital standards have already been implemented in 11 (out of 28) Basel Committee member jurisdictions, seven of which are emerging market economies (China, Hong Kong (China), India, Mexico, Saudi Arabia, Singapore and South Africa), with Argentina, Brazil and the Russian Federation planning to implement them by the end of 2013 (BIS, 2013).

Capital requirements are the main aspect of the strengthened rules. Proposals negotiated at Basel III aim to revise and extend the existing Basel I and II capital requirements and establish a simple leverage ratio between assets and capital.[17] Microprudential regulations of this kind are to be supplemented with an additional macroprudential overlay, such as the use of capital buffers, so that in the event of the prices of their assets falling, banks will not find themselves in non-compliance with capital requirements and having to demand extra capital when credit growth develops too rapidly. Also, for the first time, Basel rules will include liquidity requirements, but there is still a debate about their precise definition as banks are not in agreement over these new requirements.

The main idea behind these refurbished and strengthened rules is to reduce risks of bank failure and the need for public bailouts by containing excessive leveraging. They also seek to deter banks from funding medium- and long-term lending by resorting to the wholesale market for very short-term borrowing, rather than using a stable deposit base.

Critics argue that Basel III regulations are still procyclical, and remain geared to evaluating risk as estimated by the markets, which have repeatedly been seen to fail in this most important task. They are also considered to be overly complex, even for developed countries, and probably more so for developing countries. In addition, very little progress has been made concerning the "too-big-to-fail" institutions or in coping with the "shadow banking" part of the financial system. With regard to the latter, there is a complex debate about how to exercise greater supervision of derivative markets' over-the-counter (OTC) operations, including requiring public registration and clearing mechanisms.

Whether the regulatory capital framework of the Basel accords should be applied in developing countries is an open question. In fact, Basel accords, starting from Basel I in the late 1980s, were supposed to establish a level playing field for large internationally active institutions. For instance, in the United States, only a few institutions were supposedly required to follow those rules, while the rest of the system would continue to be regulated in the traditional way. From the point of view of the international financial system, there is no reason why banks from developing countries should follow the same rules as large international banks. Progressively, however, Basel rules have become a general standard: every country is supposed to apply them, even if none of their banks is a major active international player. More specifically, Financial Sector Assessment Programs (FSAPs) conducted jointly by the IMF and the World Bank are supposed to check whether the countries are following Basel rules. In addition, the supposition is that the developing countries belonging to the G20 – and therefore automatically to the Financial Stability Board[18] – should set an example to other developing countries by promptly applying whatever is decided in those various committees, even if they do not exercise any formal authority on countries.

In fact, in many developing countries that have experienced serious banking crises since the 1980s, capital and liquidity requirements have been much higher than those prescribed by Basel rules (in what used to be called Basel+ rules). Experience in the application of those rules indicates that there was a generalized restriction on lending, in particular to small and medium-sized enterprises.

The recent financial crisis has also led to new thinking about the structure of banking. One main feature of the proposed reforms is the separation of commercial from investment banking activities. The idea is to insulate retail banking that is vital for the normal functioning of the economy (as it receives deposits and savings, delivers loans and manages payment mechanisms) from riskier activities related to securities trading (Gambacorta and Van Rixtel, 2013). In particular, the non-deposit-taking side will not have access to lender-of-last-resort facilities from the central bank. Hence, separating banking activities may also help to improve transparency in the financial sector, which would facilitate market discipline and supervision, and – ultimately – support efforts to recover from the present crisis, while also reducing risks of further crises.

Ongoing or proposed reforms are less radical than their notorious predecessor, the Glass-Steagall Act, adopted in 1933 in response to an even larger banking crisis. In the United States, the Volcker Rule prohibits proprietary trading by banks operating in the country, and it also restricts private equity activity. However, although the rule became law in 2012, banks were given two years to comply. In the United Kingdom, the Vickers Commission recommended placing a ring-fence around retail banking activities, separating them from the investment banking activities of financial institutions. Legislation is planned for 2015, and banks would have until 2019 to comply. In Europe, the Liikanen plan was announced in October 2012, which proposed that the investment banking activities of universal banks be placed in a separate entity from other banking activities, but there are no plans at present to legislate on these proposals.

The need to separate different banking activities is also closely related to concerns about bank size, in particular with the rise of very large universal banks that cover an extremely broad range of financial activities in many countries and jurisdictions. Hence, regulation seeking legal, financial and operational separation of different banking activities would help to avoid the eventuality of certain financial institutions growing so large and assuming such a diversity of activities that their performance becomes systemically important (Viñals et al., 2013). Developing countries, where financial systems are still in the process of taking shape and where there is considerable scope for an expansion of commercial banking activities may be well advised to draw lessons from the experience of the developed countries in this regard.

Other measures envisaged in developed countries, especially those aimed at improving banking governance and resolution in case of bank failure may also be of importance in developing countries. Such measures could possibly be easier to implement in countries whose banking systems are still relatively small but may expand as their economies grow. An important objective in this context is to reduce incentives for highly risky behaviour of market participants who can obtain large financial profits without having to bear the consequences of incurring losses. Resolution mechanisms must allow authorities to wind down bad banks, recapitalize institutions through public ownership, and force the bail-in of creditors that have become much more important than depositors in the funding of systemically important institutions. All this would help return banks to productive activities as quickly as possible, without having to use enormous amounts of scarce public revenue in bailout operations (Borio, 2012).[19]

In summary, these different categories of regulatory approaches reflect a welcome new political willingness to grapple with long-standing issues that stand in the way of sustainable economic recovery. However, their "one size fits all" approach is not necessarily the most appropriate for developing countries. A major limitation is that they tend to narrowly focus more on the stability of the financial system than on its efficiency in terms of serving the real economy. Yet this latter aspect is particularly important for developing countries, much more so than for developed countries. Much still remains to be done to help align the incentives of the financial sector more closely with the needs of productive investment, job creation and sustainable economic growth.

3. Orienting the financial sector towards serving the real economy

In order to support development strategies that give a greater role to domestic demand for driving growth, it is essential for developing countries to strengthen their domestic financial systems. They need to focus on the financial sector's key role in economic growth, which is the financing of fixed capital formation that boosts production and generates employment.

In most countries, investments in real productive capacity are financed primarily from retained profits (internal financing) or by resorting to bank credit (table 3.3). The observation that internal financing is the main source for the financing of investment highlights the importance of strengthening a profit-investment nexus. This is important not only because of the decisive role of rising demand for making additional investment in productive capacity profitable, as discussed in chapter II, but also because of the need to finance private investment. This runs counter to the conventional idea that higher household savings, and thus lower consumption, are preconditions for greater investments. Indeed, a policy that aims at increasing those savings as a means to raising the rate of investment, rather than viewing savings as resulting from higher investment, weakens demand and economic activity, with a negative impact on profits, which are a major source of investment finance.

Moreover, financing by banks can enable firms to accelerate their capital formation over and above what is possible from retained profits. For potential investors to borrow for this purpose, financing by banks must be available in sufficient amounts and at a cost that is commensurate with the expected profitability of the investment project. Again, aiming at increasing the availability of financing for investment by encouraging an increase in savings deposits in the banking system would be counterproductive, because higher interest rates also mean higher costs of bank financing for potential investors, in addition to the demand-reducing effect of higher household savings.

Therefore, a more promising approach to increase both the propensity to invest and the availability of financial resources for investment is to support demand, encourage the reinvestment of profits and facilitate access to long-term, low-cost bank loans. New loans do not require an increase in savings deposits; they can be made available through the central bank's provision of adequate liquidity to the banking system and by keeping the policy interest rate as low as possible.

In developing countries, since the financial systems are mainly bank-based, banking reform should be a priority. The following section describes

Table 3.3

SOURCES OF INVESTMENT FINANCE, SELECTED COUNTRY GROUPS, 2005–2012

	Number of countries	Number of firms	Internal finance	Bank finance	Trade credit	Equity or stock sales finance	Other
			(Per cent)				
All countries	136	70 781	68.4	17.2	4.8	3.8	5.7
Developed Europe	5	3 354	57.7	20.5	3.3	4.9	13.6
Emerging Europe	10	3 196	58.4	25.2	5.0	6.8	4.6
Africa	44	17 971	81.1	9.4	3.4	1.5	4.5
Latin America and the Caribbean	31	14 657	59.0	21.0	10.1	4.4	5.6
Developing Asia	24	20 477	67.1	20.3	2.8	2.8	7.0
Developing Oceania	5	619	53.3	25.8	3.2	9.0	8.7
Transition economies	17	10 507	69.4	15.6	4.3	7.4	3.3

Source: UNCTAD secretariat calculations, based on World Bank, *Enterprise Survey* database.
Note: Developed Europe comprises Germany, Greece, Ireland, Portugal and Spain. Emerging Europe comprises Bulgaria, Czech Republic, Estonia, Hungary, Latvia, Lithuania, Poland, Romania, Slovakia and Slovenia.

a broad range of bank-related policy instruments and institutions which would enable a more effective distribution of credit that supports real growth.

(a) Measures for orienting bank financing to serve the real economy

Various measures could be considered for orienting bank financing to support the real economy. To begin with, banks could be encouraged, or obliged, to undertake a more reasonable amount of maturity transformation operations (i.e. deliver long-term credits matched by short-term deposits). In the past, commercial banks in developing countries often preferred to grant mainly short-term personal loans or buy government securities because they considered the risks involved in maturity transformation to be too high. However, these risks may have been exaggerated, since, even during severe financial crises, withdrawals of deposits from banks never exceeded 25 per cent of their deposit base. A revised regulatory framework could include elements that encourage a different allocation of bank assets and credit portfolios, accompanied by requirements for provisioning and for adequate collateral to take into account the additional risks related to the longer maturity of a proportion of their assets. Moreover, public guarantees for commercial bank credit for the financing of private investment projects or their

co-financing with national development banks may encourage banks to provide more lending for such purposes. By reducing the credit default risk, such measures would also lower the risk premiums on such long-term investment loans. The resulting lower interest cost for investors would further reduce the probability of defaults, and thus reduce the likelihood of governments having to cover such losses under the guarantee scheme.

Central banks could support maturity transformation in their role as lenders of last resort (LLR) and by providing deposit insurance. The latter measure would reduce the risk of sudden withdrawals of deposits that could result in liquidity constraints for banks, while the former would address liquidity shortages, should they occur. These arrangements are of course not new: the LLR principle was proposed in the early nineteenth century and also advocated by Bagehot in 1873, while deposit insurance has been progressively implemented worldwide since the 1930s. But such arrangements have seldom succeeded in encouraging banks to provide a significant amount of long-term financing to the real economy. A more hands-on approach by the monetary authorities is therefore required.

Historically, central banks have used a wide variety of instruments to channel long-term finance in support of development objectives (Epstein, 2005), including direct financing of non-financial firms. For instance, before the First World War and in the inter-war period, the Bank of England supported different industrial sectors, including textiles, metallurgy, shipbuilding, aluminium, rayon and wood-pulp industries. Indeed, the Bank became heavily involved in some industries, taking equity stakes and participating directly in their management. In 1929, the Securities Management Trust was instituted as a holding company for managing the stakes acquired by the bank in various firms. Similarly, the Bank of Italy got involved in the financing and indirect management of different industrial firms (O'Connell, 2012).

Central bank and government intervention in credit allocation became widespread in the immediate post-war period in developed and developing countries alike. For example, France nationalized the main deposit banks and established the National Credit Council, which was in charge of allocating credit in accordance with national interests and priorities (Coupaye, 1978). Credit policy was partly implemented by a number of public, semi-public and specialized cooperative institutions, which financed agricultural activities and the development of rural infrastructure as well as regional and municipal investments, social housing and industrial and commercial investments in small and medium-sized enterprises (SMEs) at preferential rates. In addition, France's central bank influenced the lending decisions of the commercial banks through selective rediscounting at preferential rates, the conditional release of mandatory reserves, and the exemption of certain activities (e.g. export credits, medium-term loans for investment) from quantitative credit ceilings (*encadrement du crédit*) that were in place until 1986, as well as through a multitude of credit lines for specific uses at preferential rates. Other European countries, including Belgium, Germany, Italy, the Netherlands and the United Kingdom, also used similar instruments, not only to support some sectors and activities, but also to discourage credit-financed personal consumption, imports and inventory accumulation (Hodgman, 1973; O'Connell, 2012).

In several Asian and Latin American countries, the predominance of bank credit in firms' debt financing provided the basis for proactive credit policies aimed at influencing the allocation of bank credit and moderating the costs of interest. These policies played a decisive role in fostering the process of industrialization, especially between the 1950s and 1980s.

Specialized institutions, including national development banks and other State-owned banks, channelled long-term credit to selected industries, agriculture and housing. Credit distribution by commercial banks, some of which were State-owned,[20] was also subject to government policies, or central bank regulations. For instance, in Indonesia, Malaysia, the Republic of Korea, Thailand and Taiwan Province of China, loans to SMEs had to constitute a given share of banks' assets. In addition, central banks introduced differential reserve requirements, rediscounting and access to central bank loans at regulated interest rates in order to orient credit allocation. These schemes played a central role in the rapid industrialization of many countries. However, they did not always deliver the expected outcomes, and in several countries they were misused, as State-owned banks sometimes provided credit to other public entities for purposes that were not related to productive investment. As a result, non-performing loans burdened their balance sheets and undermined their lending capacities. On the other hand, it was the privatization of State-owned banks and deregulation of financial systems that paved the way for major financial crises in Latin America and East and South-East Asia.

In light of these different experiences, developing countries need to carefully weigh the pros and cons of the different systems when shaping or reforming their domestic financial sectors. They should also ensure that public and private financial activities are undertaken by institutions equipped with appropriate governance structures and that they operate in the interests of the economy and society as a whole.

At present, flaws in credit allocation by deregulated private banks and difficulties in reestablishing the supply of credit for the real sector in developed economies (despite expansionary monetary policies) have led to a renewed interest in credit policies. For instance, in July 2012 the Bank of England established a temporary Funding for Lending Scheme, with the goal of incentivizing banks and building societies to boost their lending to the country's real economy. Under this scheme, the Bank of England provides low-cost funding to banks for an extended period of time, and both the price and quantity of funding provided are linked to their lending performance (increased net lending to SMEs, for instance, gives them access to a greater amount of cheap funding) (Bank of England, 2013). The Bank of Japan had launched a similar initiative in 2010 (Bank of

Japan, 2010). In the same vein, several initiatives aim to increase lending by public institutions to SMEs. For instance, the German development bank (KfW Entwicklungsbank) is to lend €1 billion to the Spanish development bank (Instituto de Crédito Oficial, ICO), so that it can channel loans to SMEs in Spain at German lending rates. In addition, in June 2013 the European Council launched an Investment Plan with the support of the European Investment Bank, whose capital was increased by €10 billion. The plan envisages the provision of additional credit to provide SMEs with better access to finance and foster job creation, especially for the young (EIB, 2013).

However, these initiatives are frequently introduced as extraordinary measures for dealing with exceptional circumstances. There are strong arguments in favour of central bank and government intervention to influence the allocation of credit in normal times, especially in developing countries. Such credit should aim at strengthening the domestic forces of growth and reducing financial instability, since long-term loans for investment and innovation and loans to micro, small and medium-sized enterprises are extremely scarce even in good times (*TDR 2008*, chap. IV). Some recent reforms have sought to encourage this kind of intervention by the central banks, thereby reinforcing or restoring their historical developmental role.[21] In addition to the objectives of monetary and financial stability, central banks should complement other government efforts and policies aimed at economic development in general, with an emphasis on improving productivity and generating employment.

Such policies would mainly involve commercial banks rather than investment banks, as part of a "social contract" between the former and the central bank. According to such a contract, the central bank would provide deposit insurance and liquidity support if needed (as an LLR), while commercial banks would assume the task of maturity transformation following guidelines by central banks, in addition to providing lines of credit under certain conditions. This is an additional reason for differentiating between deposit-taking institutions and investment banks which intermediate between investors willing to run higher risks and non-financial companies demanding long-term finance, and which would not have access to LLR facilities and liability insurance.

Managing a banking system with development objectives is not a purely technical matter; it also involves political choices, and therefore calls into question the rationale for keeping a central bank independent of elected authorities. Strictly speaking, policy intervention aimed at securing monetary and financial stability is also political in nature, as illustrated by the way the crisis was managed. In the process, central banks had to distribute gains and losses, redistribute income and wealth, decide for or against bailouts and dictate rescue conditions, not only to private financial and non-financial agents, but also, as with the countries in the euro-zone periphery, to sovereign States. If it is accepted that the mandate of central banks should be broadened to include development objectives, the purely supposedly "technical" character of their activities becomes even more illusory. If the monetary authorities are to implement monetary, financial and credit policies as part of a development strategy, they need to coordinate their actions with the other economic authorities.

(b) Towards more diversified financial systems

Besides a growing awareness of the need to review the role of central banks and the structure of commercial banking, as discussed above, there is also a renewed interest in the scope and role of development banks. These typically State-owned banks can take deposits (although not as much as normal commercial banks), raise funds in capital markets and provide loans for projects that are intended to contribute to overall economic development. Historically, governments established development banks to provide financial services that private financial institutions were unable or unwilling to provide to the extent desired. Even today, despite decades of criticism of the public sector and a widespread belief that privatization of State-owned institutions would accelerate growth and raise productivity, a large number of development banks still exist. About 40 per cent of these were established between 1990 and 2011. More recently, new ones have been created in a number of developing and emerging market economies, including in Angola, Bulgaria, India, Oman and Thailand. In the United Kingdom, a Business Bank is in the process of being established, as well as a new "Green Bank" to finance environmental projects; in France a development bank was recently created and there are also plans for a new development bank in the United States. This indicates that governments still consider national development banks to be useful institutions for promoting economic growth and structural change (de Luna-Martínez and Vicente, 2012).

State-owned financial institutions are estimated to account for, on average, 25 per cent of the total assets of the world banking system and for 30 per cent of the total financial system of the EU. In Latin America, 56 public development banks distribute $700 billion a year – some 10 per cent of total credit – and hold assets amounting to 25 per cent of the region's GDP (IADB, 2013). One of the benefits of having a sizeable alternative source of credit creation and intermediation became clear during the latest crisis, as development banks played an important countercyclical role, increasing their lending portfolios just as many private banks were scaling back theirs. According to a recent World Bank survey of 90 development banks across developed and developing countries, between late 2007 and late 2009 these banks increased their loan portfolios by 36 per cent compared with an increase of just 10 per cent by private banks operating in the same countries (de Luna-Martínez and Vicente, 2012).

Because they add diversity to the financial system and have a broader range of objectives than the private banking system, development banks may also be seen once again – alongside more active central banks – as normal contributors to a healthy and robust financial system in good times as well as during crises.

For potential entrepreneurs seeking to pursue new and innovative activities, financing options are particularly scarce, because they constitute a credit risk that is especially difficult for ordinary banks to evaluate. This is why smaller, more specialized sources of finance also have an important role to play in the overall dynamics of the development process. Typical examples include publicly sponsored incubators that are mandated to finance activities which have the potential to enhance diversification and structural change but would not normally have access to private banking support. Research and development (R&D) activities or creative industries, for example, are often publicly supported in most developed countries.

Other non-bank-based solutions to the problems of accessing credit have also emerged in recent years. For example, new forms of finance have developed through the social media, such as crowd-sourcing loans and payment mechanisms that operate through peer-to-peer networks. Networks such as the New York-based Kickstarter, which has channelled over $600 million to thousands of projects over the last four years, or the United Kingdom's Lending Club, suggest that innovative new mechanisms are emerging where traditional financial markets are failing to deliver. Certainly, there are many historical examples of institutional solutions that were innovative once but are now considered mainstream, such as workplace-based credit unions or corporate structures of cooperatives. However, such models would not be appropriate for all enterprises, and must been seen as part of a diverse range of choices existing within a broader financial structure that serves a variety of needs.

Within this broad argument for a more diversified financial system made up of many different banking and financial institutions of different sizes, objectives and mandates, it is clear that today's paradigm of universal banking involving very big institutions needs to be reconsidered. This is not only because of the "too-big-to-fail" problem, but also because there is a need to facilitate access to credit for specific needs and to provide stability to the system by not allowing closely correlated portfolios to spread contagion. Even if much of the directed credit is still channelled through commercial banks (for instance, under a funding for lending scheme), a proactive policy for directing credit to productive uses may need to resort to a network of specialized institutions, including cooperative and development banks. Building (or restoring) such a financial structure clearly exceeds the immediate concern of credit scarcity in troubled times. In addition, the development of a financial structure that would facilitate the allocation of credit to the real sector and to productive investment would also help avoid some of the negative effects of foreign capital flows feeding bubbles and consumption booms. On the contrary, the economy would be able to profit from long-term capital inflows by channelling them to investment projects that require imports of capital goods.

E. Summary and conclusions

The adjustment of productive capacities to changes in the composition of aggregate demand is not just a matter of reallocating existing resources; in most developing and transition economies, it also requires accelerating the pace of capital accumulation. This necessitates the provision of reliable and low-cost finance to producers for productive investment through appropriate monetary and credit policies, as well as access to external sources of finance.

While many developing countries have had limited access to international capital markets, others have been recurrently affected by massive capital inflows followed by their sudden stops and reversals. Frequently, such inflows have not served to support long-term growth and productive investment. Moreover, their size and volatility have often tended to create macroeconomic and financial instability. Therefore, the extent to which financial resources contribute to growth and structural change depends on their composition, their allocation among different groups of users, and how they are used by the recipients.

The latest financial crisis, like previous ones, has shown that unregulated financial markets have a strong potential to misallocate resources and generate economic instability. Since private capital flows are inherently unstable and often unproductive, active intervention by economic authorities is indispensable for preventing destabilizing speculation and for channelling credit to productive investment. A cautious and selective approach towards cross-border capital flows, including pragmatic exchange-rate management and capital-account management, would reduce the vulnerability of developing and transition economies to external financial shocks and help prevent lending booms and busts. Such an approach could also include measures aimed at using foreign capital for development-enhancing purposes, especially for financing imports of essential intermediate and capital goods that are not yet produced domestically and that cannot be financed by current export earnings. This could be particularly important in many least developed countries with a view to increasing their overall productivity and economic diversification.

Perhaps more importantly, developing and transition economies must increasingly rely on domestic sources of finance. As retained profits constitute the most important source of finance for investment in real productive capacity, followed by bank credit, strengthening the profit-investment nexus and influencing the behaviour of the banking system in the way it allocates credit are of particular importance. The market mechanism alone cannot be relied upon to achieve this; a variety of fiscal and regulatory measures can also be used, as demonstrated by many successful industrializing countries.

Moreover, monetary policy alone is not sufficient to stimulate investment, as evidenced by the policy response to the ongoing financial and economic problems in developed countries. Monetary expansion in these countries has failed to increase bank lending to private firms for reviving investment in real productive capacity. This points to the need for a credit policy as well. Central banks could support maturity transformation in the banking system and encourage, or oblige, banks to provide more lending for the financing of productive investment. There is nothing radically new in such a policy. There are numerous examples from both developed and developing countries of central bank involvement in orienting credit through, for example, direct financing of non-financial firms, selective refinancing of commercial loans at preferential rates, and exempting certain types of bank lending from quantitative credit ceilings.

Credit policy can also be partly implemented by other public, semi-public and cooperative institutions for financing agricultural and industrial investment, in particular by SMEs, at preferential rates. National and regional development banks may provide loans and financial services that private financial institutions are unable or unwilling to provide. More generally, a network of specialized domestic institutions may be more effective in channelling credit for development-enhancing purposes than big universal banks. There is also the danger that these banks may eventually expand to an extent that they become not

only "too big to fail" but also "too big to manage" and "too big to regulate".

Thus, for supporting development and structural change what is needed is not only better regulation of the financial system aimed at achieving monetary and financial stability, but also a restructuring of the financial – particularly the banking – system to ensure that it serves the real economy better than in the past. Monetary and financial stability and sustained growth are complementary goals: without the first two, stable growth of investment, output and employment would be difficult to achieve, and without sustained growth, there is the risk that corporate failures and non-performing bank loans will undermine monetary and financial stability.

Notes

1   The term emerging economies (or emerging market economies) refers to a number of countries typically belonging to the middle-income group, that private financial institutions consider to be potential clients. They are also seen as offering higher profits than developed economies, but they also present higher risks. This group of countries includes several new entrants into the EU which previously were classified as transition economies.

2   This corresponds to the global stock of debt and equity outstanding, as estimated by Lund et al., 2013.

3   For instance, an increase of the exposure of United States institutional investors, such as pension funds, to emerging market debt from the current average of 4 per cent to 8 per cent of their portfolio (as recommended by some investment advisers) would funnel into emerging market bonds $2 trillion, about twice the total amount of bonds sold by emerging market corporations and sovereign States in 2012 – a record year (Rodrigues and Foley, 2013).

4   UNCTAD secretariat calculations, based on IMF, *Balance of Payments Statistics* database and UNCTADstat.

5   These countries are: Afghanistan, Burkina Faso, Burundi, Djibouti, the Gambia, Grenada, the Lao People's Democratic Republic, Maldives, Sao Tome and Principe, Saint Lucia, Saint Vincent and the Grenadines, Tajikistan, Tonga and Yemen.

6   *Net* capital inflows correspond to gross inflows (e.g. an increase of inward FDI or a new credit received) minus the reduction of foreign liabilities (for instance, through disinvestment of inward FDI or the paying back of a foreign loan). It does not take into consideration capital outflows, such as outward FDI or the granting of credit to a non-resident.

7   UNCTAD secretariat calculations, based on IMF, *Balance of Payments Statistics* database and UNCTADstat.

8   Such a belief, popularized at the end of the 1980s in the United Kingdom by Nigel Lawson, the then Chancellor of the Exchequer (and often referred to as "Lawson's Law"), ended in the "sterling crisis" in 1992 and that currency's withdrawal from the ERM.

9   The intermediation of the banking system also allowed the ECB to circumvent its statutory lending limits in financing its member States. This was also

convenient for the banks that could obtain ECB loans at an interest rate of 1 per cent and acquire sovereign bonds with much higher returns.

10 Data from the ECB, Euro Area Accounts, *Statistical Data Warehouse*; available at: http://www.ecb.int/stats/html/index.en.html.

11 Data from the Bank for International Settlement, *Consolidated Banking Statistics* database.

12 In particular, if central banks sterilize money creation resulting from the accumulation of international reserves by increasing their liabilities, a financial cost arises if interest earnings from international reserves are smaller than the interest payments resulting from the new debt issuances.

13 In this respect, the recent ability of some LDCs to access private capital markets should be exercised with caution. Since 2007, several sub-Saharan African countries, such as Angola, the Democratic Republic of the Congo and Senegal, have issued sovereign bonds. However, while such foreign-currency denominated government debt allows them some room for manoeuvre, it carries significant maturity and currency risks, and makes those countries vulnerable to the destabilizing impact of private capital movements (Stiglitz and Rashid, 2013).

14 The case of the Argentinean "Convertibility Plan" between 1991 and 2001 was, in that sense, a harbinger for what is happening to the euro-zone periphery. In Argentina, policymakers sought monetary stability as the main macroeconomic target by adopting a currency board scheme with an irrevocably fixed exchange rate. At the same time, they deregulated both the domestic financial system and capital flows. As exchange-rate risk seemed to have disappeared, capital inflows of the carry-trade type spurred domestic credit and raised asset prices, leading to some years of rapid GDP growth, although it also led to increasing current account deficits. The subsequent loss of competitiveness eventually hurt economic growth and made the country dependent on ever-increasing capital inflows. Any slowdown of capital inflows led to economic recession, as in 1995 and 1998–2001. After several years of economic depression and increasing difficulties in maintaining the exchange-rate peg, a reversal of capital flows led to the collapse of the Convertibility Plan. The Government tried to restore the confidence of financial markets with a law that sought to eradicate fiscal deficits (through the so-called Zero-deficit Act) by requiring that current expenditures (except interest payments) be adjusted quarterly to expected fiscal revenues. This led to an across-the-board reduction of 13 per cent in public servants' salaries and pensions, among other expenditures, which actually aggravated the economic depression and, as a consequence, also affected public revenues. Meanwhile, the fiscal deficit remained static. As deposits were increasingly withdrawn from banks and used for buying United States dollars, the illusion that "every peso is backed by a dollar" proved to be false, and the currency board had to be abandoned. There followed a huge devaluation and default of a large proportion of the external debt. These two unplanned and undesired outcomes set the foundations for economic recovery, as they restored competitiveness and led to debt restructuring and reduction.

15 This topic has been extensively discussed in previous *TDR*s (see, for instance, *TDR 2009*, chap. IV and *TDR 2011*, chap. VI).

16 In addition, the IMF introduces what amounts to a kind of conditionality by subjecting the countries that exercise their prerogative to introduce capital controls (established in Article VI, sec.3 of the Articles of Agreements) to surveillance disciplines, as stated in Article IV.

17 The proposal was put forward early in the reformulation process, but has gained strength after tests applied by the Basel Committee on Banking Supervision showed that there is huge variation between different banks' estimations of their risk-weighted assets, leading to significant "savings" in the amount of capital required to be set aside to support their activities.

18 Since 2009, all G20 members are represented on the Basel Committee on Banking Supervision (BCBS) and the Financial Stability Forum (FSF), and consequently on the Financial Stability Board (FSB).

19 In the United States, the Dodd-Frank Act seeks to impose a bail-in of creditors in the event of bank failure and prevent a government bailout of banks.

20 Until the 1980s, the bulk of deposits and loans was concentrated in State-owned commercial banks in Indonesia, the Republic of Korea and Taiwan Province of China, and these banks still play a major role in China and India.

21 For example, in 2010, the central bank of Bangladesh set commercial banks a target for loan disbursements to SMEs and women entrepreneurs, and the target is supported by a refinancing scheme. Achievement is a condition for the approval of new branches of the concerned bank. In addition, it required all private and foreign banks to direct 2.5 per cent of their total loans to agriculture (Bangladesh Bank, 2013). In India, the Reserve Bank of India established that 40 per cent of adjusted net bank credit must be targeted to the following priority sectors: agriculture, SMEs, micro credit, education, housing, off-grid energy solutions for households and export credit (for foreign banks only) (Reserve Bank of India, 2012). Several other central banks in Asian countries, including Cambodia, China, Malaysia, Nepal, Pakistan and Viet Nam, direct credit to priority sectors, areas or borrowers (typically SMEs), either by setting lending targets to commercial banks or through refinancing programmes (Bhattacharayya,

2012). In Latin America, most central banks abandoned their development mandates in the 1990s, and focused on inflation targets. However, a policy reorientation seems to be under way. For instance, in March 2012 Argentina reformed its Central Bank Charter, which increased its ability to implement credit policies. Under the new regulation, in July 2012 the central bank determined that all commercial banks must lend to productive investment at moderate interest rates – at least the equivalent of 5 per cent of their deposits – and at least half of those credits must be directed to SMEs. This scheme complements the rediscount line which was made available to banks that finance new investment projects under the Bicentennial Financing for Production programme launched in June 2010. Between July 2012 and May 2013, the credit granted through these two credit schemes accounted for more than 50 per cent of the total credit delivered to private firms during this period (BCRA, 2013). This should gradually reduce banks' strong bias in favour of short-term financing and facilitating access to credit by SMEs.

References

Aglietta M and Brand T (2013). *Un New Deal pour l'Europe*. Paris, Odile Jacob.

Akyüz Y (2012). The boom in capital flows to developing countries: Will it go bust again? *Ekonomi-tek*, vol. 1: 63–96.

Bagehot W (1873). *Lombard Street: A Description of the Money Market*. London, Henry S. King and Co; reprinted by Wiley, New York, 1999.

Bangladesh Bank (2013). *Annual Report 2011-2012*. Dhaka, 7 March.

Bank of England (2013). Funding for lending scheme; available at: http://www.bankofengland.co.uk/markets/Pages/FLS/default.aspx.

Bank of Japan (2010). Financial System Report. Tokyo, September.

BCRA (Banco Central de la Republica Argentina) (2013). Informe Macroeconómico y de Política Monetaria, Buenos Aires, July.

Bhagwati J (1998). The capital myth: The difference between trade in widgets and dollars. *Foreign Affairs*, May/June.

Bhattacharyya N (2012). Monetary policy and employment in developing Asia. ILO Asia-Pacific Working Paper Series. Bangkok.

BIS (2013). Report to G20 Finance Ministers and Central Bank Governors on monitoring implementation of Basel III regulatory reform. Basel, April.

Blanchard O (2013). Rethinking macroeconomic policy. *Voxeu*, 9 May; available at: www.voxeu.org.

Borio C (2012). The financial cycle and macroeconomics: What have we learnt? BIS Working Paper No 395, Bank for International Settlements, Basel.

Borio C (2013). Macroeconomic and the financial cycle: Hamlet without the Prince? *Voexu*, 2 February; available at: www.voxeu.org.

Brunnermeier MK, de Gregorio J, Lane P, Rey H, Shin HS (2012). Banks and cross-border capital flows: Policy challenges and regulatory responses. *Voexu*, 7 October.

Coupaye P (1978). Les banques françaises: bilan d'une réforme. Paris, La Documentation Française.

De Luna-Martínez J and Vicente CL (2012). Global survey of development banks. World Bank, Policy Research Working Paper No. 5969. Washington, DC, February.

Dullien S (2009). Central banking, financial institutions and credit creation in developing countries. UNCTAD Discussion Paper No. 193, Geneva, January.

EIB (European Investment Bank) (2013). Increasing lending to the economy: Implementing the EIB capital increase and joint Commission-EIB initiatives. Joint Commission-EIB report to the European Council, 27–28 June.

Epstein GA (2005). Central banks as agents of economic development. Helsinki, United Nations University World Institute for Development Economics Research (UNU-WIDER), April.

Galbraith JK (1994). *A Short History of Financial Euphoria*. New York, Penguin Books.

Gambacorta L and van Rixtel A (2013). Structural bank regulation initiatives: Approaches and implications.

BIS Working Papers No 412, Bank for International Settlements, Basel, April.

Goff S and Jenkins P (2011). UK banks cut periphery Eurozone lending. *Financial Times*, 17 November.

Haldane AG (2011). The big fish small pond problem. Speech delivered at the Institute for New Economic Thinking Annual Conference, Bretton Woods, New Hampshire, 9 April 2011; available at: www.bankofengland.co.uk/publications/speeches.

Haldane AG (2012). On being the right size. Speech delivered at the Institute of Economic Affairs, The 2012 Beesley Lectures, 22nd Annual Series, 25 October.

Hodgman DR (1973). Credit controls in Western Europe: An evaluative review. In: *Credit Allocation Techniques and Monetary Policy*, Conference Series 11, Federal Reserve Bank of Boston, September.

IADB (2013). Bancos públicos de desarrollo ¿hacia un nuevo paradigma? (Edited by Fernando de Olloqui). Washington, DC, Inter-American Development Bank.

IMF (2010). Preserving debt sustainability in low-income countries in the wake of the global crisis. Washington, DC.

Jeanne O, Subramanian A and Williamson J (2012). *Who Needs to Open the Capital Account?* Washington, DC, Peterson Institute for International Economics.

Keynes JM (1936/1973). The general theory of employment, interest and money. In: *The Collected Writings of John Maynard Keynes*, Vol. VII. London, Macmillan and St. Martin's Press, for the Royal Economic Society.

Kindleberger CP (1978). *Manias, panics and crashes: A history of financial crises*. London and Basingstoke, Macmillan.

Koo RC (2011). The world in balance sheet recession: Causes, cures, and politics. *Real-world Economics Review*, (58): 19–37.

Lund S, Daruvala T, Dobbs R, Härle P, Hwek J-H and Falcón R (2013). Financial globalization: Retreat or reset? *Global Economic Watch*, McKinsey Global Institute, McKinsey & Company.

O'Connell A (2012). Financial reform for development and the role of central banks. Presented to the Seminar on The State and Perspectives of Financial Reforms Worldwide, Sardinia, 7–8 September.

Pollin R, Heintz J, Garrett-Peltier H and Wicks-Lim J (2011). 19 million jobs for US workers: The impact of channeling $1.4 trillion in excess liquid asset holdings into productive investments. Amherst, MA, Political Economy Research Institute, University of Massachusetts.

Prasad E, Rajan R and Subramanian A (2007). Foreign capital and economic growth. *Brookings Papers on Economic Activity,* (1): 153–209.

Prasad E, Rogoff K, Shiang-Jin W and Kose MA (2003). The effects of financial globalization on developing countries: Some empirical evidence. IMF Occasional Paper No. 220, International Monetary Fund, Washington, DC.

Reinhart C and Rogoff K (2009). *This Time is Different. Eight Centuries of Financial Folly*. Princeton, NJ, Princeton University Press.

Reserve Bank of India (2012). *Annual Report 2011-2012*. New Delhi, August.

Rodrigues V and Foley S (2013). Concerns over high demand of EM bonds. *Financial Times*, 27 March.

Schumpeter JA (1954/2006). *History of Economic Analysis*. London and New York, Routledge.

Shin HS (2011). Global banking glut and loan risk premium. Mundell-Fleming Lecture, delivered at the IMF Annual Research Conference, 10–11 November; available at: www.princeton.edu/~hsshin/www/mundell_fleming_lecture.pdf.

Stiglitz J (2013). The lessons of the North Atlantic crisis for economic theory and policy. *Voxeu*, 9 May; available at: www.voxeu.org.

Stiglitz J and Rashid H (2013). Sub-Saharan Africa's eurobond borrowing spree gathers pace. Project Syndicate, 26 June.

UNCTAD (2012). *Least Developed Countries Report 2012*. New York and Geneva.

UNCTAD (*TDR 2008*). *Trade and Development Report, 2008. Commodity Prices, Capital Flows and the Financing of Investment*. United Nations publication, Sales No. E.08.II.D.21, New York and Geneva.

UNCTAD (*TDR 2009*). *Trade and Development Report, 2009. Responding to the Global Crisis: Climate Change Mitigation and Development*. United Nations publication, Sales No. E. 09.II.D.16, New York and Geneva.

UNCTAD (*TDR 2011*). *Trade and Development Report, 2011. Post-crisis Policy Challenges in the World Economy*. United Nations publication, Sales No. E.11.II.D.3, New York and Geneva.

Viñals J, Pazarbasioglu C, Surti J, Narain A, Erbenova M and Chow J (2013). Creating a safer financial system: Will the Volcker, Vickers and Liikanen structural measures help? Staff Discussion Note 13 April, International Monetary Fund, Washington, DC.

Wicksell K (1935). *Lectures on Political Economy*. London, Routledge and Keagan.

UNITED NATIONS CONFERENCE
ON TRADE AND DEVELOPMENT

Palais des Nations
CH-1211 GENEVA 10
Switzerland
(http://unctad.org)

Selected UNCTAD Publications

Trade and Development Report, 2012
Policies for Inclusive and Balanced Growth

United Nations publication, sales no. E.12.II.D.6
ISBN 978-92-1-112846-8

Trade and Development Report, 2011
Post-crisis policy challenges in the world economy

United Nations publication, sales no. E.11.II.D.3
ISBN 978-92-1-112822-2

Trade and Development Report, 2010
Employment, globalization and development

United Nations publication, sales no. E.10.II.D.3
ISBN 978-92-1-112807-9

Trade and Development Report, 2009

Responding to the global crisis

Climate change mitigation and development

United Nations publication, sales no. E.09.II.D.16

ISBN 978-92-1-112776-8

Chapter	I	The Impact of the Global Crisis and the Short-term Policy Response
		Annex: The Global Recession Compounds the Food Crisis
Chapter	II	The Financialization of Commodity Markets
Chapter	III	Learning from the Crisis: Policies for Safer and Sounder Financial Systems
Chapter	IV	Reform of the International Monetary and Financial System
Chapter	V	Climate Change Mitigation and Development

Trade and Development Report, 2008

Commodity prices, capital flows and the financing of investment

United Nations publication, sales no. E.08.II.D.21

ISBN 978-92-1-112752-2

Chapter	I	Current Trends and Issues in the World Economy
		Annex table to chapter I
Chapter	II	Commodity Price Hikes and Instability
Chapter	III	International Capital Flows, Current-Account Balances and Development Finance
		Annex: Econometric Analyses of Determinants of Expansionary and Contractionary Current-account Reversals
Chapter	IV	Domestic Sources of Finance and Investment in Productive Capacity
Chapter	V	Official Development Assistance for the MDGs and Economic Growth
		Annex: Details on Econometric Studies
Chapter	VI	Current Issues Related to the External Debt of Developing Countries

Trade and Development Report, 2007

Regional cooperation for development

United Nations publication, sales no. E.07.II.D.11

ISBN 978-92-1-112721-8

Chapter	I	Current Issues in the World Economy
		Statistical annex to chapter I
Chapter	II	Globalization, Regionalization and the Development Challenge
Chapter	III	The "New Regionalism" and North-South Trade Agreements
Chapter	IV	Regional Cooperation and Trade Integration Among Developing Countries
Chapter	V	Regional Financial and Monetary Cooperation
		Annex 1 The Southern African Development Community
		Annex 2 The Gulf Cooperation Council
Chapter	VI	Regional Cooperation in Trade Logistics, Energy and Industrial Policy

Trade and Development Report, 2006

Global partnership and national policies for development

United Nations publication, sales no. E.06.II.D.6

ISBN 92-1-112698-3

Chapter	I	Global Imbalances as a Systemic Problem
		Annex 1: Commodity Prices and Terms of Trade
		Annex 2: The Theoretical Background to the Saving/Investment Debate
Chapter	II	Evolving Development Strategies – Beyond the Monterrey Consensus
Chapter	III	Changes and Trends in the External Environment for Development
		Annex tables to chapter III
Chapter	IV	Macroeconomic Policy under Globalization
Chapter	V	National Policies in Support of Productive Dynamism
Chapter	VI	Institutional and Governance Arrangements Supportive of Economic Development

Trade and Development Report, 2005

New features of global interdependence

United Nations publication, sales no. E.05.II.D.13

ISBN 92-1-112673-8

Chapter   I   Current Issues in the World Economy

Chapter   II   Income Growth and Shifting Trade Patterns in Asia

Chapter   III   Evolution in the Terms of Trade and its Impact on Developing Countries

        Annex: Distribution of Oil and Mining Rent: Some Evidence from Latin America, 1999–2004

Chapter   IV   Towards a New Form of Global Interdependence

* * * * * *

Trade and Development Report, 1981–2011

Three Decades of Thinking Development

United Nations publication, sales no. E.12.II.D.5

ISBN 978-92-1-112845-1

Part One   Trade and Development Report, 1981–2011: Three Decades of Thinking Development

1.   Introduction

2.   Interdependence

3.   Macroeconomics and finance

4.   Global economic governance

5.   Development strategies: assessments and recommendations

6.   Outlook

Part Two   Panel Discussion on "Thinking Development: Three Decades of the *Trade and Development Report*"

Opening statement
    by Anthony Mothae Maruping

Origins and evolving ideas of the *TDR*
    Introductory remarks by Richard Kozul-Wright
    Statement by Rubens Ricupero
    Statement by Yılmaz Akyüz

The *TDR* approach to development strategies
    Introductory remarks by Taffere Tesfachew
    Statement by Jayati Ghosh
    Statement by Rolph van der Hoeven
    Statement by Faizel Ismail

The macroeconomic reasoning in the *TDR*
    Introductory remarks by Charles Gore
    Statement by Anthony P.
    Statement by Carlos Fortin
    Statement by Heiner Flassbeck

Evolving issues in international economic governance
    Introductory remarks by Andrew Cornford
    Statement by Jomo Kwame Sundaram
    Statement by Arturo O'Connell

The way forward
    Closing remarks by Alfredo Calcagno

Summary of the debate

* * * * * *

The Financial and Economic Crisis of 2008-2009 and Developing Countries

United Nations publication, sales no. E.11.II.D.11
ISBN 978-92-1-112818-5

Edited by Sebastian Dullien, Detlef J. Kotte,
Alejandro Márquez and Jan Priewe

Introduction

The Crisis – Transmission, Impact and Special Features

Jan Priewe
What Went Wrong? Alternative Interpretations of the Global Financial Crisis

Daniela Magalhães Prates and Marcos Antonio Macedo Cintra
The Emerging-market Economies in the Face of the Global Financial Crisis

Jörg Mayer
The Financialization of Commodity Markets and Commodity Price Volatility

Sebastian Dullien
Risk Factors in International Financial Crises: Early Lessons from the 2008-2009 Turmoil

The Crisis – Country and Regional Studies

Laike Yang and Cornelius Huizenga
China's Economy in the Global Economic Crisis: Impact and Policy Responses

Abhijit Sen Gupta
Sustaining Growth in a Period of Global Downturn: The Case of India

André Nassif
Brazil and India in the Global Economic Crisis: Immediate Impacts and Economic Policy Responses

Patrick N. Osakwe
Africa and the Global Financial and Economic Crisis: Impacts, Responses and Opportunities

Looking Forward – Policy Agenda

Alejandro Márquez
The Report of the Stiglitz Commission: A Summary and Comment

Ricardo Ffrench-Davis
Reforming Macroeconomic Policies in Emerging Economies: From Procyclical to Countercyclical Approaches

Jürgen Zattler
A Possible New Role for Special Drawing Rights In and Beyond the Global Monetary System

Detlef J. Kotte
The Financial and Economic Crisis and Global Economic Governance

* * * * * *

The Global Economic Crisis: Systemic Failures and Multilateral Remedies

United Nations publication, sales no. E.09.II.D.4
ISBN 978-92-1-112765-2

*Report by the UNCTAD Secretariat Task Force
on Systemic Issues and Economic Cooperation*

Chapter   I   A crisis foretold

Chapter   II   Financial regulation: fighting today's crisis today

Chapter   III   Managing the financialization of commodity futures trading

Chapter   IV   Exchange rate regimes and monetary cooperation

Chapter   V   Towards a coherent effort to overcome the systemic crisis

* * * * * *

These publications may be obtained from bookstores and distributors throughout the world. Consult your bookstore or write to United Nations Publications/Sales Section, Palais des Nations, CH-1211 Geneva 10, Switzerland, fax: +41-22-917.0027, e-mail: unpubli@un.org; or United Nations Publications, Two UN Plaza, DC2-853, New York, NY 10017, USA, telephone +1-212-963.8302 or +1-800-253.9646, fax: +1-212-963.3489, e-mail: publications@un.org. Internet: http://www.un.org/publications.

Regional Monetary Cooperation and Growth-enhancing Policies:
The new challenges for Latin America and the Caribbean

United Nations publication, UNCTAD/GDS/2010/1

Chapter   I   What Went Wrong? An Analysis of Growth and Macroeconomic Prices in Latin America

Chapter   II   Regional Monetary Cooperation for Growth-enhancing Policies

Chapter   III   Regional Payment Systems and the SUCRE Initiative

Chapter   IV   Policy Conclusions

* * * * * *

Price Formation in Financialized Commodity Markets: The role of information

United Nations publication, UNCTAD/GDS/2011/1

1. Motivation of this Study

2. Price Formation in Commodity Markets

3. Recent Evolution of Prices and Fundamentals

4. Financialization of Commodity Price Formation

5. Field Survey

6. Policy Considerations and Recommendations

7. Conclusions

* * * * * *

These publications are available on the website at: http://unctad.org. Copies may be obtained from the Publications Assistant, Macroeconomic and Development Policies Branch, Division on Globalization and Development Strategies, United Nations Conference on Trade and Development (UNCTAD), Palais des Nations, CH-1211 Geneva 10, Switzerland; e-mail: gdsinfo@unctad.org.

UNCTAD Discussion Papers

No. 210	Dec. 2012	Giovanni Andrea CORNIA and Bruno MARTORANO	Development policies and income inequality in selected developing regions, 1980–2010
No. 209	Nov. 2012	Alessandro MISSALE and Emanuele BACCHIOCCHI	Multilateral indexed loans and debt sustainability
No. 208	Oct. 2012	David BICCHETTI and Nicolas MAYSTRE	The synchronized and long-lasting structural change on commodity markets: Evidence from high frequency data
No. 207	July 2012	Amelia U. SANTOS-PAULINO	Trade, income distribution and poverty in developing countries: A survey
No. 206	Dec. 2011	André NASSIF, Carmem FEIJÓ and Eliane ARAÚJO	The long-term "optimal" real exchange rate and the currency overvaluation trend in open emerging economies: The case of Brazil
No. 205	Dec. 2011	Ulrich HOFFMANN	Some reflections on climate change, green growth illusions and development space
No. 204	Oct. 2011	Peter BOFINGER	The scope for foreign exchange market interventions
No. 203	Sep. 2011	Javier LINDENBOIM, Damián KENNEDY and Juan M. GRAÑA	Share of labour compensation and aggregate demand discussions towards a growth strategy
No. 202	June 2011	Pilar FAJARNES	An overview of major sources of data and analyses relating to physical fundamentals in international commodity markets
No. 201	Feb. 2011	Ulrich HOFFMANN	Assuring food security in developing countries under the challenges of climate change: Key trade and development issues of a fundamental transformation of agriculture
No. 200	Sep. 2010	Jörg MAYER	Global rebalancing: Effects on trade flows and employment
No. 199	June 2010	Ugo PANIZZA, Federico STURZENEGGER and Jeromin ZETTELMEYER	International government debt
No. 198	April 2010	Lee C. BUCHHEIT G. MITU GULATI	Responsible sovereign lending and borrowing
No. 197	March 2010	Christopher L. GILBERT	Speculative influences on commodity futures prices 2006–2008
No. 196	Nov. 2009	Michael HERRMANN	Food security and agricultural development in times of high commodity prices
No. 195	Oct. 2009	Jörg MAYER	The growing interdependence between financial and commodity markets
No. 194	June 2009	Andrew CORNFORD	Statistics for international trade in banking services: Requirements, availability and prospects
No. 193	Jan. 2009	Sebastian DULLIEN	Central banking, financial institutions and credit creation in developing countries
No. 192	Nov. 2008	Enrique COSIO-PASCAL	The emerging of a multilateral forum for debt restructuring: The Paris Club
No. 191	Oct. 2008	Jörg MAYER	Policy space: What, for what, and where?
No. 190	Oct. 2008	Martin KNOLL	Budget support: A reformed approach or old wine in new skins?

* * * * * *

UNCTAD Discussion Papers are available on the website at: http://unctad.org. Copies of *UNCTAD Discussion Papers* may be obtained from the Publications Assistant, Macroeconomic and Development Policies Branch, Division on Globalization and Development Strategies, United Nations Conference on Trade and Development (UNCTAD), Palais des Nations, CH-1211 Geneva 10, Switzerland; e-mail: gdsinfo@unctad.org.

G-24 Discussion Paper Series
Research papers for the Intergovernmental Group of Twenty-Four
on International Monetary Affairs and Development

No. 59	June 2010	Andrew CORNFORD	Revising Basel 2: The Impact of the Financial Crisis and Implications for Developing Countries
No. 58	May 2010	Kevin P. GALLAGHER	Policy Space to Prevent and Mitigate Financial Crises in Trade and Investment Agreements
No. 57	December 2009	Frank ACKERMAN	Financing the Climate Mitigation and Adaptation Measures in Developing Countries
No. 56	June 2009	Anuradha MITTAL	The 2008 Food Price Crisis: Rethinking Food Security Policies
No. 55	April 2009	Eric HELLEINER	The Contemporary Reform of Global Financial Governance: Implications of and Lessons from the Past
No. 54	February 2009	Gerald EPSTEIN	Post-war Experiences with Developmental Central Banks: The Good, the Bad and the Hopeful
No. 53	December 2008	Frank ACKERMAN	Carbon Markets and Beyond: The Limited Role of Prices and Taxes in Climate and Development Policy
No. 52	November 2008	C.P. CHANDRASEKHAR	Global Liquidity and Financial Flows to Developing Countries: New Trends in Emerging Markets and their Implications
No. 51	September 2008	Ugo PANIZZA	The External Debt Contentious Six Years after the Monterrey Consensus
No. 50	July 2008	Stephany GRIFFITH-JONES with David GRIFFITH-JONES and Dagmar HERTOVA	Enhancing the Role of Regional Development Banks
No. 49	December 2007	David WOODWARD	IMF Voting Reform: Need, Opportunity and Options
No. 48	November 2007	Sam LAIRD	Aid for Trade: Cool Aid or Kool-Aid
No. 47	October 2007	Jan KREGEL	IMF Contingency Financing for Middle-Income Countries with Access to Private Capital Markets: An Assessment of the Proposal to Create a Reserve Augmentation Line
No. 46	September 2007	José María FANELLI	Regional Arrangements to Support Growth and Macro-Policy Coordination in MERCOSUR
No. 45	April 2007	Sheila PAGE	The Potential Impact of the Aid for Trade Initiative
No. 44	March 2007	Injoo SOHN	East Asia's Counterweight Strategy: Asian Financial Cooperation and Evolving International Monetary Order
No. 43	February 2007	Devesh KAPUR and Richard WEBB	Beyond the IMF
No. 42	November 2006	Mushtaq H. KHAN	Governance and Anti-Corruption Reforms in Developing Countries: Policies, Evidence and Ways Forward
No. 41	October 2006	Fernando LORENZO and Nelson NOYA	IMF Policies for Financial Crises Prevention in Emerging Markets
No. 40	May 2006	Lucio SIMPSON	The Role of the IMF in Debt Restructurings: Lending Into Arrears, Moral Hazard and Sustainability Concerns
No. 39	February 2006	Ricardo GOTTSCHALK and Daniela PRATES	East Asia's Growing Demand for Primary Commodities – Macroeconomic Challenges for Latin America

* * * * * *

G-24 Discussion Paper Series are available on the website at: http://unctad.org. Copies of *G-24 Discussion Paper Series* may be obtained from the Publications Assistant, Macroeconomic and Development Policies Branch, Division on Globalization and Development Strategies, United Nations Conference on Trade and Development (UNCTAD), Palais des Nations, CH-1211 Geneva 10, Switzerland; e-mail: gdsinfo@unctad.org.

QUESTIONNAIRE

Trade and Development Report, 2013

In order to improve the quality and relevance of the Trade and Development Report, the UNCTAD secretariat would greatly appreciate your views on this publication. Please complete the following questionnaire and return it to:

Readership Survey
Division on Globalization and Development Strategies
UNCTAD
Palais des Nations, Room E.10009
CH-1211 Geneva 10, Switzerland
Fax: (+41) (0)22 917 0274
E-mail: tdr@unctad.org

Thank you very much for your kind cooperation.

1. What is your assessment of this publication?

	Excellent	*Good*	*Adequate*	*Poor*
Overall	☐	☐	☐	☐
Relevance of issues	☐	☐	☐	☐
Analytical quality	☐	☐	☐	☐
Policy conclusions	☐	☐	☐	☐
Presentation	☐	☐	☐	☐

2. What do you consider the strong points of this publication?

   _____
   _____
   _____

3. What do you consider the weak points of this publication?

   _____
   _____
   _____

4. For what main purposes do you use this publication?

   Analysis and research ☐   Education and training ☐
   Policy formulation and management ☐   Other (*specify*) _____

5. Which of the following best describes your area of work?

   Government ☐   Public enterprise ☐
   Non-governmental organization ☐   Academic or research ☐
   International organization ☐   Media ☐
   Private enterprise institution ☐   Other (*specify*) _____

6. Name and address of respondent (*optional*):

   _____
   _____
   _____

7. Do you have any further comments?

   _____
   _____
   _____